Taboo or not Taboo

Taboo or not Taboo

Sexuality and Family in the Hebrew Bible

Ilona N. Rashkow

FORTRESS PRESS
MINNEAPOLIS

TABOO OR NOT TABOO
Sexuality and Family in the Hebrew Bible

Cover art: Guercino, *Abraham Expelling Hagar and Ismael* (1657), Pinacoteca di Brera, Milan, Italy. Scala/Art Resource, New York. Used by permission.
Cover design: Derek Herzog
Interior design: Beth Wright

Library of Congress Cataloging-in-Publication Data

Rashkow, Ilona N. (Ilona Nemesnyik)
    Taboo or not taboo : sexuality and family in the Hebrew Bible / Ilona N. Rashkow.
        p.   cm.
    Includes bibliographical references and index.
    ISBN 0-8006-3085-8 (alk. paper)
        1. Problem families in the Bible. 2. Sex in the Bible. 3. Bible. O.T.—Psychology.
    4. Psychoanalysis and religion. I. Title.
    BS680.F3 R37 2000
    221.8'3067—dc21
                                                                                    99-048079

The paper used in this publication meets the minimum requirements of American National Standard for Information Sciences — Permanence of Paper for Printed Library Materials, ANSI Z329.48-1984.

Manufactured in the U.S.A.   AF1-3085
04   03   02   01   00   1   2   3   4   5   6   7   8   9   10

טוֹבִים דֹּדֶיךָ כְוֹיָּיו

To Bruce

Contents

Acknowledgments

I am not a psychoanalyst, nor have I received formal training in psychology. My education and my expertise are in Comparative Literature; my primary subjects have been feminist literary theory, psychoanalytic literary theory, and the Hebrew Bible. My acquaintance with psychoanalysis derives from reading the works of Freud and his followers, particularly Lacan, and correspondence with psychiatric professionals.

The readers of this book, I assume, will include Bible scholars and those interested in psychoanalytic literary theory. I also hope that these will not be its only readers. I have therefore taken pains to make the book accessible to all interested persons and to write so that the only prerequisites for understanding my arguments are curiosity and an open mind. I have attempted to avoid technical language wherever possible and to make the discussions intelligible to the nonspecialist. Translations of biblical passages are my own, in consultation with the major modern Bible translations.

Many have helped me with this project. I have profited from responses to presentations given before the American Academy of Religion Mid-Atlantic Conference (February 1999), the Society of Biblical Literature National Conferences (1997 and 1998), and the Association for the Psychoanalysis of Culture and Society National Conference (1997). Earlier versions of parts of chapters 2 and 4 were included in *Reading Bibles, Writing Bodies: Identity and the Book* (Beal and Gunn, 1972) and *Genesis: A Feminist Companion to the Bible* (Brenner, 1998), respectively. I thank the editors for permission to include revisions of this material.

Generous and wise colleagues and friends have been ready and willing to read different parts of my book, offering encouragement and thoughtful criticism. They have devoted precious time and care to these pages. Louise Vasvari, Sandy Petrey, Lillian Klein, and Wayne Rollins graciously read early drafts of the book and made detailed and very useful comments. Jesse Rubin, M.D., was always ready to guide me through the unfamiliar world of medical literature, to help me locate pertinent sources and interpret them once I had found them. A skilled and caring psychiatrist, he has heard ideas presented in this book since I first began to formulate them, and often his responses have influenced the shapes they were to take. I am grateful for the time and attention all have given to me. They have flavored my thinking and significantly strengthened my book, although, of course, they are not responsible for any errors in the finished product.

Professor Adele Berlin has my gratitude for taking me on as a graduate student many years ago and training me in biblical studies with care and precision. May her wisdom and insight continue to shape my scholarly efforts.

I am glad for the opportunity to express my deep gratitude to my parents. I thank my mother, Helen, for standing by me throughout this long, sometimes difficult process and demonstrating once again the strength of maternal love. I wish my father John (of blessed memory) could have been alive to see the book in its final form. Although he did not fully understand (and certainly did not always agree with) all of my ideas, he never swerved in offering encouragement. My two nephews, Tyler and Jonathan Warden, have, wittingly or not, inspired some of my interpretations, perhaps to the chagrin of their parents.

None of this would have been possible, however, without my husband, Bruce, the best reader I know. He listened to my theories, gave me support and encouragement, lightened my discouragements, and helped me with all my revisions. Bruce is my friend, my companion, my love, and my husband. I dedicate this book to him.

Chapter 1 ————————————

Psychoanalytic Literary Theory and the Hebrew Bible: What Hath Freud Wrought?

Background

Sigmund Freud once acknowledged that most of his discoveries about the unconscious mind had been anticipated by the poets of the past. Thus, it should not be surprising that psychology has been used in an effort to explain the origins, character, and effects of literature, including *biblical* literature.

What makes a reading of a literary work psychoanalytic? As I have discussed more fully elsewhere,[1] to call a reading psychoanalytic or Freudian immediately introduces ambiguity, because such an expression can refer either to the use of Freudian themes or to Freudian methods. That is, an interpretation of a literary work can be called Freudian or psychoanalytic with respect either to the substance of the text (*what* it reads) or to the interpretive procedures and techniques a reader uses (*how* it reads).

Generally speaking, there are three points at which psychoanalysis can enter the study of a literary work: examining the mind of the author, the minds and behavior of the author's characters, or our own minds. There is a long tradition of Freudian criticism that examines the text for buried motives and hidden neurotic conflicts that generated the writer's art: in writing *Hamlet,* for example, Shakespeare was working over the death of his son (Jones 1949); and in writing *The Gambler* Dostoevsky was drawing upon the prohibitions placed upon masturbation in his childhood (Freud 1928). Because the hazards of examining an author's mind are inversely proportional to the amount of material available on the writer's life and private thoughts, it is never completely safe to guess at the psychic significance of a work of art, even that of a candid living author, and for some major writers (like Chaucer, Shakespeare, and the biblical writers), we have only the most minimal sense of what their private lives may have been. Thus, this form of psychoanalytic literary criticism generally is viewed as mere speculation.

1

Most of Freud's own ventures into literature were the analyses of literary characters. His initial remarks on the Oedipus complex were literary, involving both Hamlet and Oedipus Tyrannis. Hamlet, according to Freud, is "the hysteric" who delays because he is paralyzed by guilt over Claudius's enactment of his own unconscious wishes (1916–17:335). A stream of essays by other analysts followed, mostly on fictitious textual characters. They wrote what might be described as case studies of literature, dealing with those authors or characters whom they categorized as neurotic. Most of them emphasized such analytic themes as the Oedipus complex, analytic, schizoid tendencies, latent or expressed homosexuality, guilt, etc., and the roles they played in the works of the writers or among their other literary characters.

Analyzing literary characters has not fallen into as deep a disrepute as concentrating on the writer, in great part because fictional characters are viewed as representatives of life and as such can be understood only if we assume that they are "telling a truth." This assumption allows us to find "unconscious" motivations, albeit in fictitious characters. For example, Abraham's actions and language reveal a great deal about him, despite the fact that all we will ever know is contained in the 1,534 verses of Genesis.

On the other hand, literary characters are both more and less than real persons. This presents a problem. While one aspect of narrative characterization is to provide a *mimetic* function (to represent human action and motivation), another aspect is primarily *textual* (to reveal information to a reader or to conceal it). This situation has no precise parallel in life (although it can be argued that real persons often resemble literary characters in the masks they present to the world). As a result, examining a narrative character is not risk-free either. For instance, contradictions in Abraham's character may result from the psychic complexities the biblical writer imagined; or they may result from the fact that Abraham is an agent in a literary narrative with a highly developed system of conventions—his "traits" may be more a function of the requirements of the story line than of his personality.

Since authors may not provide much material for the theorists and since characters are not real persons, many scholars have shifted their focus from the interpretation of meanings embedded within a text to the processes of writing and reading. This is true of the French structuralists and post-structuralists (for example, Roland Barthes), psychoanalytically influenced critics (see Norman Holland), and of other proponents of reader-response criticism (such as Stanley Fish, Wolfgang Iser, Hans Georg Gadamer). Rather than attempting to determine *objective* meanings hidden within a text (meanings a reader needs to extricate) these scholars concentrate on the *subjective* experience of the reader (interactions between reader/text/author) and the values and premises with which a reader approaches interpretation of a text. As within psychoanalysis itself, their foci are problems of indeterminacy, uncertainty, perspective, hermeneutics subjective (and communal) assumptions, and agreements.

The Bible and Psychoanalytic Literary Theory

Until recently, reading the Bible was thought to be a rather straightforward procedure. The goal was to respond properly by trying to understand the text and grasp *the* meaning. This changed once psychoanalytic literary theory gained wide acceptance within biblical studies.[2]

Of course, psychoanalytic literary theory is no more a conceptually unified critical position in biblical studies than in literary studies generally. The term is associated with scholars who examine the writer (David Halperin), the biblical characters (David Clines, Shoshana Feldman, Ilona Rashkow, Dorothy Zeligs), or the reader (David Clines et al.). Further, the approaches are neither monolithic nor mutually exclusive. But biblical scholars who use psychoanalytic literary theory seem to agree that meaning does not inhere completely and exclusively in the text and that the effects of reading Scripture, psychological and otherwise, are essential to its meaning. Ultimately, this type of literary criticism yields in biblical studies a way of looking at biblical narratives *and* readers that reorganizes both their interrelationships and the distinctions between them. As a result, recognizing the relationship of a reader to a text leads to a more profound awareness that no one biblical interpretation is intrinsically true. That is, the meaning of biblical narratives is not waiting to be uncovered but evolves, actualized by readers (and interpreters).

Objections to Psychoanalytic Literary Theory

One of the primary objections to psychoanalytic literary theory (among biblical scholars and others) is the Freudian idea of penis envy.[3]

Torok, for example, argues that penis envy is not based on biological fact but is a misconception: a common phallic phase does not characterize the infantile development of both sexes. One psychoanalyst who seems to bridge the Freudian and anti-Freudian schools of thought is Jacques Lacan who reinterprets Freud in light of structuralist and post-structuralist theories of discourse. Since Lacan focuses on the mutual interaction among society and the self with the use of language as intermediary—that is, language is the pivotal concept linking self and society—he shifts from Freud's biological penis to the phallus as signifier, and as a result, many scholars find his writings more relevant to both males and females.

Lacan, the French psychoanalyst whose thought has had such a broad influence on literary theory since the 1960s, considered psychoanalysis as much a part of philosophy as of medicine. Ironically, although Lacan deviated from the mainstream of psychoanalytic thought and was expelled from the International Psychoanalytic Association, he believed himself to be returning *to* Freud rather than departing *from* him.

Briefly, where Freud views the mechanisms of the unconscious as generated by libido (sexual energy), Lacan centers the theory of the unconscious on the sense within us of something being *absent*. Lacan describes two levels of absence: the less intense awareness of absence that can take the form of mere lack (*manque*) or of need (*besoin*), the perception of an unmet need or an unmet desire that is more profound and hence more urgent. Both of these levels of absence force the psyche to make demands. A deeper feeling of absence takes the higher form of desire (*désir*). Lacan defines *désir* as twofold: first, it is an unconscious feeling toward an object; second, this object can and does desire us in return. Lacan's terms for the universal symbol, or signifier of *désir* is the *Phallus*. It is important not to confuse the Phallus in this sense with the male sexual organ, the penis. According to Lacanian theory, *both* sexes experience the absence of and desire for the Phallus—which may be one reason Lacan's restructuring of Freud has appealed to feminists such as Hélène Cixous and Luce Irigaray. Indeed, the sexually critical and liberatory potential of Lacan is that although one sex has an anatomical penis, neither sex can possess the Phallus. As a result, sexuality is incomplete and fractured for *both* sexes. Moreover, although men and women must line themselves up on one or another side of the linguistic/sexual divide, they need not align themselves with the side that is anatomically isomorphic.

Lacan's theory of psychosexual development is also a revision of Freud's in that Lacan shifts the description of mental processes from a purely biological model to a semiotic one. For example, Freud discusses the first phase of childhood as the oral phase, in which the child's pleasure comes largely from suckling; the anal phase follows, when the child learns to control and to enjoy controlling the elimination of feces. For Lacan, the analogue of the oral phase is the "Mirror-Stage," from six to eighteen months, in which the child's image of its bodily self changes from mere formlessness and fragmentation to an identification with a unified shape it can see in the mirror. During this development, the child experiences itself as "*le Désir de la Mère*," the desire of the mother (in both senses—as an object that is itself unconscious and can desire us in return). That is, the baby not only knows that it needs its mother but also feels itself to be what completes and fulfills the mother's desires. From this phase Lacan derives the psychic field of the "Imaginary," the state in which a person's sense of reality is grasped purely as images and fantasies of the fulfillment of his or her desires. This stage, begun during the child's second year of life, continues into adulthood.

In Lacanian thought, repression and thus unconscious content occur together with the acquisition of language, at around eighteen months (when Freud's anal stage begins). Lacan derives his ideas of language and the unconscious from the semiotician Ferdinand de Saussure, as he was interpreted by the structuralist anthropologist Claude Lévi-Strauss. Briefly, Lévi-Strauss considered the unconscious as "reducible to a function—the symbolic function," which in turn was merely "the aggregate of the laws" of language (1967:198). The primary laws of language in structural linguistics are those of the selection and combination of primary basic elements. *Metaphor* is a mode of symbolization in which one thing is signified by another that is like it that is part of the same paradigmatic class (for example, "a sea of troubles" or "All the world's a stage"). Lacan sees metaphor as equivalent to the Freudian defense of "condensation" (in which one symbol becomes the substitute for a whole series of associations). *Metonymy*, on the other hand, is a mode of symbolization in which one thing is signified by another that is associated with it but *not* of the same class (for example, the use of "Washington" for "the United States government" or of "the sword" for "military power")—a syntagmatic relationship that Lacan regards as equivalent to Freudian "displacement."

As the child learns the names of things, his or her desires are no longer met automatically; now the child must ask for what he or she wants and cannot request things that do not have names. As the child learns to ask for a signified by pronouncing a signifier, he or she learns that one thing can symbolize another and has entered what Lacan calls the "field of the Symbolic." As Muller and Richardson describe: "From this point on the child's desire, like an endless quest for a lost paradise, must be channeled like an underground river through the subterranean passageways of the symbolic order, which make it possible that things be present in their absence in some ways through words" (1982:23).

At this stage, desires can be repressed, and the child is able to ask for something that metaphorically or metonymically replaces the desired object. Lacan punningly calls this stage of development "*le Nom-du-Père*"—the Name-of-the-Father—because language is only the first of the negations and subjections to law that now will begin to affect the child. (In French the phrase *le Nom-du-Père* is pronounced exactly the same as *le Non-du-Père*—the no-of-the-Father—hence its connection to negation and subjection to law.)

Another Lacanian field, less discussed in his writings than the others, is that of the "Real." By this Lacan refers to those incomprehensible aspects of experience that exist beyond the grasp of images and symbols through which we think and constitute our reality. That is to say, adult humans are always inscribed within language, but language does not constitute the ultimate reality. Since in Lacan's dialectic of desire one object may symbolize another (which is itself a substitute for still another), Lacan says that "the unconscious is structured like a language" (1977:34).

Like Freud, Lacan approaches literature primarily as material that properly interpreted illustrates the major concepts of his psychology. His indirect influence on literary theory and criticism has been considerable, primarily because his psychology has affected the philosophy and literary theory of the many French scholars who attended his seminars (and then by extension, British and American scholars who were influenced by the French). But a strain of direct Lacanian criticism has begun to appear as well in the past several years, in separate essays and in collections such as those edited by Shoshana Felman (1981) and Robert Con Davis (1983). Many of these works have taken the form of interpenetrative readings of Lacan and a literary text, which inevitably find the basic themes of Lacan's psychology within the text. This seems to be a workable compromise while Lacan's ideas are still relatively unfamiliar and is, in great part, the approach that I have used throughout this book. I suspect, however, that as Lacanian criticism becomes more widely accepted, the focus will change. Like Lacanian analysis itself, Lacanian-based readings will be centered more intensely on "the Word" and the chain of associations that are developed within the text—an approach that may be particularly relevant for biblical scholars.

In any event, whether Freudian, Lacanian, feminist, or any combination thereof, as David Clines observes, "what has happened . . . in the last three decades can be represented . . . as a shift in focus that has moved from *author* to *text* to *reader*" (1990:9–10); readers "*use* the Bible today . . . in terms of *their values, attitudes, and responses*" (McKnight 1988:14–15, emphasis added). Dissenters notwithstanding.

The Remainder of This Book

There has been a significant amount of work done recently in various disciplines on the family, particularly with regard to sexual relationships. However, most of what has been written by sociologists and psychoanalysts is of a highly theoretical nature generally not accessible to those not already steeped in the field. Within the area of biblical studies, books and articles are beginning to appear, including, for example, Halperin's *Seeking Ezekiel: Text and Psychology* (1993). The centerpiece of Halperin's argument is a reexamination of Edwin C. Broome's 1946 article "Ezekiel's Abnormal Personality" (1946). Broome's basic premise is that certain puzzling features of the Book of Ezekiel could be rendered intelligible only if taken as symptoms of a recognizable mental illness.

Another recent book, Carmichael's *Law, Legend, and Incest in the Bible: Leviticus 18–20,* deals specifically with incest (1997). His assumption is that the biblical lawgivers (that is, the writers of Leviticus 18–20) "set out to tackle the ethical and legal problems they encountered in their reading of these tales" and that the biblical laws "constitute a commentary upon matters arising in the national folklore" (1997:5).

In addition to these book-length studies there have been a few shorter articles by biblical scholars that use Lacanian theory in examining the Genesis 1–3 narrative. Both Anna Piskorowski's "In Search of Her Father: A Lacanian Approach to Genesis 2–3" (1992) and Fodor's "The Fall of Man in the Book of Genesis" (1954), for example, discuss the prohibition of not eating of the tree of knowledge of good and evil as "the law of the Name-of-the-Father" or the "Phallus" (see p. 4). In addition, Kim Parker's "Mirror, Mirror on the Wall, Must We Leave Eden, Once and for All?" (1999) suggests that the maturation theme as discerned in the Eden narrative has certain affinities with modern psychoanalytical theory, and, in particular, with the work of Lacan. He sees the expulsion from Eden as necessary and just as painful, as a child's maturation and socialization through Lacan's Oedipal stage.

This book differs from these works in several respects. First, rather than concentrate on one narrative (see Piskorowski, Fodor, and Parker) or even one book (see Halperin and Carmichael), I include narratives, laws, and poetry throughout the Hebrew Bible that focus on the representation of the "dysfunctional" family construct. I wish to make it quite clear that I am not using the term *dysfunctional* as a clinical term of art. Clinically, the term is used to describe a situation in which the psychopathology of individual family members and the psychopathology of the family unit interact in such a way that neither the individual nor the family is able to function. That is to say, the family unit does not promote and nurture the needs of the individual members, and therefore the individual family members are unable to function in society. Rather, I am using the term here to refer to those family relationships that are proscribed in the text and hence contrary to the societal norms embedded within the Hebrew Bible. As a result of this premise, a second difference between my work and that of Halperin's is that I view deviations from these norms as *deviations* rather than as "symptoms of a recognizable mental illness." Third, I examine the intertextuality of biblical literature with other contemporaneous works. My thesis is that the Hebrew Bible, despite its reputation as the preeminent monotheistic religious document, echoes with incest themes and narratives common to polytheistic literature including a strong earlier matriarchal polytheism, wars between rival deities, and an eventual supplanting of the goddesses with a single male deity. Fourth, I include plastic representations of many of the relevant biblical texts as alternative (and supportive) readings of my own that highlight the psychoanalytic interpretations, particularly those that are Oedipal in nature.

There are several aspects to my approach that should be stated at the outset.

First and foremost, I take my own feminist stance as an explicit starting point and as Freud stated in the preface to the Hebrew translation of his *Introductory Lectures on Psychoanalysis*, "much [of this text] contradicts traditional opinions and wounds deeply-rooted feelings . . . it is bound . . . to provoke" (1916–17:11).

Second, unlike many biblical scholars who see the Hebrew Bible in terms of discrete strands that they identify as "sources," "traditions," or "literary forms," I approach the Hebrew Bible as a single literary work. While it is tempting to resolve textual ambiguities by resorting to the common assumption that narrative "problems" are a result of the conflation of these sources, my concern is their *literary* effect.

Third, my theoretical approach is literary, albeit *influenced* by psychoanalytic theory. Unfortunately, the relationship between literature and psychoanalysis usually implies a relationship of subordination rather than coordination. Literature is submitted to the "authority," to the "prestige," of psychoanalysis (Felman 1980:5). The literary text is considered as a body of language to *be* interpreted, while psychoanalysis is a body of knowledge used *to* interpret. What I have tried to do throughout this book is to read psychoanalytic literary theory and the Bible concurrently rather than to provide a hierarchical positioning. That is, I have not been reading the Bible *in light* of Freud and Lacan, but rather *while reading* these theorists. Certainly, I do not consider either a biblical scholar. Rather, I appropriate their psychoanalytic *approaches* as tools for biblical interpretation.

Thus, the remainder of this book is devoted to a few of the many Hebrew Bible narratives that depict dysfunctional familial relationships (often in a positive manner), and the approach I use is psychoanalytic literary theory, notwithstanding some modifications. A short description of the chapters to follow seems to be in order at this point. Chapter 2 is an overview of the laws that deal with "acceptable" and "unacceptable" biblical sexual practices, mores, and societal prohibitions. These laws are significant in that they have had a major effect on Western civilization. For example, the Levitical prohibitions (with the addition of rules from Roman law in some instances), became the law governing incestuous relations in those countries where the church was most influential. For centuries, not only were the prohibitions of Leviticus 18 and 20 in force but also a great many others derived from them.[4]

As I discuss in chapter 2, sex-determined biological difference, gender difference, and difference in sexual orientation and/or sexual practice are mainstays in the definition of patriarchal biblical societies where power lies in the hands of heterosexual males. Thus, in order to maintain authority, it is necessary for heterosexual males to define themselves as the norm by marking all others as different. Other sexual practices viewed as deviations from the accepted biblical sociosexual mores include: incest, bestiality, adultery, rape, prostitution, and homosexuality. (I have retained the traditional term *homosexuality*, here used without gendering or activity specification. Further elaboration, including the question of what is meant by homosexuality in the Hebrew Bible is discussed in chapter 2.) With the exception of bestiality, the descriptions, prohibitions, and penalties for participating in these acts differ for males and for females.

Chapter 3 explores the narrative in Gen 1:26—3:24, one of the best known and most explicated biblical texts. I realize that any attempt to examine this story yet again is dangerous. This reservation notwithstanding, I approach the story of Adam, Eve, and the Deity as the first (among many) accounts of dysfunctional families depicted in the Hebrew Bible, particularly as relating to father-daughter relationships. Many questions arise when looking at this "family constellation." Who/where is the mother? Who is the father? What is the familial relationship of Adam and Eve? How well do the family members get along? Why is the Deity/father angry enough to punish so severely? I suggest that the "missing" mother in this narrative can help answer these questions. Apparent lack of primal mother notwithstanding, I see Mom lurking *somewhere* in the garden.

Chapter 4 examines issues dealing with paternal identification in biblical texts and the attendant impact of the covenant of circumcision. The society that created biblical literature is undoubtedly phallic.

Characterizing biblical Israel as a phallocentric society is by no means an empty generalization: the Hebrew Bible posits the human penis as the explicit, emblematic, and exclusive symbol of religious identity and membership of the communal order. The penis symbolizes the special link between this society's deity and the members of the community. It serves as a physical reminder of both inclusion in the community and exclusion from it. Circumcision defines males and males only as the full members of the covenant community. Such a characterization, however, does not imply that males, because they have a penis, are the owners of the Phallus (in the Lacanian sense). As I discuss, while biblical scholars have discussed the political and religious implications of this covenant, they have not paid much attention to the "token" that seals the arrangement.[5] Why the penis?

The book of Genesis relates two episodes of a father drinking wine to excess, having a sexual encounter with his offspring, and subsequently condemning not his offspring but his grandchildren. Genesis 9:18-27 narrates the tale of an inebriated Noah and Genesis 19 relates the story of Lot. Most commentators have excused the fathers' behavior and censured the children. Chapter 5 is an alternative reading—one in which neither father is blameless. I see the stories as related in that under the influence of alcohol, Lot and Noah acted upon repressed desires or frustrations and knowingly engaged in incestuous acts.

The Lot story exemplifies the most common type of incest and has many similarities to clinical reports of father-daughter incestuous relationships: the disintegrated family, the father who has lost his patriarchal role, the abuse of alcohol, the mother who looks away, and the involvement of more than one daughter. The usually unconscious desire of the father toward the daughter is, in this instance, consciously acted out. Similarly, psychoanalytic literary theory, other literary representations of the incest motif, and clinical situations involving father-son incest allow the Noah narrative to be read as involving either Noah's *fantasizing* about a homosexual activity or possibly even actually *initiating* such a liaison with his son Ham.

Many ancient mythologies contain tales of two brothers, one of whom is killed or defeated by the other in some way. Often, one of the brothers is of heroic character, sometimes immortal, while the other is of human origin, weaker, and *very* mortal. Often fated to perish young, he leads a diminished existence beside his heroic brother, as in the relationships of Heracles and Iphicles, of Agamemnon and Menelaus, and of Hector and Paris. Certainly, the tragic theme of feuding brothers is one of the most frequent conflicts in biblical literature. The first biblical murder is fratricide, and the subsequent relationships of Esau and Jacob, Joseph and his brothers, Jehoram and his brothers, and Absalom and Amnon are far from harmonious. Freud relates the frequency and powerful elemental effect of the sibling conflict to our first impressions of childhood: siblings are our first potentially *conquerable* rivals. Chapter 6 examines the relationship of Jacob and Esau in light of Freud's brother/brother scenario and the transference of the Oedipal construct from father to brother. In chapter 7 I use Freud's theories on brother/brother/sister relationships with regard to Absalom/Amnon/Tamar and Cain/Abel/unnamed sister. In both chapters 6 and 7 sibling love evolves into hatred and is informed with Lacanian theory.

In sum, the relationships discussed in the following chapters run the full gamut of familial ties: father/daughter; mother/son; father/son; brother/sister; brother/brother. Indeed, the Hebrew Bible is replete with consanguineous sex! Abraham twice acknowledges his wife to be his sister, and his son, Isaac, marries his father's brother's daughter. Isaac's son, Jacob, acquires two wives, sisters who constitute a lineal double of each other. That is to say, Jacob marries two of his father's father's brother's son's son's daughters, who are simultaneously his mother's brother's daughters and thereby are connected back to Abraham. In the next generation, Reuben sleeps with his father's second wife's maid, symbolically violating family purity laws, and Judah sleeps with his daughter-in-law. (Certainly Jacob views Reuben's act as a violation of family purity laws. In Gen 49:4, Jacob censures Reuben for "going up to" his father's bed and "defiling" it. The verb Jacob uses, *ʿālîtā*, is from the stem *ḥ-l-t* ("pollute, defile, profane") and is used in connection with sexual depravity (see, e.g., Lev 19:29; 21:9). The list of prohibited yet consummated sexual relations is quite impressive: Adam-Eve, Noah-Ham, Lot-his daughters, Reuben-Bilhah, and Jacob-Tamar all involve parent-child incestuous congress or exposure, while Adam-Eve and Abraham-Sarah are brother-sister unions (as is Amnon-Tamar in 2 Samuel), and Isaac-Rebecca and Jacob-Leah-Rachel are cousin marriages. As the chart on the following page indicates, contra Lévi-Strauss, familial and

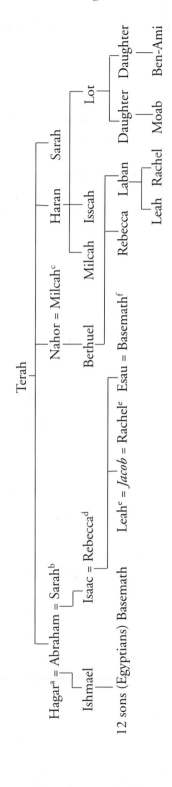

a. Hagar is Sarah's handmaid.
b. Sarah is Abraham's half-sister (both children of Terah).
c. Milcah is Nahor's niece.
d. Rebecca is Isaac's first cousin, once removed.
e. Leah and Rachel are Jacob's second cousins, once removed.
f. Basemath is Esau's first cousin.

sexual integrity in Genesis alone seem to be observed more in the breach than in the maintenance.

And the theme of forbidden relationships does not end with Genesis! The Hebrew Bible is replete with banned sexual behavior. Significantly, this same text has been used as a paradigm of righteous behavior, and throughout history the Bible has also been used as a justification for various societal abuses such as slavery, misogyny, and child abuse. The following chapters examine the influence of the biblical text's representations of the dysfunctional family on later literature and the plastic arts in order to explicate the power of this "seminal" text.

Chapter 2 ———————————————

Sin and Sex, Sex and Sin:
The Hebrew Bible and Human Sexuality

> There is a well-known comic anecdote according to which an intelligent
> Jewish boy was asked who the mother of Moses was. He replied without
> hesitation: "The Princess." "No," he was told, "she only took him out of
> the water." "That's what *she* says," he replied. (Freud 1916–17:161)

Psychoanalysis *and* the Hebrew Bible deal with many aspects of
human sexuality. Throughout this book I juxtapose some psychoanalytic writings with biblical narratives that deal with the sexual life of
human beings.[1] This chapter provides some background material on
what the Hebrew Bible deems "acceptable" and "unacceptable" sexual
practices and societal prohibitions.

What Is/Is Not "Acceptable Sex" . . . and Why?
Biblical references to male and female erogenous zones, primary and
secondary, are generally euphemistic, and the culture reflected in the
Bible protects the penis and its physical environs with vigor. The phallic, phallocentric society that created biblical literature posits the
human penis as the explicit characteristic of religious identity. The
penis is the special link between its god and the members of the community. As I discuss more fully in chapter 4, circumcision, imported
from other cultures and reinterpreted, defines males as members of the
community. By this token, women are excluded a priori from that
symbolic order, and bonding with the (male) god is stamped on the
(male) body.

Sex-determined biological difference, gender difference, and difference in sexual orientation and/or sexual practice are characteristics of
patriarchal societies in which power lies in the hands of heterosexual
males. Heterosexual males in such societies reinforce their authority by
defining themselves as the norm and marking all others as different. Sexual practices viewed as so-called deviations from the accepted biblical
sociosexual mores include, in addition to homosexuality (see page 10),

incest, bestiality, adultery, rape, and prostitution. With the exception of bestiality, the descriptions, prohibitions, and penalties for participating in these acts differ for males and for females. Since it is questionable whether masturbation is considered a category of "negative" sexual activity in the Hebrew Bible, I shall not discuss masturbation. (The sin of Onan [Genesis 38] is not necessarily that of masturbation; otherwise, oblique references to seminal emission, such as "a man, when an emission of semen comes out of him" [Lev 15:16], refer to the emission rather than its circumstances. Female masturbation is never mentioned in the Hebrew Bible.)

The Laws

Biblical sexual prohibitions are significant since they have had a major effect on Western law. The Levitical prohibitions (with the addition of rules from Roman law in some instances), became the law governing incestuous relations in those countries where the church was most influential. For centuries, not only were the prohibitions of Leviticus 18 and 20 in force but also a great many others derived from them.[2]

In the Hebrew Bible, Leviticus (chap. 12 and following) is primarily a code of moral and ritual laws whose motivation is "holiness." (In this context, holiness refers to the entire people, not just to the priestly tribe.) Since a major concern of the writers of the Levitical and Deuteronomical text(s) seems to have been the creation of rules that would shape the identity of the emerging nation, these passages state over and over again a claim that the Israelites are different from the surrounding cultures. As a result, they established incest rules by which Israelites could and should define themselves. It is possible, however, that the Israelites were not as "different" as they proclaimed themselves to be. According to the rabbis,[3] the Israelite attitudes toward sexuality were similar to those of the Persians. Indeed, the *Babylonian Talmud Berakhoth* 8b notes that the Zoroastrians were equally chaste in sexual matters:

> It has been taught: R. Akiba says: "For three things I like the Medes [Persians]: When they cut meat, they cut it only on the table; when they kiss, they kiss only the hand; and when they hold counsel, they do so only in the field." . . . R. Gamaliel says: "For three things do I like the Persians: They are temperate in their eating, modest in the privy, and chaste in another matter [in sexual matters]."

However, certain cultural similarities with their surrounding neighbors notwithstanding, within the biblical construct, segregation of both persons *and* things is a primary consideration. For instance, Lev 19:19

and Deut 22:11 prohibit the wearing of *sha'atnez*, cloth combining wool and linen. (The Levitical passage defines the prohibition as *beged kil'ayim*—cloth made from a mixture of two kinds of material; the Deuteronomical text is more specific and prohibits wearing *ṣemer ûpištîm yaḥdāw*—wool and linen together.) The clothing of the priests was notably exempt from the prohibition of *sha'atnez*. Exodus 28:6, 8, 15, and 39:29 prescribe various pieces to be made of linen and colored wool interwoven. Although seemingly irrelevant to the discussion at hand, this prohibition is considered a prime example of a divine statute that has no rational explanation, and Jewish philosophers have attempted to rationalize its intent in ways that are reminiscent of both incest prohibitions and dietary laws. Maimonides explains that the wearing of mixed garments was forbidden since heathen priests wore such garments (*Guide for the Perplexed* 3:37).

In other words, since biblical writings emphasize the differences between the Israelite community and all others, prohibitions against and penalties for illicit relations, homicidal cult practices, and magic probably exist for the same reason as the *sha'atnez* and food prohibitions: separation and distinction from the neighboring tribes whose perceived idolatrous and immoral practices were to be avoided. The Levitical verses that deal with illicit sexual relations, for example, are encased by an introduction that castigates the Egyptians and Canaanites for the depravity of their sexual practices: "You shall not do as they do in the land of Egypt, where you dwelt, and you shall not do as they do in the land of Canaan, to which I am bringing you. You shall not walk in their statutes" (Lev 18:3).

Total destruction and exile is the threat if these laws are not followed: "Lest the land vomit you out, when you defile it, as it vomited out the nation that was before you. For whoever shall do any of these abominations, the persons that do them shall be cut off from among their people" (Lev 18:28-29). For the purposes of this book, I would like to concentrate on those aspects of holiness that refer to human sexuality. Within this context, I am defining sexuality according to the laws in the three juridical texts (Leviticus 18, 20 and Deut 27:20, 22-23).

Of the list of prohibitions of sexual relations in Leviticus, that of chapter 18 is the most unified. After an introduction that attributes abhorrent sexual practices to Egypt and Canaan (vv. 1-5), a superscription (v. 6), and the prohibition against a man "uncovering the

nakedness" of his father, a list of twelve categories of forbidden females
is presented (vv. 7b-18):

mother (v. 7)
father's wife (v. 8)
maternal and/or paternal sister, from the household or outside
    it (v. 9)
son's or daughter's daughter (v. 10)
stepmother's daughter by the same father (v. 11)
paternal aunt (v. 12)
maternal aunt (v. 13)
uncle's wife (v. 14)
daughter-in-law (v. 15)
brother's wife (v. 16)
woman and her daughter, and their female descendants (v. 17)
woman and her sister (v. 18)

Other sexual prohibitions follow (vv. 19-23):

intercourse with menstruating women (v. 19)
adultery (v. 20)
sacrifice of "seed" to Moloch (v. 21)
male homosexuality (v. 22)
bestiality of male and female (v. 23)

The list of Leviticus 20 is of a somewhat different nature, although
males (again) are addressed. In addition, the terminology differs slightly
as do the punishments. Seven categories of forbidden females are included within other categories of sexual transgressions:

father's wife (v. 11)
daughter-in-law (v. 12)
woman and daughter (v. 14)
maternal and/or paternal sister (v. 17)
maternal or paternal aunt (v. 19)
uncle's wife (v. 20)
brother's wife (v. 21)

Other sexual prohibitions are interspersed:

male homosexuality (v. 13)
bestiality of male and female (v. 15-16)
intercourse with menstruating women (v. 18)

Unlisted here (by comparison to Leviticus 18) are:

adultery
sacrifice of "seed" to Moloch

man's granddaughter
stepmother's daughter by the same father
woman and her sister

The remainder of this chapter examines various legal aspects of forbidden relationships.

Abomination Number One: Incest

Incest[4] taboos in the ancient world were not universal. Indeed, sexual relations among blood relatives were directly encouraged in many ancient cultures, often based upon divine example. Most of these societies were tribal, and sibling marriages formed the simplest types of kinship systems. That the historical works and literature of the ancients are filled with tales of incest and that the practice occurred among ancient people is validated further by the especially strict customs, taboos, and punishments that eventually evolved to prohibit their continuance.

Incest rules have fascinated scholars of various disciplines—anthropologists, ethnographers, historians, philosophers, sociologists, psychologists, and theologians, among others—and attempts to explain the prohibitions are associated with writers as diverse as Philo, Plutarch, Augustine, Maimonides, Jeremy Taylor, Hugo Grotius, David Hume, Charles Montesquieu, Jeremy Bentham, Lewis Morgan, Émile Durkheim, James Frazer, Sigmund Freud, Bronislaw Malinowski, and Claude Lévi-Strauss (Carmichael 1997:3). Yet, despite all of the scholarly attention, there is little consensus over the *origin* of the incest taboo. According to some behavioral psychologists, for example, prohibitions against incest are "uniquely human," an instinctive safeguard against the consequences of inbreeding. Behavioral psychologists who argue otherwise, however, note the lack of universality in attitudes toward incest. That is, different societies have different taboos concerning paternal versus maternal sisters as well as extensions of the taboo from blood to marital kin.

Some sociological theories form a correlation between sex and power and posit incest prohibitions as exogamy/endogamy rules that help regulate socioeconomic forces. This school of thought holds that woman is the basic social currency. As such, she establishes and regulates both the economy and the hierarchy, and that, therefore, all male members of the clan must outbreed. In other words, incest prohibitions provide a collective male sanction against aggressive males who might attempt to seize power over society's basic commodity (women), beginning with their own female relatives. This explanation might apply to the biblical taboos discussed below since, as is well recognized, biblical society was by and large patriarchal, and the "father's house" was the basic family unit. Since typically the nuclear unit encompassed two to three generations of blood kin, marital kin, and dependents, incest laws helped set boundaries.

Thus, Lévi-Strauss's well-known analysis of kinship systems seems particularly relevant to biblical literature. Lévi-Strauss argues that the most significant rule governing any family structure is the ubiquitous existence of the incest taboo that imposes the social aim of exogamy and alliance upon the biological events of sex and procreation. Indeed, as I discuss in chapter 1, Genesis alone nearly constitutes a meditation on the questions that concern from where wives for the patriarchy should come, how closely they should be related to "us," or how "other" they should be (Pitt-Rivers 1977:128, 165). Is there a pattern here? Certainly, the numerous examples of incestuous unions indicate that at least among the major characters of the Hebrew Bible the incest prohibitions seem to be observed more in the breach than in the maintenance.

Other sociologists write that incest prohibitions might have evolved from a concern with procreation, not in terms of defective births but rather in terms of the inability to produce children by certain unions. For example, the (observed) difficulty of postmenopausal conception may have led to a prohibition against sexual relations involving a man with a *woman* relative of an older generation but not between a woman and an older *male* relative (as in the case of Isaac and Sarah). Certainly, the astonishment expressed by Sarah and Abraham when she becomes pregnant in her old age points in this direction. In Gen 17:17, "Abraham fell upon his face and laughed" (*wayyippōl 'abrāhām 'al-pānāyw*) when he heard that Sarah was to have a child. Later, the narrator emphasizes the absurdity of that prediction: "Abraham and Sarah are old and coming in years. For Sarah, it had ceased to be after the manner of women" (Gen 18:11).

Not surprisingly, the postmenopausal Sarah, hearing of the prediction does not believe it: "Sarah laughed inwardly and said, "After I am shriveled! I shall have pleasure? My lord is old!'" (Gen 18:12).

As is apparent from the lists quoted on page 18–19, the Levitical and Deuteronomical incest laws are quite specific, and some of the prohibitions differ from those of today. For example, although biblical notions of incest *include* marital restrictions, biblical concepts of incest are broader than specific marital prohibitions. In fact, marital ties are seldom mentioned explicitly.

It should be noted that the law of levirate marriage (Deut 25:5-10) contradicts the incest prohibition of sexual intercourse with a sister-in-law. According to the Deuteronomical requirement, if a married man dies childless, his brother *must* marry the widow, and their firstborn child will be the heir of the deceased man (any subsequent children will be heirs of the second husband). If the brother refuses his obligation, the widow must humiliate him publicly.[5]

I would like to highlight that the Levitical list contains no express prohibition against intercourse with a full sister (as compared to maternal or paternal sister). Nor is there a prohibition against a father having intercourse with a daughter, as I discuss in subsequent chapters. By contrast, both the Hittite Code[6] and the Code of Hammurabi[7] prohibited both a son having intercourse with his mother and a father having intercourse with his daughter. (Compare Article 199 of the Hittite Code, which says that a citizen may not have sexual intercourse with his mother, his daughter, or his son. Compare also Article 154 of the Code of Hammurabi, which says that if a citizen has sexual intercourse with his daughter, then he is exiled from the city; and Article 157, which says that if a citizen has intercourse with his mother after the death of his father, then both are to be burned at the stake [*Ancient Near Eastern Texts* 1958:196]). The lack of biblical prohibition of brother-sister incest and father-daughter incest is particularly curious since the sexual abuse of a son or daughter (or a sister by a brother) is the most prevalent in the world of experience (Herman and Hirschman 1981).

Nudity and/or Uncovering the Nakedness

One salient feature of all of these biblical laws is that the juridical texts are addressed exclusively to *males:* males are subjects of the incest prohibitions, and for the most part females are objects. That is to say, specific blood-kindred and marriage-kindred females are cited as forbidden to the relevant *males.* The prohibitions that refer to a marriage kinship are often referred to as "exposing the nakedness" of some male relative (Lev 18:7-8, 14, 16). For example, in the list of forbidden relations, sex with one's father's wife is referred to as "exposing the nakedness of one's father." The implication is that when a son has relations

with his father's wife, a woman who may or may not be his biological
mother, he is trespassing upon the spot where the nakedness of his
father has already been exposed. G. Wenham arrives at a similar analysis: "Foreign to our way of thinking is the idea that a wife's nakedness
is her husband's nakedness and vice versa. In other words, marriage or
more precisely marital intercourse, makes the man and wife as closely
related as parents and children. In the words of Gen 2:24, 'they
become one flesh'" (1979:255). Similarly, when incest occurs with a
father's brother's wife or a brother's wife, the nakedness of these men is
exposed, since the kinship tie through marriage is metaphorically a
man's nakedness. In other words, it is the nakedness of a male relative
that has made these women kin.

Despite a definition of incest based on the term *nakedness*, the
Hebrew Bible, by and large, seems to lack evidence of either a social
understanding of nakedness or its more common uses. For example,
when Tamar dresses as a prostitute to seduce Judah, she covers herself
completely (see chap. 4 for a discussion of this narrative): "She put off
her widow's garments, and put on a veil, wrapping herself up, and sat
at the entrance to Enaim, which is on the road to Timnah; for she saw
that Shelah was grown up, and she had not been given to him in marriage" (Gen 38:14). Similarly, Joseph is attractive to Potiphar's wife,
although he always remained clothed: "She caught him by his garment, saying, 'Lie with me.' But he left his garment in her hand, and
fled and got out of the house" (Gen 39:12). And Tamar is dressed in
a tunic (the narrative is careful to tell us) when Amnon rapes her:
"Now she was wearing a long robe with sleeves; for thus were the virgin daughters of the king clad of old. So his servant put her out, and
bolted the door after her" (2 Sam 13:18; see chap. 5 for a further discussion). It is only Bath-Sheba's nakedness that is portrayed as sexually
tempting to a male: "It happened, late one afternoon, when David
arose from his couch and was walking upon the roof of the king's
house, that he saw from the roof a woman bathing; and the woman
was very beautiful" (2 Sam 11:2).[8]

Significantly, the Hebrew Bible does not seem to use nakedness as a
marker of either character or marital status, but it does indicate vulnerability, as the exchange between Michal and David upon his success
in bringing the ark into Jerusalem indicates: "And David returned to
bless his household. But Michal the daughter of Saul came out to meet
David, and said, 'How the king of Israel honored himself today,

uncovering himself today before the eyes of his servants' maids, as one of the vulgar fellows shamelessly uncovers himself!'" (2 Sam 6:20). In this narrative, as David's procession enters the city, Michal watches the proceedings from a window and observes her husband "leaping and dancing before YHWH." Michal speaks with authority, with an assumed voice of strength, and her speech concerns "hônor." Her sarcastic comment indicates clearly that she regards David's behavior as inappropriate—instead of conducting himself as a king, David shamelessly frolics before his servants' maids and the weight of her criticism lies entirely in the fact that David has "uncovered" himself. (Since David is wearing only a loincloth [2 Sam 6:14] it is more than likely that David is exposing himself, and not just "some part of his thighs or legs.")

This aversion to male nakedness in antiquity appears to have been to a large degree unique to the Israelites (the ancient Persians' apparently chaste sexual practices notwithstanding [see p. 16]). From the ancient Near East to Greek and Roman cultures, there was little squeamishness about the display of the phallus in sacred contexts or in the representation or description of the genitalia of the gods. Sumerian art, for example, regularly portrayed naked male divinities, and their literature did not refrain from description of their genitalia.[9] Much later representations in Greek and Roman art of naked male divinities, especially Pan, are of course quite common; Greek and Roman art depict soldiers going into battle wearing only a loincloth as well as priests of mystery cults performing their duties while naked in further attempts to ward off evil.

Surprisingly, there are very few rabbinic comments on Greek and Roman portrayals of the genitalia of their male gods. One exception is a references in the *Babylonian Talmud* that describes how a queen used the phallus on a statue of a god to satisfy herself sexually:

> "But has it not been stated, 'And also Maacah the mother of Asa the king, he removed her from being queen, because she had made an abominable image. . . .' What means [abominable image]?—Rab Judah said: '[An object that] intensifies licentiousness as R. Joseph taught: "It was a kind of phallus with which she had daily connection."' ('Abod. Zar. 44a)

Despite the paucity of evidence, however, there can be little doubt that the rabbis would have seen the statues of Hermes and Priapus as ridiculous. According to *'Abod. Zar.* 33.8, 43a for example: "Ba'al: His head was a penis, and it was like a pea." In other words, the rabbis mock the biblical Ba'al not only because he was represented as a penis, but a small one at that!

Abomination Number Two: Adultery

Adultery, as defined in the Hebrew Bible, is the voluntary sexual intercourse between a married woman (or a "free" woman engaged by payment of a brideprice) and a man other than her husband. (The payment of a brideprice established a marriage tie only in the case of a free woman; slave women were "designated" for marriage by their masters [Exod 21:8], and therefore no marriage tie existed before the woman had been redeemed or freed.) It should be noted that the extramarital intercourse of a married man is *not* viewed as adulterous unless the woman involved is married or engaged. Adultery is prohibited in Exod 20:14 and 5:18 (*lō' tin'ap*), where it is listed between murder and theft, and in Jer 7:9; Ezek 16:38; Hos 4:2; Ps 50:18; Prov 6:30 ff.; and Job 24:14-15, where it is listed as one among many offenses against society. As with all of the biblical sexual prohibitions, adultery "defiles" those who commit it: "You shall not lie carnally with your neighbor's wife, and defile yourself with her" (Lev 18:20). Indeed, adultery is such a grave offense that it is punishable by stoning, a procedure specifically prescribed for crimes that threaten the well-being of the nation as a whole, although there is no indication within the Hebrew Bible as to whether the severe provisions of the law were ever actually carried out. (Again, there is a difference in the case of a slave woman: a sexual relationship between a man and a designated slave woman is not punishable by stoning, but rather the male must pay an indemnity and bring a guilt offering [Lev 19:20–22]. The question of the slave woman's consent is not raised in the law, presumably because she is even less a "legal person" than a free woman and her consent is, therefore, legally immaterial.)

While other ancient Near Eastern law collections also prescribe the death penalty for adulterers, they treat adultery as an offense against the husband alone, and they permit the aggrieved husband to waive or mitigate the punishment. (Compare Article 19 of the Code of Hammurabi, which states that if a wife of a citizen commits adultery, then she and her partner are to be tied up and tried by ordeal in the river. If, however, the woman's husband pardons her, then the monarch can pardon her partner. Compare also Article 15 of the

Middle Assyrian Code,[10] which allows that if the aggrieved husband asks to have his wife go free, then the ruler or the elders shall let the defendant go free [Matthews and Benjamin 1997:104, 116].) Biblical law, however, allows no such mitigation. Because the marriage bond is described as "divinely sanctioned" (Prov 2:17; Mal 2:14), the prohibition of adultery is of divine origin, and God as well as the husband is described as "offended" by adultery: "Then God said to him [Abimelech] in the dream, 'Yes, I know that you have done this in the integrity of your heart, and it was I who kept you from sinning *against me;* therefore I did not let you touch her'" (Gen 20:6, emphasis added). As an offense against God, adultery cannot be pardoned by humans. (It does appear, however, that at one point it was the husband's right to punish his adulterous wife *himself,*[11] that it was only when adultery was elevated to the rank of a grave offense against *God* as well that the husband was required to resort to the priests or to the courts.)

Deuteronomy 22:23–27 presents a set of circumstances that mitigate the law in some instances:

> If there is a betrothed virgin, and a man meets her in the city and lies with her, then you shall bring them both out to the gate of that city, and you shall stone them to death with stones, the young woman because she did not cry for help though she was in the city, and the man because he violated his neighbor's wife; so you shall purge the evil from the midst of you. But if in the open country a man meets a young woman who is betrothed, and the man seizes her and lies with her, then only the man who lay with her shall die. But to the young woman you shall do nothing; in the young woman there is no offense punishable by death, for this case is like that of a man attacking and murdering his neighbor; because he came upon her in the open country, and though the betrothed young woman cried for help there was no one to rescue her. (Deut 22:23-27)

In other words, if the sexual act between a man and an engaged woman takes place in the open country where no help would be available in response to a cry from her, she is presumed to have been forced and only her attacker is stoned; if the sexual act occurs in the city, however, help would presumably have been afforded her had she cried out, and she is presumed to have consented, and therefore she is stoned with the male. Unfortunately for raped wives, no such presumptive distinction is made in passage regarding the married woman: she and the male must die regardless of circumstance: "If a man is found lying with the wife of another man, both of them shall die, the man who lay with the woman, and the woman; so you shall purge the evil from Israel" (Deut 22:22).

The theme of adultery appears in several biblical narratives that are discussed in greater detail in subsequent chapters. For example, Abraham's and Isaac's wives are taken or nearly taken into the harems of foreign rulers who believe them to be the patriarchs' sisters (Gen 12:10–20; 20:2ff.; 26:6–11). As I have discussed elsewhere, it is noteworthy that these passages seem to assume that these foreigners would sooner commit murder than adultery, "the great sin" (Rashkow 1993:26–64). In addition, Tamar's fornication (Genesis 38) is viewed as adulterous, at least by Judah, since she had already been assigned for Shelah because of the law of the levirate marriage (see p. 21). Further, Potiphar's wife attempts to seduce Joseph, who refuses to sin against his master (see p. 35) and David commits adultery with Bath-Sheba, wife of Uriah the Hittite (2 Samuel 11).

In the Hebrew Bible, adultery is used often as a metaphor for idolatry, and the exclusive loyalty that Israel must give God is analogous to the exclusive fidelity a wife owes her husband. Indeed, the metaphor of marriage to express Israel's relationship with God employs adultery language to describe worship of other gods. That is to say, according to the texts, Israel literally "whores" after other gods: "You take of their daughters for your sons, and their daughters whore after their gods and make your sons whore after their gods" (Exod 34:16). And as a result of Israel's adultery, YHWH becomes "jealous" (*qannā'*):[12] "I the LORD your God am a jealous God, visiting the iniquity of the fathers upon the children to the third and the fourth generation of those who hate me" (Exod 20:5).

Adultery is one of the crimes with which the prophets, particularly Hosea (4:2; etc.) and Jeremiah (7:9; 23:10, 14; etc.), charge Israel. Indeed, Hosea's own wife is described as adulterous, and the book of Proverbs warns extensively against the seductions of the adulterous woman (2:16-19; 5:1-14; 6:24-35; 7:5-27; cf. 30:20). The adulterous woman rarely is found in her own home (Prov 7:11-12), a frequent description of promiscuous women throughout the ancient Near East. (Compare Article 141 of the Code of Hammurabi, which describes an adulterous wife as one who "leaves the house of her husband on her own business" [Matthews and Benjamin 1997:105]). According to the book of Proverbs, the adulterous wife uses a "smooth tongue" to lure the foolish "like oxen to the slaughter" to her bed (2:16; 5:3; 6:24; 7:13ff.). Adulterers seek the protection of darkness (Prov 7:9; Job 24:15; Eccl 23:18) and are more foolish than a thief, who will at least escape with his life (Prov 6:30ff.). Dealings with the adulterous woman lead inevitably to loss of wealth (Prov 5:9-10) and life (Prov 2:18-19, 5:5; 6:32-35; 7:22-23, 26-27). Instead, one ought to drink water from one's own cistern (*šᵉtēh-mayim mibbôrekā*) (Prov 5:15) and not from another's.

Abomination Number Three: Prostitution

Prostitution, sexual intercourse for payment or for religious purposes, was practiced by males and females within the Hebrew Bible. The Hebrew Bible discusses two types of prostitute: the secular prostitute (*zonah*) and the cult prostitute (*kᵉdeshah*). Although the two types of prostitution are similar in that they both involve sexual activity outside the bounds of matrimony, there are certain differences between them. Only women appear to have been secular prostitutes in the Hebrew Bible; on the other hand, both men are women are referred to as cult prostitutes. As discussed below, although the secular prostitute is viewed as an inferior occupation, secular prostitution was tolerated (and apparently was quite prevalent) as long as the woman was not married, in which case her prostitution became the more serious crime of adultery. Cult prostitution, however, was rejected on both moral and religious principals and totally prohibited.

As with the adulterer, the word *zenut*—"prostitution"—is applied both to common and sacred prostitution and often is used metaphorically.

Cultic sexual service by men and women appears to date back to the Neolithic period and to various cults of the Mother-Goddess or of the so-called Great Goddess in her many manifestations (Gimbutas 1982; James 1959; Lerner 1986). The archaeological evidence of the existence of female figurines, with exaggerated breasts, hips, and buttocks, is abundant throughout the Mediterranean, and many were found in what archaeologists have interpreted as shrines. In addition, there is a significant amount of linguistic, literary, pictorial, and legal evidence from which scholars have reconstructed the worship of female goddesses and the lives and activities of priests and priestesses in the ancient Near East during the Neo-Babylonian period.

Cult prostitution came into being in the ancient Near East because the Babylonians and Canaanites, for example, thought of the gods and goddesses as actually dwelling in the temple, not as symbolically represented there. The staff of the temple, the various ranks of priests and priestesses, artisans, workers, and slaves, all worked to care for and feed the god/goddess. Daily meals were prepared and set out for the deity; a bed was prepared; and music was played for his or her entertainment. For people who regarded fertility as sacred and essential to their own survival, caring for the gods and goddesses included, in some cases, offering them sexual services (Oppenheim 1964:187–92). Thus, a class of temple prostitutes—male and female—developed, and sexual activity for and on behalf of the deity was considered beneficial to the people as a whole and therefore sacred. The practices varied according to the god or goddess, the place, and the period, and it appears that commercial (common) prostitution flourished near or within the temple as well.

Two "historic" accounts of sexual activities in and around the Babylonian temples have influenced modern historians. One was that of Herodotus (fifth century BCE), which describes religious prostitution in the temple of the goddess Mylitta:

> Every woman born in the country must once in her life go and sit down in the precinct of Venus [Mylitta], and there consort with a stranger. . . . A woman who has once taken her seat is not allowed to return home till one of the strangers throws a silver coin into her lap, and takes her with him beyond the holy ground. . . . The silver coin may be of any size. . . . The woman goes with the first man who throws her money, and rejects no one. When she has gone with him, and so satisfied the goddess, she returns home, and from that time forth no gift however great will prevail with her. Such of the women . . . who are ugly have to stay a long time before they can fulfill the law. Some have waited three or four years in the precinct. (Herodotus 1920:199)

The other account was that of the Roman geographer Strabo four hundred years later, which confirms Herodotus. No other confirmation of Herodotus's account appears to exist, and there do not seem to be any known laws regulating or even referring to this practice.

The common ancient Near Eastern understanding of the sexual act as holy (or at least potentially so) was emphatically rejected by Israel, although the Canaanite terms *k̆deshim*—masculine—and *k̆deshot*—feminine—("holy/consecrated ones") were used to refer to illicit cult prostitutes. Since sex in Israel belonged to the order of the profane (that is, not religious or holy), its proper uses included both enjoyment and procreation. Emphasis upon the former accounts for literature such as the Song of Songs and also explains Israel's concession (in the male interest) to common prostitution. For the most part, however, extramarital sex was discouraged for practical, moral, and religious reasons.

Sacred prostitution, because of its association with idolatry, was the object of numerous attacks in the Bible, especially in the historical and prophetic books (cf., e.g., 2 Kgs 23:4-14; Jer 2:20; Ezek 23:37ff.). Terms connected with harlotry are used figuratively to characterize unfaithfulness toward the Deity (Num 25:1-2; Judg 2:17; 8:27, 33; Jer 3:6; Ezek 6:9; Hos 4:12; passim). However, various biblical passages (Deut 23:18; Hos 1–3; 14:14; Jeremiah 2; Ezekiel 23; Numbers 25; 1 Kgs 14:24; 15:12; 22:47; 2 Kgs 23:7; passim) illustrate that fertility rites were extensively practiced in ancient Israel and that there were male and female prostitutes in Israel and Judah during the monarchy. In Judah, cult prostitutes were, from time to time, the object of royal decrees of expulsion (cf. 1 Kgs 14:24; 15:12; 22:47; 2 Kgs 23:7; Hos 4:14), and Deut 23:18-19 forbids Israelites, men and women alike, to become sacred prostitutes, and states that their wages must not be used for paying vows. "There shall be no cult prostitute of the daughters of Israel, neither shall there be a cult prostitute of the sons of Israel. You shall not bring the hire of a harlot, or the wages of a dog, into the house of the LORD your God in payment for any vow; for both of these are an abomination to the LORD your God" (Deut 23:17-18). Although members of the religious establishment tried to fight these practices as a foreign threat that needed to be eliminated, cult prostitution was apparently difficult to contain. The prophets, in particular, issue repeated warnings and admonitions as to the dire consequences that would be levied upon Israel by the Deity if cult prostitution continued. (It has been supposed that "the women who performed tasks at the entrance to the Tent of Meeting," mentioned in 1 Sam 2:22, were sacred prostitutes—although this hardly suits their other appearance in Exod 38:8.)

The common or secular prostitute (*zonah*) was an accepted member of the Israelite society, both in urban and rural life (Gen 38:14;

Josh 2:1ff.; 1 Kgs 3:16-27). Indeed, there are no overtones of moral judgment in the narratives of Tamar's temporary harlotry, the professional harlotry of Rahab, or the visits of Samson to the harlot of Gaza (Judg 16:1). Prostitutes had the same access to the king's tribunal as other people (1 Kgs 3:16ff.) and might be encountered in the streets and squares, and on street corners, calling out to passersby (Prov 7:10-23); they sang and played the harp (Isa 23:16), and bathed in public pools (1 Kgs 22:38). Their glances and smooth talk were dangers against which the immature were warned (Jer 3:3; Prov 2:16; 5:3; 6:24-25; 7:5; etc.). Despite the fact that harlots appeared to be quite numerous and relatively accepted by society, harlotry was a shameful profession, and to treat an Israelite girl like a prostitute was considered a grave offense (as in the story of the rape of Dinah in Gen 34:31; see chap. 7). The Israelites were warned against prostituting their daughters (Lev 19:29), and priests were not allowed to marry prostitutes (Lev 21:7). The punishment of a priest's daughter who became a prostitute (thereby degrading her father) was death through fire (Lev 21:9).

Abomination Number Four: Homosexuality

For a patriarchal system to be sustained, not only must men endeavor to control women's sexual behavior (and the social understanding of women's sexuality, discussed below and in subsequent chapters), but they must police and (preferably) prohibit all forms of sexual expression that fall outside the binary world of heterosexuality (which therefore do not maintain the status quo), specifically (male) homosexuality. For example, Article 20 of the Middle Assyrian Code, which says that if one citizen has homosexual intercourse with another, then, following due process, the defendant is castrated. The Hebrew Bible has a similar prohibition: "You shall not lie with a male as with a woman; it is an abomination" (Lev 18:22). The punishment for this transgression is found in Deut 24:7, which says that if a man kidnaps and "abuses" a fellow Israelite, he must receive the death penalty. Since the reflexive tense of this verb (*hit'ammer*) can involve sexual possession and domination (as is clear from an analogous usage in the case of a captured foreign woman [Deut 21:14], where the punishment in the Hebrew Bible is death), it can be argued that the penalty here is perhaps even worse than that of the Middle Assyrian Code (or maybe not?).

David Daube has argued that the curious formulation of this rule may be an invective against anal intercourse, since the language is not "to uncover the nakedness" (as in the incest prohibitions) or "to lie," but "to lie with a male [as if it were] the lying with a woman," and the only way a man can penetrate another man as he might a woman is by anal intercourse (1986:447–48). Thus, Daube suggests that the view of male homosexuality in Israelite society may have been similar to the Greek condemnation of anal intercourse but not of other forms of homosexual activity.[13] Biblical examples and prohibitions/fears about male homosexuality will be discussed more fully in chapters 5 and 6.

Like incest prohibitions, the prohibition against homosexuality applies only to men, and there is no corresponding prohibition against female homosexuality. To be sure, if anal intercourse is the issue, the practice envisaged is obviously *inapplicable* to women. Of course, there are probably additional reasons why we find no rules about lesbian sex. (Since Article 20 of the Code of Hammurabi [see p. 30] specifically restricts homosexual activities to "citizens," by implication the Babylonian code does not address lesbian relationships either.) For example, it is virtually inconceivable that a woman would have been asked about her sexual preference when the issue of a marital arrangement arose between a prospective husband and her father or guardian. Perhaps another reason we find no rule about lesbian sex in the Hebrew Bible is that the traditions with which the lawgivers worked simply did not discuss the topic.[14] Significantly, in the Talmud, lesbian conduct is compared to adultery by the rabbis (Talmud—Mas. Sotah 26b) and to women's joining in when men sing (Talmud—Mas. Sotah 48a)!

Lack of overt prohibition notwithstanding, lesbianism is assumed by many modern authors to be implied in Leviticus 18 and 20. The eighteenth chapter is introduced with a general prohibition against subscribing to the practices of Egypt and Canaan: "Say to the people of Israel, 'I am the LORD your God. You shall not do as they do in the land of Egypt, where you dwelt, and you shall not do as they do in the land of Canaan, to which I am bringing you. You shall not walk in their statutes'" (Lev 18:2-3). Most of the exegetical material on these verses tries to recover the reasons why Egypt and Canaan are addressed in this section, and the curious verse against following "their laws." A Midrash in *Sifra Aharei Mot* 8:9 offers one solution—it is the practices of the ancestors of Egypt and Canaan that lie behind this phrase: "And what did they do? One man marries another man, a woman marries a woman, and a man marries a woman and her daughter, and a woman marries two [men]." Similarly, the *Jerusalem Talmud* includes a debate between the schools of Hillel and Shammai over whether female homosexual intercourse invalidates virginity and thus disqualifies such women from marrying priests: Shammai disqualifies them, but Hillel permits them to marry priests. (Note the bisexual assumption underlying this controversy.)

Baruch Levine writes that "in due course, Rabbinic interpretation added this prohibition [of lesbianism] as well [as to homosexuality in this verse]" (1989:123), although Maimonides claims that the punishment for lesbianism is neither biblical nor rabbinic (Commentary to Mishnah Sanhendrim 7:4). Maimonides addresses the topic more fully in the Mishneh Torah:

> Women are forbidden to be *mesolelot* with one another. This is the practice of the Land of Egypt, against which we have been warned, as it is said: "Like the practice of the Land of Egypt etc. you shall not do." The Sages said: "What did they do? A man marries a man, a woman marries a woman, and a woman marries two men." Although this practice is forbidden, no flogging is imposed, since there is no specific negative commandment against it, nor is there any intercourse at all. Consequently, [such women] are not forbidden to the priesthood on account of harlotry, nor is a woman prohibited to her husband on account of it, since there is no harlotry in it. However, a flogging for disobedience (*mardut*) should be given, since they have performed a forbidden act. A man should be strict with his wife in this matter, and should prevent women who are known to engage in this practice from visiting her, and prevent her from going to them.

Female Sexuality Is Problematic

The biblical concept of sexuality is problematic. Although in the Bible males do "lie with" females in the context of "legitimate" sexual relations (Uriah's reference to spending the night with his wife, 2 Sam 11:11, and the conception of Solomon, 2 Kgs 12:24, are two examples), the vast majority of the uses of the verb *shakab* refers to rape (as in the rape of Dinah, Genesis 34), incest (e.g., Lot and his daughters, Gen 19:32, 34, 35, discussed in chap. 5), promiscuity (the activities of Eli's sons, 1 Sam 2:22), seduction (the attempts of Potiphar's wife to seduce Joseph, Gen 39:10, 12, 14, discussed on page 35), adultery (the punishment of David that others will lie with his wives, 2 Sam 12:11), and forbidden relationships (such as an unclean woman, father's wife and daughter-in-law, aunt, and homosexuality, Lev 20:11-19, discussed above).[15]

Shakab also has numerous associations with death and defeat. To die is to lie with one's ancestors (1 Kgs 1:21; 2 Kgs 14:22; etc.), and the dead are those who lie in the grave (Ezek 32:21, 29; Ps 88:6; etc.). Certainly, associations of eroticism and destruction/death have a long literary tradition. Emily Vermeule points to the "ambiguity of slaughter and sex" and notes that Homer has "a habit, at mocking moments, of treating enemies as lovers, fusing the effects of Eros and Thanatos" (1979:157). Death itself has been described as a lover (McClelland 1964:182–216) and, significant for this book, as a sexually potent *goddess* (Good 1982; Coogan 1978).

Attraction and revulsion, longing and fear, are coexisting images of sexuality and death in biblical literature as well. Song of Songs 8:6 is particularly interesting in this regard: "Set me as a seal upon your heart, as a seal upon your arm: for love is strong as death, passion is hard as Sheol. Its flashes are flashes of fire, fiercer than any flame." Commenting on this verse, Marvin Pope notes the association of love with death (1977:228–29); Francis Landy points out that because of the grammatical construction of the verse, "Death inevitably engage[s] Love" (1983:123); and Susan Niditch emphasizes the metaphoric equation, reading this verse as an assertion that on some level "love is death and death love" (1989:43n.5).

There seems to be a philological tradition tying eroticism to death as well. In many languages, the word translated as "to die" is used also to mean "have a sexual climax," especially for a man (e.g., Lat. *morticula*; Fr. *la petite mort*). As Louise Vasvari observes, it is possible that the associations are multiple: deathlike spasms in the moment of orgasm and vice versa; men about to die often experience an erection; the male organ "dies" after climax; etc. (1990).

Within the Hebrew Bible, women (in general) and female sexuality (in particular) are perceived as threats to the desirable (male) social order.[16] That is to say, male sexual appropriation of females (dependent and otherwise) is a socially conditioned response, a reaction designed to exercise control over all women. The intimate connection between homophobia and patriarchy's suppression of women is well recognized. Indeed, the story of Lillith highlights the fear of female sexual desire:

> After the Holy One created the first human being, Adam, He said: "It is not good for Adam to be alone." He created a woman, also from the earth, and called her Lillith.
>
> They quarreled immediately. She said, "I will not lie below you." He said, "I will not lie below you, but above you. For you are fit to be below me and I above you." She responded, "We are both equal because we both come from the earth."
>
> Neither listened to the other. When Lillith realized what was happening, she pronounced the Ineffable Name of G–D and flew off into the air.
>
> Adam rose in prayer before the Creator, saying, "The woman you gave me has fled from me." Immediately the Holy One sent three angels after her.
>
> The Holy One said to Adam, "If she wants to return, all the better. If not, she will have to accept that one hundred of her children will die every day."
>
> The angels went after her, finally locating her in the sea, in the powerful waters in which the Egyptians were destined to perish. They told her what G–D had said, and she did not want to return.[17]

The biblical laws pertaining to women place them firmly under male control, first by fathers (or brothers), then husbands. Women's sexuality is controlled by males even beyond the grave as in the case of the law of levirate marriage, which requires Tamar to remain widowed and regulates her sexuality for the sake of a dead husband and his line (Deut 25:5-10). (Article 193 of the Code of Hammurabi has a similar provision, although more detailed: if a citizen dies, then his brother marries his widow; if a citizen and his brother die, the citizen's father marries the widow; if a citizen, his brother, and his father die, then one of his brother's sons marries the widow.) Other biblical legislation concerning female sexuality, such as laws about adultery (Num 5:11-31; Deut 22:23) and virginity (Deut 22:13-21) speak also to male advantage. For example, a man can bring his wife to trial merely on suspicion of adultery (Num 5:11-31), but that right is not reciprocal. (Again, there is a great similarity between this law and that of Articles 131 and 132 of the Code of Hammurabi. These articles provide that if a citizen falsely accuses his wife of adultery and she swears an oath of innocence before the divine patron of her household, she may return home. In addition, if a citizen charges a woman with adultery but has no evidence, then she is to be tried by ordeal in the river to restore the honor of her husband. If she survives, then she must pay a fine.)

A girl whose lack of virginity shames her father on her wedding night can be stoned to death (Deut 22:13-21), and an unbetrothed virgin who is raped *must* marry her assailant (Deut 22:28-29). (Article 55 of the Middle Assyrian Code requires marriage as well; however, the Assyrian law goes even further. It provides that if a marriageable woman who is the daughter of a citizen, living in her father's house, not engaged or married, and is not collateral for any of her father's debts, is kidnapped and raped by another citizen, either in the city, in the country, in the street at night, in a granary, or at a city festival, then the father of her household is to kidnap and rape the wife of his daughter's assailant. If the assailant has no wife, the father of the daughter who was kidnapped and raped may also give his daughter to her assailant in marriage, and the assailant must pay one-third more than the standard brideprice in silver to her father as the brideprice for a marriageable woman and he must marry her without the opportunity for divorce. If the father does not wish to marry his daughter to the assailant, he is to accept one-third more than the standard brideprice in silver as a fine and marry his daughter to whomever he wishes.) Although the subject of all of these ancient laws is women, the Bible does not address or even acknowledge the reactions of a raped girl married to her attacker or the feelings of a wife accused of adultery by an unfaithful husband.

Even the sexual desires of non-Israelite childless wives such as Potiphar's wife are condemned. Joseph, like his mother, Rachel, is described as "doubly beautiful" (*yᵉpēh-tô'ar wîpēh mar'eh*—literally, "good-looking and good to look at" (Gen 39:6). Even more importantly, her husband is a eunuch. At the very least, he is sterile and may possibly even be incapable of normal marital relations.[18] Yet the text shows neither sympathy for nor understanding of the Egyptian woman's sexual needs. This is not surprising since female sexuality is the focus of only one biblical text, Song of Songs.

This anxiety about female sexuality is most clear in the complicated ritual and ideological systems of *tûmah* and *tahor*, terms usually translated as "uncleanliness" and "cleanliness," although more accurately described as "taboo" and "ritual purity." A woman with a normal menstrual period, for example, is "unclean" or "taboo" for seven days after the flow has ceased as well as during the flow itself (Lev 12:2); and after childbirth, for forty-one days in the case of a male child and eighty days in the case of a female child (Lev 12:2-6). From the perspective of patriarchal hierarchy and social control, the separation and confinement of women in general (especially those laws concerning menstruation, female genital discharge, and postnatal condition) as well as incest prohibitions serve to maintain social order and stability. In other words, when women's lives seem to clash with their socially inferior status (that is, when they do something that men cannot, such as give birth), they are confined, and any contact with them is suspended until they are once again perceived as inferior to males. (Although seminal emission also renders males taboo, it is only for one day.) It is no doubt unfair to impose twentieth-century standards of "dirtiness" on the biblical construct of ritual purity; however, there is equally no doubt that these laws had the effect of preventing women from participating in sexual activities for a significant portion of their lives.

While Hebrew Scriptures describe various instances of harnessing women's sexuality, there seem to be few biblical constraints on male sexual needs. Indeed, female sexuality is depicted as negative in relation to positive or neutral male standards. The one exception is the Song of Songs, where positive female sexual imagery and potency abound, depicted as analogous to nature in general and the land in particular, the language of gardens, hillsides, plants, and animals predominating. Throughout the rest of the Hebrew Scriptures, however, male sexuality is accepted as a natural part of hu-*man* life and there is little denunciation of specific male sexual behavior, in contrast to female sexual prohibitions (Plaskow 1990:47).[19] Indeed, few transgressions are punished more severely than female sexual offenses. *Promiscuity,* a word that is repeated eighty-four times in the Hebrew Bible, is likened to "a woman out of control" (Setel 1985). Apparently, this means "out of the control of *males,*" and therefore dangerous. Hosea 2:2-4 is a typical example:

> Plead with your mother, plead—for she is not my wife, and I am not her husband—that she put away her harlotry from her face, and her adultery from between her breasts; lest I strip her naked and make her as in the day she was born, and make her like a wilderness, and set her like a parched land, and slay her with thirst. Upon her children also I will have no pity, because they are children of harlotry.

In this metaphor, not only is the promiscuous female to be physically punished, but there are broader implications as well. By using the promiscuous female as a metaphor for Israel, female sexual promiscuity is set in opposition to fertility (see chap. 4).

Athalya Brenner has highlighted what is perhaps the essence of biblical views on female sexuality:

> The Hebrew word for "male"—human (Gen 1:27), animal (Deut 15:19) or inanimate (of an image, Deut 4:16) is . . . from a root denoting "to remember." The more general and superordinate term "man" . . . can sometime serve in the narrower sense of "human male"—as for instance in Judg 11:39, where Jephthah's daughter "has never known a man." A female, human (Gen 1:27) or animal, is . . . derived from a root denoting "hole," "cavity," "opening," "orifice." . . . A "female" is sexed rather than gendered: she is an "orifice," orifices and holes require that they be filled. A "male" is gendered: he is the carrier of memory, the one "to be remembered," thus a social agent. The female is there to be penetrated and to be receptive; the term . . . implies that socially there is no difference between biological and social functions. The male agent carries the burden of social continuity, of culture ("remembrance"); he is there to "give," that is, penetrate the female "hole" or receptacle. (1997b:11–12)

Brenner's insight fits beautifully within the Lacanian context, that is, the linkages between "remembering" and the system of laws represented by the phallic symbolizer associated with the *Nom-du-Père*. In effect, throughout the Hebrew Bible the biblical female is treated like a "hole" or "cavity." That is to say, the female is an "absence," or what Lacan calls "a lacuna."

Thus, while the biblical concept of sexuality is problematic in general, female sexuality is particularly so. Simplistic as it may seem, beginning with Genesis 1–3, female sexuality appears to be the chief source of male anxiety in the Hebrew Bible. Indeed, the sexually promiscuous female is the most common prophetic metaphor for a nation's disaster. In describing Israel, for example, Jeremiah states: "You [female] are destroyed.[20] What will you do? Because you dressed in scarlet, because you decked yourself with golden ornaments, because you widened your eyes with paint, in vain you make yourself beautiful. Your lovers despise you, they will seek your life" (4:30).

And in Isaiah, Babylon, the virgin, will become the unhappy spoils of war, sexually humiliated and abused: "Take millstones and grind flour; uncover your hair; expose your skirt; uncover your leg; pass over the rivers. Your nakedness will be uncovered and your shame will be seen" (47:2-3).

In Judg 5:27 images of vulnerability, petitions, and ignominious defeat in battle intertwine, bringing together the association of female sexuality with defeat and death. There Jael lures the enemy with gentle promises of comfort. Sisera, the warrior, "between her legs, destroyed—fallo" In the sexual posture of a would-be lover, a vulnerable petitioner.[21] And this ambivalent role of woman as potential nurturer is not unique to Jael; the sexually active biblical woman invariably represents a fusing of Eros and Thanatos.

Incest and Food

Howard Eilberg-Schwartz sees an interesting correspondence between the incest prohibitions and rules about cooking, hunting, or sacrificing (1990). He disagrees with Mary Douglas, who argues that in biblical religion "we seek in vain a statement, however oblique, of a[n] . . . association between eating and sex" (1975:262). Instead, Eilberg-Schwartz argues that the rule against boiling a kid-goat parallels the prohibition against a male child having intercourse with his mother:

> The first of the first fruits of your ground you shall bring into the house of the Lord your God. You shall not boil a kid in its mother's milk. (Exod 23:19; 34:26)
>
> You shall not eat anything that dies of itself; you may give it to the alien who is within your towns, that he may eat it, or you may sell it to a foreigner; for you are a people holy to the LORD your God. You shall not boil a kid in its mother's milk. (Deut 14:21)
>
> You shall not uncover the nakedness of your father, which is the nakedness of your mother; she is your mother, you shall not uncover her nakedness. (Lev 18:7)
>
> Cursed be he who lies with his father's wife, because he has uncovered her who is his father's. And all the people shall say, "Amen." (Deut 27:20)

Similarly, laws that prevent certain kinds of acts (for example, "taking" a mother bird and her fledglings and then sending away the mother bird) correspond to the prohibitions against a man "taking" a woman and her mother:

> If you chance to come upon a bird's nest, in any tree or on the ground, with young ones or eggs and the mother sitting upon the young or upon the eggs, you shall not take the mother with the young. (Deut 22:6)
>
> If a man takes a wife and her mother also, it is wickedness; they shall be burned with fire, both he and they, that there may be no wickedness among you. (Lev 20:14)
>
> "Cursed be he who lies with his mother-in-law." And all the people shall say, "Amen." (Deut 27:23)

But the question arises as to *why* incest rules should find their parallel in rules about hunting, cooking, or sacrificing. As I discuss in other chapters, food and eating often serve as metaphors for sexual activity, and such metaphors can and do structure human behavior. Thus, in interpreting the prohibition against cooking a kid-goat in its mother's milk, Jean Soler translates this rule into the following statement: "You shall not put a mother and her son into the same pot, any more than into the same bed" (1979:29). In other words, just as an Israelite man may not be "stirred up" by his mother, it is forbidden to "stir" a kid-goat in its mother's juices.[22]

Perhaps specific examples might be useful to elucidate this relationship, and there are a number of biblical narratives in which the role of the kid-goat serves as a symbolic substitute for a male child. By way of illustration, in the story of Jacob and Esau (Genesis 27, discussed in chap. 6), Jacob outfoxes his blind father by pretending to be Esau, quite a trick, for Esau was a hairy man and hunter while Jacob was smooth-skinned. To effect the substitution, Jacob kills two kid-goats, which are used for a stew that tastes like freshly captured game. The hides of the kids are used to cover his arms, thus replicating the hairy arms of his brother. The substitution of kid-goats for wild game parallels the displacement of one (kind of) young man for another. Just as Isaac expects to eat a dish prepared from wild game but instead is served one made from a domesticated animal, so too he intends to bless Esau the hunter but instead blesses Jacob the homebody.

The displacement of a male by a kid-goat is a theme in several other narratives as well. For example, in the story of Judah and Tamar (Genesis 38), Tamar is married in succession to two of Judah's sons, each of whom subsequently dies. By Israelite law, Tamar should marry her dead husbands' brother, but in this case the only surviving brother is too young to marry. Judah promises that when his son matures he will carry out the levirate duties. But when the child grows up, it is clear that Judah has no intention of living up to his promise. Out of desperation, Tamar deceives Judah into thinking she is a harlot so that she can produce a child of his seed. Significantly, when Judah asks to sleep with her, he promises to send her a kid from the flock as a fee. "He answered, 'I will send you a kid from the flock.' And she said, 'Will you give me a pledge, till you send it?'" (Gen 3:17). So while Judah actually owes Tamar his son, he tries to satisfy her by substituting a kid-goat, once again the animal serving as a metaphoric equivalent to a male child. (Sadly for Tamar, just as she never gets Judah's youngest son, she also never gets the kid-goat.)

Similarly, when Jesse sends his son David to King Saul, he sends along a kid-goat. Perhaps he is signaling that just as Saul would "eat" this kid, he would attempt to "consume" David: "And Jesse took an ass laden with bread, and a skin of wine and a kid, and sent them by David his son to Saul" (1 Sam 16:20). The goat also figures prominently in the story in which Mano'ah and his wife are informed by an angel that they will shortly conceive a male son. They reciprocate by offering the angel a . . . kid-goat! "Mano'ah said to the angel of the LORD, 'Pray, let us detain you, and prepare a kid for you'" (Judg 13:15). And when Joseph's brothers sell Joseph into slavery, it is not a kid- but a male goat that acts as a metaphoric substitute. The brothers dip Joseph's coat into the blood of the animal and thus the goat serves as a symbolic replacement for the boy. When Jacob sees the coat he exclaims, "Joseph was devoured by a wild beast," when in fact it was the goat who was devoured by Joseph's brothers (Gen 37:33).

Of course, the most famous displacement of an animal for a human is in the "scapegoat" ritual of Yom Kippur: "And he shall take from the congregation of the people of Israel two male goats for a sin offering, and one ram for a burnt offering" (Lev 16:5). Leviticus 16 contains distinctive "rites of riddance" designed to remove and destroy impurity. The transgressions of the Israelites and their priests, which produce impurity, are dramatically transferred to the scapegoat that is driven into the wilderness, never to return. Although sin offerings on behalf of the entire community usually consisted of large cattle, as in, for example, Lev 4:1-21, those offered by individuals were usually from the flocks (as in Lev 4:22-23.). The Yom Kippur ritual was an exception since he-goats from the flocks served as sin offerings for the entire people.

There is a convergence of the issues of female sexuality, sexual taboos, and food in the narrative of Miriam's mysterious disease. Numbers 12 reports that Miriam spoke against Moses. As a result, she was stricken with a somewhat mysterious affliction. Childless, her disease (*ṣōra'at*) is the same as the venereal discharge described in Lev 22:4.[23] Her "offense" extends beyond discussing her brother Moses' sexual behavior; indeed, it is replete with its own sexual allusions.

Although there is a reluctance among some biblical scholars to read the book of Numbers in its final form, Fewell's and Gunn's argument for reading Judges 4 and 5 sequentially are just as valid here: "why not do the obvious thing and try reading . . . [it] . . . as a single story"

(1991:390). If we do, Miriam's punishment follows the account of those who left Egypt having "lusted a lust," leading one to search for a deeper dynamic in the desert than a churning stomach. Certainly, that for which they "lusted"—meat—has a double meaning today, and the word apparently has the same sexual innuendo for Ezekiel who chastises Israel with this sexual imagery: "You have harloted with the sons of Egypt, your neighbors of large *meat*" (Ezek 16:26). Equally graphic is Ezek 23:20: "She lusted after her lovers whose *meat* was like those of asses and seed like that of horses" (Ezek 23:20). And the Deity seems to view Miriam's offense as having a sexual origin. YHWH compares Miriam to the young woman who is publicly humiliated by her father and has to "bear her shame for seven days," an expression used often in the context of humiliation for a sexual offense.

Moses also considers his sister's illness venereal. His warning to the Israelites that they must follow certain procedures in dealing with this disease begins with a reminder that Miriam was similarly afflicted, and follows three legal sections, each having sexual ramifications for women.

The first legal section decrees that a man who divorces a woman may not remarry her after the death or divorce of her second husband, because she is now sexually defiled: "Her former husband, who sent her away, may not take her again to be his wife, after she has been defiled; for that is an abomination before the LORD, and you shall not bring guilt upon the land which the LORD your God gives you for an inheritance" (Deut 24:4).

The second legal section states that a "handmill" must not be taken in pawn, for that would be taking someone's life in pawn (Deut 24:6). Since this word (*rehayim*) is also the dual form of *rehem* ("uterus"), the word *handmill*—a pair of stones with holes in their centers is a metaphorical off-color colloquialism referring to a female with a sexual function, perhaps a concubine or a childbearing slave, thus making "woman" and "vulva" synonymous. And in rabbinic literature, the rabbis quip that a man's wife is a "millstone around his neck":

> Our Rabbis taught: "If one has to study Torah and to marry a wife, he should first study and then marry. But if he cannot [live] without a wife, he should first marry and then study." Rab Judah said in Samuel's name: "The *halachah* is, [A man] first marries and then studies." R. Johanan said: "[With] a millstone around the neck, shall one study Torah! Yet they do not differ: the one refers to ourselves [Babylonians]; the other to

them [Palestinians]." Rashi reverses the interpretation: "The Babylonian scholars used to travel to Palestine, the home of the Mishnah; hence they were free of household worries, and so might marry before study. But the Palestinians, studying at home and bearing family responsibilities, could make no progress if married, and so they were bound to study first. (Kiddushin 29b)

This reading seems to be reinforced by Job, who uses "grinding" as a sexual metaphor: "Then let my wife grind for another, and let others bow down upon her" (Job 31:10).

Conclusion: Phallocentrism and Logocentrism

Throughout this chapter I have been examining biblical sexual prohibitions. As stated in chapter 1, my approach in this book is to read psychoanalytic literary theory and the Bible concurrently. Reading the biblical laws regarding human sexuality and Freud simultaneously, it seems difficult to distinguish their respective ideas: "We might lay it down," writes Freud, "that . . . sexuality . . . is of a wholly masculine character" (1905d:217–18). In biblical narratives, as in Freud, female sexuality is explicitly subordinated to and subsumed by the male.[24] As Simone de Beauvoir argues, heterosexual men have established an absolute human type, the heterosexual male, against which all others are measured. Men are always the definers, women the defined (1961:xv–xvii). Likewise, the Hebrew Bible makes phallocentrism synonymous with logocentrism, as I discuss through the rest of the book. Within the Scriptures, it is primarily the male characters who have defined "woman" and "man," and in the more than two thousand years of biblical interpretation, it is male-dominated discourse that has "cast in stone" these constructs. The laws of Leviticus and Deuteronomy, symbolized by the circumcised heterosexual penis, has resulted in the "erection" of a paternal logos through the denial, or misnaming, of alternative sexual experience(s). Reconstructing biblical sexuality reveals the textual struggle within and against this patriarchy.

Chapter 3

Throw Momma from the Garden a Kiss: Or Paradise Revisited

The narrative in Gen 1:26 —3:24 is one of the best known and most explicated biblical texts. I realize that any attempt to examine this story yet again is dangerous. This reservation notwithstanding, I would like to discuss the narrative as the first (among many) accounts of dysfunctional "families" depicted in the Hebrew Bible, particularly as relating to father-daughter relationships.

So much has been written about the Garden of Eden that I shall begin with an alternate reading.

* * *

A four-year-old boy asked his aunt to tell him a story. "Once upon a time there was a little boy (about your age) who lived on a beautiful farm. The farm was almost perfect: there was lots and lots of room to jump and run and ride a bicycle, trees to climb, flowers to smell (and even pick!), and a perfect-sized lake in which he could swim and splash to his heart's content. But the little boy was lonely. His daddy said that maybe he needed some animals to play with, so he brought him some pets. First, Daddy brought him a fish, but that didn't work because all the little boy could do was watch the fish swim. Next, Daddy brought him a bird, but the bird wasn't much of a playmate because the little boy had to keep it in a cage or it would fly away. Daddy brought him a horse and a cow, and although the little boy liked to ride the horse and milk the cow, he wanted someone with whom he could laugh and read stories. And even though he really liked his new puppy dog and kitty, they did not know how to talk, and so they couldn't play with him. What the little boy really wanted was a baby brother or sister!

"About nine months later Daddy surprised him. Daddy brought home a baby sister for the little boy. At first the baby couldn't do very much, but soon she was able to talk and giggle and play games. The two children loved each other and were very, very happy (especially when they romped outside). But Daddy had a new rule: although the children could continue to play with the animals, and jump and run and ride bicycles, and climb trees, and smell (and even pick!) flowers, and swim and splash to their hearts' content in the perfect-sized lake, they were not allowed to go near the *great big* cookie jar that was in the middle of the garden. No matter how hungry they got. Daddy said they could eat anything else on the farm that they wanted (peaches, plums, pears, broccoli, asparagus, brussels sprouts . . . anything at all) but *they could not go near that cookie jar!* Daddy said that if they *did* eat the cookies from the jar, they would get very, very sick, and he would get very, very angry.

"One day, the children were outside playing, and suddenly they were *starving.* They walked into the garden and they smelled the most wonderful smell coming from *the cookie jar.* Chocolate chip cookies! For some silly reason, none of the fruits and vegetables appealed to them. They were tired of peaches, plums, pears, broccoli, asparagus, and brussels sprouts. All they wanted was a cookie. So the little girl said, 'Let's try one!' The little boy said to her, 'But Daddy said we shouldn't or we would get very, very sick and he would get very, very angry.' The little girl thought about that for a few minutes and then asked her brother, 'Why would Daddy put something right in the middle of the garden where we could reach it if it would make us sick? Daddy loves us. He would not put those cookies here if they really were dangerous. After all, he did put all of the knives on high shelves so we wouldn't cut ourselves, and he put a fence around the well so we wouldn't stumble in. Daddy always takes good care of us. Let's try just one little cookie.' 'Okay,' said the little boy. 'But you go first.' (Apparently, even though the little boy loved his sister, he wanted to wait to see if his sister would get very, very sick before he tried the cookie!) The little girl ate a cookie and it tasted *delicious!* (Certainly better than the brussels sprouts she had for dinner the night before.) And she didn't get very, very sick. She didn't get sick at all! In fact, suddenly she felt really happy (it must have been all that chocolate). So she gave one to her brother who was with her, and he didn't get sick either. (He loved the chocolate so much he even wanted two cookies—but that's another story.)

"Later that afternoon, Daddy came outside while the two children were playing and said to the little boy, 'Did you have any cookies?' The little boy said, 'My baby sister (the one *you* gave to me)—*she* gave me a cookie.' Daddy was furious and he said, 'From now on neither of you may play outside. You may not play with the animals, and jump and run and ride bicycles, and climb trees, and smell (and even pick!) flowers, and swim and splash to your hearts' content in the perfect-sized lake. You, my son, must weed the garden, mow the lawn, and dig irrigation ditches. You, my daughter, must cook, wash, clean, iron, sew, and make pickles!'"

When the aunt was finished telling the story, her nephew thought for a few minutes. Then he said, "Where was the Mommy?" "I don't know," replied the aunt. "Where do *you* think she was?" "The Daddy sent her away because the children loved her and the Daddy wanted them to love only him. But first she baked the cookies."

* * *

Back to Genesis. Many questions arise when looking at this family constellation. Who is the father? Who/where is the mother? What is the familial relationship of Adam and Eve? How well do the family members get along?

Before proceeding with my reading of this narrative, I would like to establish a few parameters. First, since I am approaching this text from a psychoanalytic literary perspective rather than a theological one, I am consciously and assiduously avoiding any theological discussions such as predestination and/or freedom of choice on the part of Adam and Eve. Second, I am treating the Deity as a literary representation of a father. Indeed, in classic psychoanalytic theory, God is thought of as the projection of the father's image (Freud 1913:147) and Rank has noted how the Greek gods were modeled on the image of the paterfamilias ([1912] 1992:230). In other words, I am not ascribing an automatic assumption of perfection to God; rather, I am dealing with the Deity as a literary character with many anthropomorphic features, both good and bad, much as I would deal with Zeus in discussing Hesiod's *Theogony*. Third, I would like to emphasize what I stated in chapter 1: my using a psychoanalytic literary construct does not mean that I agree with all of Freud's or Lacan's views, nor that I consider them biblical scholars. Instead, throughout this chapter I am reading Genesis 1–3 in conjunction with psychoanalytic literary theory in an attempt to bring an anterior text out of a subsequent one. Freud and Lacan come to me not as authorities but as Iser's "foreshortened" text.[1]

In brief, both the Genesis version of this story and the alternative reading seem to portray God as a rather benevolent, albeit tyrannical, male parent. Although he is a progenitor who provides life, a carefree existence, and suitable playmates, in return he demands total obedience (secured by threats), practices constant supervision over his children and tests the children's loyalty (the tree/cookie jar: forbidden yet desirable and flourishing in the middle of the garden). Indeed, the father not only denies his children, the freedom of choice (awareness/ innocence, or viewed alternatively, adulthood/eternal childhood) but also the *knowledge* of good and evil. Generally speaking, the Deity seems to act as a domineering parent who uses a combination of favors and threats, or carrots and sticks, in order to secure filial devotion.

And the children? Not surprisingly, the children rebel. But the children must pay a price for this rebellion: divine/parental anger and the loss of physical and emotional comfort. (Unfortunately, the primeval children are not alone. This story is recapitulated frequently in the tales of adolescent development throughout the Hebrew Bible, particularly with regard to daughters, as I discuss in this and other chapters.)

Why is the Deity/father angry enough to punish so severely? Perhaps the unmentioned mother in this narrative can help answer this question. My thesis is that beneath the surface of this Genesis narrative lie two interwoven subtexts. The first is a father-daughter narrative in which the Adam material appears merely as a re-narration. The second is the Deity's/father's repressed fear of emasculation. Just as the father on the farm was threatened by his children's love of/by Momma ("The Daddy sent her away because the children loved her and the Daddy wanted them to love only him. But first she baked the cookies"), the biblical father fears that the relationship of mother and child (goddess and son) will cause his downfall. As a result, God, the male Deity, banishes his wife, the goddess. He is attracted to his daughter but projects that desire onto others. What makes the seemingly absent Mother so central in this otherwise emphatically masculine epic is *her* potential to threaten patriarchal power and rule.

Who/Where Is Mom?

The ancient Hebrews (like virtually every other ancient civilization) had its own creation/fertility myth,[2] a narrative that has a purely sexual significance and explains (in terms of the intentions and actions of deities and other supernatural beings) why the world is as it is and things happen as they do. But the Hebrew Bible seems to be unique in that most of these other creation stories involve the myth of world *parents*. That is, according to the prototypical myth, an original *female* deity creates itself and then creates a mate from her own body. Most often, in the following generation, parents continue mating with their children and sibling incest occurs as well.

When humans began to cultivate the earth, these myths were extended to the bearer (earth mother) and producer (seed father) of fertility in nature. An African Yoruba myth, for example, relates that Odudua, the earth, created Obatala, the sky, and they lie "tightly pressed upon one another in a gourd. An argument arises, and the noble husband strikes out Odudua's eye, whereupon the gourd separates and the sky rises upward." They produce two children, a boy, Aganyu (the firmament), and a girl, Yemaya (the water goddess), who mate and produce a son, Orungan. Orungan mates with his mother and they produce fifteen additional deities (Rank [1912] 1992:225).

Similarly, the Egyptian myth of world parents relates that "in the beginning, the universe filled a boundless primordial expanse of water (Nun), which held in its womb the male and female seeds, the beginnings of the future world. The first act of creation began with the formation of the egg out of the primordial water, from which daylight, Ra, the immediate source of life in the realm of the earth, sprang forth" (Rank [1912] 1992:226). Like Gaia in the Greek cosmogony (discussed below), Ra parthenogenetically produces the first gods, Shu and Tefent (air and water), a pair of sibling mates who produce Keb and Nut (earth and sky), again sibling spouses. Shu, their father, mates with his daughter Nut and produces still more deities.

Likewise, the Babylonian creation myth relates that the first world arises from the incestuous union of mother and son. "In the beginning there was chaos, called 'ocean' as a man and 'sea' as a woman [Apsu and Tiamat]. . . . Their son Mummu . . . presses between them and engenders a new generation, that is, a new universe, with his mother Tiamat" (Rank [1912] 1992:227). Otto Rank reports also that, according to Japanese mythology, the first human beings were the brother and sister Izanagi and Izanami, who paired according "to the example of the birds" (1932:53), and legends of the ancient Peruvians relate that the children of the first Inca married each other (Schiller-Tietz 1892:7ff.).

But how do the incestuous relationships that occur in the majority of the myth of world *parents* relate to Genesis 1–3, where no female deity seems to be present? One answer seems to emerge if the absent mother of the Genesis narrative is read alongside Hesiod's *Theogony*.[3]

Like the Hebrew Bible, which states that "the earth was without form and void"[4] (Gen 1:2), Hesiod's *Theogony* begins with Chaos (or Void). Chaos reproduces parthenogenetically: first "broad-bosomed" Earth, then Eros (Desire), Darkness, Night, and other children who are primarily deifications of the features of the physical world (for example, Mountains and Sea). In the next generation, Earth (also without any mate) gives birth to Sky, whom she sets "over and against herself" to "cover her on all sides." Finally, Earth and Sky (together) reproduce the elemental deities and the Titans.

Earth's husband, Sky (who is also her son), hates his children and hides them "deep within Earth." Earth persuades her son Cronus to castrate his father (Sky) with a sickle she provides (perhaps a good mother but not the greatest wife!). From the blood of the severed testicles, the Giants and Erinyes (spirits of vengeance) are born, as well as a goddess, Aphrodite, who emerges from the white foam of the sea into which the castrated organ fell.

The story repeats itself with some modifications in the next generation of deities. King Cronus mates with his sister Rhea (Earth's daughter). Having been told by his parents, Earth and starry Sky, that like his father he was destined to be overcome by his own son, Cronus decides to swallow his offspring. Rhea appeals to her parents and Earth hides Zeus, the youngest child, in a cave in Crete, giving Cronus a stone to swallow instead. Zeus grows to adulthood, Earth induces Cronus to regurgitate his children, and Zeus, as predicted, takes his father's place as king of the universe, ruling over the world of the Olympian gods and mortals. Eventually, Zeus puts an end to the successive overthrowing of male deities by the conspiracies of female deities and their youngest sons, establishes a patriarchal government on Olympus (in lieu of the former matriarchal rule), and introduces "moral order and culture" by fathering the Hours, the Fates, the Muses, and the Graces. Eventually, the god Zeus reproduces parthenogenetically (as had the goddesses Chaos and Earth in the beginning of the myth), giving birth to a daughter, Athena, through his head and to a son, Dionysus, from his thigh.

Like most creation myths, Hesiod's themes are the nature of the divine cosmos, a rationalization of the physical cosmos (how the world and all of its features came into existence), and an explanation of the human cosmos. What I find particularly interesting in Hesiod is the evolution from the primacy of female deities to the primacy of the male deity—in virtually every respect. For example, although there is a recurrent theme of the subversion of the authority of the father by an alliance between the mother and the youngest son (Earth instigates Cronus to castrate his father, Heaven, and Rhea saves Zeus from being swallowed by his father, Cronus), in each succeeding generation the role of the mother diminishes. That is, in the first conflict, Cronus is a subordinate who executes the will of his mother, Earth; Zeus, while owing his escape to his mother, Rhea, goes on to win power by virtue of his *own* intelligence and strength in the battle against the Titans. And not only is Rhea's role more limited, but her actions portray a weaker female than her mother. Rhea, at her wits' end to save her youngest child, must turn to her parents, Earth and Heaven, to formulate the plan and execute it. It is Earth, not her daughter Rhea, who hides the infant Zeus, fools Cronus with a stone, and tricks him into regurgitating the children he had swallowed. Patriarchal power is finally consolidated when Zeus, faced with the same threat as his father, Cronus, and his grandfather, Sky, swallows his potentially dangerous consort, Metis, and averts potential disaster.

The diminution of female prominence extends even to reproduction: while Mother Earth produces children without male partnership and mates with her own sons, Zeus is "the father of gods and men." Thus the total picture in Hesiod's *Theogony* is one of a graduated *increase* in male authority and an attendant *decrease* in female authority.

Clearly, Hesiod and the biblical writer did not write the same tale. Yet despite the many differences, there are similarities—some overt, some less so. The most commonly cited difference is the apparent lack of an original female deity in Genesis. But why only an apparent lack?

Until fairly recently, scholars shared the view that the Israelite religion was completely (male) monotheistic. As Michael Fishbane points out, "if one nostrum is widely accepted it is just this: . . . the Hebrew Bible reflects a primary rupture with the world of myth and myth-making. . ." (1991:1).[5] Indeed, Israel's monotheism is usually presented as a *contrast* to that of its neighboring tribes who worshipped a pantheon of fertility goddesses (the "great mother," Ishtar, Ashtoreth, Astarte, Asherah, Inanna, and Anat are the most famous). While pre-Israelite statues of Canaanite goddesses (dated to 25,000 BCE, millennia prior to any male Canaanite figures and millennia prior to the Israelite creation story) are relatively prevalent, archaeologists have recovered *later* Canaanite goddess figures as well. The Ashdoda, for example, so-named by the archaeologist who discovered her at Ashdod, is a twelfth-century BCE figurine. She is a schematic melding of a woman and a chair covered with the black- and red-painted decoration characteristic of Philistine pottery.

Later clay figures that apparently had a cultic use in fertility rites have been found in the Chalcolithic site of Gilat (Northern Negev). One of the best-preserved of these dates from approximately 4000 BCE. The figurine is a pregnant woman seated on a stool, supporting an urn on her head with one hand and holding a vessel under her other arm. Like the Ashdoda that predates her, the urn and the stool are painted red. And like most fertility goddess figurines, the woman has prominent breasts and pubic hair. More significant for purposes of this chapter is an Asherah figure that has been dated to the time of King Solomon (c. 900 BCE), as well as the discovery of eighth-century inscriptions that mention a pair of gods—YHWH and his Asherah. At two sites, Kuntiliet Ajrud in the southwestern part of the Nesev hill region and Khirbet-el Kom in the Judea piedmont, Hebrew inscriptions have been found that mention "YHWH and his Asherah," "YHWH Teman and his Asherah," and "YHWH shomion and his Asherah."

Thus, in spite of the fact that biblical literature is often said to be distinguished from other ancient texts by its apparent break with mythology's panoply of deities, recent archaeological investigations and other lines of evidence have complicated our understanding of the origins of the Israelite religion. Although the position developed in the Hebrew Bible is that the worship of Asherah *should* have ceased when the Israelites invaded and conquered Canaan (c. 1200 BCE), apparently it did not. In fact, scholars have noted that many Hebrew Bible narratives strongly resemble the themes and language of ancient Near East mythic cycles, a prominent feature of which is the *presence* of strong fertility goddesses and the fear they generate among *male* gods (and among male humans). In addition, the history of Israel and Judah (from c. 1200 BCE to the Babylonian exile in 586 BCE) depicted within the Hebrew Bible itself is described in cycles of univocal YHWH worship *alternating* with YHWH worship that included worship of other gods and goddesses. Judges 3:7, for example, relates that "the sons of Israel did what was evil in the sight of YHWH, forgetting YHWH their God, and serving the Baals and the Asheroth." Even Solomon, the king who built the Temple in Jerusalem, worshipped Asherah: "Solomon went after Ashtoreth [in the sense of followed in order to worship], the goddess of the Sidonians, and after Milcom the abomination of the Ammonites" (1 Kgs 11:5). Clay models of Solomon's temple from that period provide us with further clues about Solomon's involvement with Asherah.

According to the biblical account, Asherah worship apparently was rather common (even in the Temple itself) and coincides with fluctuations in power politics. Raphael Patai chronicles it as shown in the following table (1967:78):

Asherah in the Temple (BCE)	*Asherah excluded from the Temple* (BCE)
928–893 (35 years)	
825–725 (100 years)	893–825 (68 years)
698–620 (78 years)	725–698 (27 years)
609–586 (23 years)	620–609 (11 years)

Although we do not know the full extent of goddess worship among the Israelites (that is, the presence of a goddess figurine may mean as little as a statue or pillar somewhere in the Temple court or it may mean that her worship was combined with that of YHWH), certainly Asherah's existence, importance, and legitimacy were acknowledged by kings, priests, and the people for most of 236 years. As popular as she may have been, however, Ashtoreth, a household goddess intended for the common folk of Israel, was called "Ashtoreth the abomination of the Zidonians" (Phoenicians) (1 Kgs 11:5) in the Hebrew Bible, and woe betide anyone who worshipped her! Apparently, the worst of these worshippers was Ahab who "did more to provoke the LORD God of Israel to anger than all the kings of Israel who were before him" (1 Kgs 16:30). For Ahab not only took "to wife Jezebel the daughter of Ethbaal king of the Zidonians" (1 Kgs 16:31); in addition, he converted to her religion. But Jezebel committed an even greater crime: advocating her Phoenician religion at the *expense* of the God of Israel. (And apparently Jezebel was quite a religious enthusiast: 450 priests of Baal

ate at her table.) Jezebel had the prophets of YHWH killed, whereupon Elijah, the "servant of the LORD," annihilated her priests. This in
turn upset Jezebel so much that she threatened to destroy Elijah. In the
end she was punished, of course, by a horrific death:

> When Jehu came to Jezreel, Jezebel heard of it; and she painted her eyes,
> and adorned her head, and looked out of the window. And as Jehu
> entered the gate, she said, "Is it peace, Zimri, murderer of your master?"
> And he lifted up his face to the window, and said, "Who is on my side?
> Who?" Two or three eunuchs looked out at him. He said, "Throw her
> down." So they threw her down; and some of her blood spattered on the
> wall and on the horses, and they trampled on her. Then he went in and
> ate and drank; and he said, "See now to this cursed woman, and bury
> her; for she is a king's daughter." But when they went to bury her, they
> found no more of her than the skull and the feet and the palms of her
> hands. When they came back and told him, he said, "This is the word
> of the Lord, which he spoke by his servant Elijah the Tishbite, 'In the
> territory of Jezreel the dogs shall eat the flesh of Jezebel; and the corpse
> of Jezebel shall be as dung upon the face of the field in the territory of
> Jezreel, so that no one can say, This is Jezebel.'" (2 Kgs 9:30-37)

Since a significant number of Ashtoreth figurines and plaques have
come to light in Israel, the cult of this goddess must have been very
popular. Like other ancient Near Eastern fertility goddesses, the archaeological finds support a strong maternal presence in goddess figures discovered in Israel (and condemned in the biblical text). Since Ashtoreth
was the nourishing mother goddess, she is usually represented as nude,
supporting her breasts. Other statues show her grasping lilies, snakes,
or both in her upraised hands, both of which were considered symbols
of female fecundity.

Almost all of the clay idols lift up their breasts for emphasis, and this
is particularly true of the pillar figures from the eighth to the sixth centuries BCE known as Astarte figurines, after the Phoenician goddess of
love and fertility. This *dea nutrix* (nourishing deity) has been described
as a "kind of tree with breasts" that was tantamount to a tangible
prayer for fertility and nourishment (Frymer-Kensky 1992:159–60).
Is it possible that this "kind of tree with breasts" might in fact have represented the "tree of knowledge"? Was the tree of knowledge an oblit-
erated mother/nature agricultural goddess?

Even the great [male] lion of Judah is linked to a goddess. Exca-
vated in 1899, this relief was created during the reign of Nebuchad-
nezzar II, king of Babylon (604–562 BCE), and the mosaic adorned the

processional way from the Ishtar Gate to the great temple of Marduk (suggested to be the Tower of Babel). In addition, the lion is associated with many ancient Near Eastern goddesses and signifies majesty, strength, and a symbol of life and death.

Thus, it seems more than likely that if idols of Asherah were accepted into the Temple, Asherah was worshiped throughout the land. Indeed, archaeological finds seem to confirm that polytheism was prevalent in early Israel as well as in Canaan. As Bernhard Lang notes,

> during the four and a half centuries of Israelite monarchy (ca. 1020–586 BCE), the dominant religion is polytheistic and undifferentiated from that of its neighbors. The religions of the Ammonites, Moabites, Edomites, Tyrians, etc., are local variants of the common Syro-Palestinian pattern which is not transcended by their individual traits and distinctive features. The original religion of Israel belongs to this group of West-Semitic cults. (1983:23)

Thus, as recent scholarship suggests, emergent Israel shared basic elements with Canaanite culture and was derived from it; indeed, views that present a sharp distinction between Israelite and Canaanite religious practices have been called into question. In other words, not only was Asherah part of Israel's Canaanite heritage but the birth of Israelite monotheism was, in fact, a laborious (if you'll excuse the pun) break with its *own* past rather than an avoidance of alien Canaanite practice or a mixing of distinct traditions.

One explanation for the popularity of Asherah (and other fertility goddesses) may be that goddesses had a particular appeal to women because of the numerous roles open to females in sacred rites that accompanied goddess worship. Indeed, women could function as singers, dancers, diviners, dream interpreters, mourners, and priestesses (Ochshorn 1981: chap. 4; Harris 1976; Stone 1976: chaps. 7, 8). Since many such figurines were found in Judean sites (many in private dwellings), some archaeologists have speculated that they may have served as amulets or to enhance fertility among *Israelite* worshipers. Certainly, if the biblical text is any witness, Jeremiah rails against goddess worship! Throughout the book (7:17-18; 44:9, 17-25 and passim) Jeremiah describes how the kings of Judah and their wives along with the men of Judah and their wives gather in the streets of Jerusalem and other cities to pay homage to the goddess, make promises by which they bind themselves to her, and offer cakes to the "queen of heaven" marked with her image. And who is this queen of

heaven? Her name, whether Ishtar, Anat, Astarte, or Isis, is not important. What *is* significant is the cultural manifestation of the great
mother goddess whose worship, the people claim, can bring peace and
economic prosperity:

> As for the word which God spoke to us in the name of the YHWH, we
> will not listen to you. But we will do everything that we have vowed,
> burn incense to the queen of heaven and pour out libations to her, as we
> did, both we and our fathers, our kings and our princes, in the cities of
> Judah and in the streets of Jerusalem; for then we had plenty of food,
> and prospered, and saw no evil. But since we left off burning incense to
> the queen of heaven and pouring out libations to her, we have lacked
> everything and have been consumed by the sword and by famine. And
> the women said, "When we burned incense to the queen of heaven and
> poured out libations to her, was it without our husbands' approval that
> we made cakes for her bearing her image and poured out libations to
> her?" (Jer 44:16-19)

In Lacanian terms, the "queen of heaven" seems to emphasize the
imaginary (discussed on page 5) and the pre-organization as tranquil,
oceanic, and not as turbulent. The sword to which Jeremiah refers is
clearly phallic and thus represents the patriarchal, symbolic realm of
the "Law" (see page 6). Thus, from a Lacanian perspective, things were
better with the imaginary, that is to say, during the worship of the
Mother Goddess.

Although archaeological evidence sufficiently indicates that the
Mosaic covenant was grafted onto an extant Canaanite tribal religion
rather than breaking from it, the indications are even stronger from a
literary perspective. For example, scholars have noted that the Canaanite god El shares several characteristics with the Israelite Deity.
Canaan's El, like the El of the Hebrew Bible, is portrayed as father and
creator, not as a nature deity. Like Israel's El, he is a warrior. Like
Israel's El, in some texts Canaan's El abides in a tent, in some a palace,
and sometimes "in the far north" at the "mountain of El," a description that fits "Eden the garden of God at the mount of God" in
Ezekiel. His epithets, "god of the covenant," "El the judge," "eternal
king," etc., carry over to YHWH, whose name, Frank Cross specu-
lates, might derive from the *Canaanite*/Proto-Hebrew verb "to be"
(1973:70). The description of the tabernacle (its curtains embroidered
with cherubim, and its cherubim throne, the proportions of which
were modeled on the cosmic shrine) "all reflect Canaanite modes, and
specifically the Tent of El and his cherubim throne" (Cross 1973:72).

Thus, just as the Hebrew language is an offshoot or dialect of Uga-ritic, biblical literature and culture appear to be the continuation of its antecedents rather than a clean break from these antecedents. Indeed, there are numerous verbal formulas including stock epithets, metaphors and similes, correlated parallelisms, formulas of transition, etc., shared by Canaanite and Hebrew texts.

Umberto Cassuto sees the biblical characterization of YHWH as an absorption and synthesis of the characteristics of *several* Canaanite gods, and notes that the struggles between the gods of heaven and the netherworld in Canaanite myth correspond to the futile rebellions of creatures against their creator in occasional "poetic" passages in the Hebrew Bible. Further, Cassuto hypothesizes that YHWH's conquest of the sea (referred to in the "Song of the Sea" in Exodus 15 as well as in a variety of passages in Psalms, Isaiah, Job, and the Apocrypha) is a primeval Hebrew myth ascribing to YHWH the victories ascribed in the Canaanite epic to the great *goddess* Anath in her battle against the netherworld god Mot and his ally, the Prince of the Sea (Cassuto 1971).[6] Similarly, John Day writes that the Hebrew Bible's use of imagery of the divine conflict with the dragon and the sea is appropri-ated directly from Canaanite mythology, deriving from the myth of Baal's conflict with the sea-god Yam and his dragon-associate Leviathan (1985:179).

Even conservative scholars generally now agree that all of the great creation stories of the ancient Near Eastern cultures (including that of the Hebrews) have at least two important things in common with Hes-iod's *Theogony:* first, all deal with the initiation and sustenance of human civilization (the securing of religious and cosmological founda-tions for the polis), and second, all presuppose or describe power strug-gles between masculine and feminine deities, usually with the masculine deities eventually gaining prominence. (It appears that a basic tenet of ancient creation mythology is that civilization could not begin or be sus-tained until the feminine, as a dominant religious power, had been mas-tered and domesticated, an ancient *Taming of the Shrew*, so to speak— that is to say, the taming of the female principal and the Lacanian imaginary realm by the male principal of the symbolic realm.) Thus, Cross has observed that the Hebrew name *Eve* may stem from the same verb "to be" as does YHWH, and that at some point prior to Eve's demotion to Adam's mate, Eve and God may even have been consorts!

Along these lines, it seems significant that the epithet whereby God identifies himself (and is referred to), "El Shaddai," derives from a word that in Hebrew means "breast." Thus, the following verses could be translated as "*God-of-the-Breasts*" rather than "God Almighty" with some rather startling differences in interpretation!

> When Abram was ninety-nine years old the LORD appeared to Abram, and said to him, "I am *God-of-the-Breasts;* walk before me, and be blameless." (Gen 17:1)
>
> *God-of-the-Breasts* bless you and make you fruitful and multiply you, that you may become a company of peoples. (Gen 28:3)
>
> And God said to him, "I am *God-of-the-Breasts:* be fruitful and multiply; a nation and a company of nations shall come from you, and kings shall spring from you." (Gen 35:11)
>
> May *God-of-the-Breasts* grant you mercy before the man, that he may send back your other brother and Benjamin. If I am bereaved of my children, I am bereaved. (Gen 43:14)
>
> And Jacob said to Joseph, "*God-of-the-Breasts* appeared to me at Luz in the land of Canaan and blessed me." (Gen 48:3)
>
> I appeared to Abraham, to Isaac, and to Jacob, as *God-of-the-Breasts,* but by my name the LORD I did not make myself known to them. (Exod 6:3)
>
> And the sound of the wings of the cherubim was heard as far as the outer court, like the voice of *God-of-the-Breasts* when he speaks. (Ezek 10:5)
>
> If you will seek God and make supplication to the *God-of-the-Breasts.* (Job 8:5)
>
> But I would speak to the *God-of-the-Breasts,* and I desire to argue my case with God. (Job 13:3)
>
> Because he has stretched forth his hand against God, and bids defiance to the *God-of-the-Breasts.* (Job 15:25)
>
> Surely God does not hear an empty cry, nor does the *God-of-the-Breasts* regard it. (Job 35:13)

Is this a remnant of the goddess? Certainly, Jacob's final blessing of Joseph, which invokes Shaddai, seems to correspond quite closely with the creation account of *Enuma Elish* in which the breasts of Tiamat become mountains with gushing springs and indicates a strong, maternal presence: "By El who will bless you with blessings of heaven above, blessings of the deep that couches beneath, *blessings of the breasts and of the womb* . . . [to] the everlasting hills" (Gen 49:25-26). There appear to be many similarities between the blessings of the breasts and the womb found in Genesis and the fertility cults of the Israelites' Canaanite neighbors. I suggest it is the influence of Canaanite goddesses, such as Asherah and Anat, whose iconography featured prominent breasts. These goddesses are referred to in the *Enuma Elish* as the "wet nurses of the gods" and "the divine breasts, the breasts of Asherah and Raham."

In summary, although the Hebrew Bible defines itself in absolute *opposition* to paganism, we know from the prophets' bitter denunciations, as well as from the historic records of Judges, 1 and 2 Samuel, and 1 and 2 Kings, that popular worship of Asherah and Anath *remained* a recurrent problem in Israel, not eradicated before the fall of the second Temple. Further, goddess worship constituted an unwanted subculture for the author of the relevant biblical passages, and the goddess cult or cults flourished in times of political and economic stress. As Athalya Brenner notes, "in such times people, especially women, seem to have turned back from the cult of the disappointing Hebrew Father to a *divine Mother* [emphasis added] in a quest for maternal love and assistance. . . . The Father's disappointment in his children appears to be mirrored by his daughters' disappointment in him" (1997:61). Indeed, sculptures are one of the most common findings at archaeological sites in the area of the Kingdom of Judea. Although some of those found were figures of horses, with or without riders, or unidentified animals, sculptures of women, used as amulets of fertility and prosperity were also common, especially in private homes.

As Raphael Patai argues, it appears that Judaism has never been without some form of goddess in disguise, whether she be figured as "wisdom," or "divine presence" or even the demonic Lillith of Jewish legend and folklore (see p. 34). Furthermore, goddess worship seemed to be a rather pleasant experience. As Robert Carroll writes, "An idyllic picture of egalitarian religion with a strong emphasis on the family worshipping together! The cakes have impressed on them the image of the queen of heaven, the mother goddess of the ancient world" (1986:212–13). With all the similarities to other ancient Near Eastern creation narratives, what *does* differentiate the Hebrew creation myth from those of its surrounding cultures? The absence of conflict (the biblical Genesis describes no overt combat among deities striving for sovereignty) and the absence of primal parent sexuality are the most conspicuous features. In the Hebrew creation myth, procreation of the universe from a divine female body has been replaced. Divine *female fecundity* becomes divine *male fiat*. Further, the positive image of the breast is eventually replaced by a negative one. Ezekiel, for example,

presents a brutal picture of divine revenge, so oral and sadistic that one
almost feels pity for the biblical commentators obliged to defend it:

> Thus says the Lord God: "You shall drink your sister's cup which is deep
> and large; you shall be laughed at and held in derision, for it contains
> much; you will be filled with drunkenness and sorrow. A cup of horror
> and desolation is the cup of your sister Samaria; you shall drink it and
> drain it out, and pluck out your hair, and tear your breasts; for I have
> spoken, says the Lord God. (Ezek 23:32-34)

It has been argued, of course, that the Deity in the Hebrew Bible is
not male and has no sex. Some feminist scholars enumerate female
images of God such as mother (for example, Num 11:12; Deut 32:11;
Isa 46:3-4, 49:15-16, 66:13; Ps 131:2; Job 38:28-29), wet nurse, and
midwife and use these attributes as a counterbalance to a masculine
characterization of YHWH (Trible 1978: chaps. 2, 3). Recently, theological literature has stressed that the terms *Father God* and *Lord God*
are not to be understood literally and naively. "God-names and prop-
erties have only symbolic significance" (Heine 1989:14). But what
does "only" mean? Feminist concerns for a female image of God seem
a little forced, especially when the gender of a word is used as proof. To
illustrate, the word *spirit* has a variety of genders depending upon the
language: in German it is male, in Greek neuter, in Hebrew feminine,
and in English, of course, none at all.

Further, there is no doubt that male designations for the divine
qualities and modes of action predominate in Hebrew Scriptures. Even
attributes and actions that are themselves gender-neutral are read
through the "filter of male language" (Plaskow 1990:123). There is
nothing intrinsically male, for example, about the strangest of all
God's names: *'ehyeh 'ăšer 'ehyeh*—I shall be who I shall be [Exod
3:14]). Yet, when the issues are justice, law, anger, punishment, and
power, God is portrayed using male terminology, male pronouns, and
in terms of male characteristics and images. As Cynthia Ozick notes,
the hand that leads Israel out of Egypt is a male hand, whether or not
it is called so explicitly (1983:122). God is a man of war (Exod 15:3),
a shepherd (most famously in Ps 23:1), a king (1 Sam 12:12; Ps 10:16),
and a father (Deut 32:6; Isa 1:2-4; 64:7; Pss 68:6; 103:13; Prov 3:12).

Apparent lack of primal mother notwithstanding, is it possible that
Mom *is* lurking somewhere in the garden? It could be argued that just
as the waters of the deep, divided by Elohim in Gen 1:6-7, 9 seem to
recall the fluid world of Tiamat, the snake figure who appears in the

garden in Gen 3:1 may allude to Tiamat's serpentlike body (cf. Rahab the dragon in Isa 51:9-10). Gerda Lerner suggests that the formless void of Genesis is related to the Babylonian void, behind which stands Tiamat, the goddess destroyed by Marduk (1986); and E. A. Speiser claims that Eve's title "Mother of all living" was the title of the goddess Araru whose priestess initiates the savage Enkidu sexually in the *Epic of Gilgamesh*[7] and makes him "wise . . . like a god," as well as teaching him to eat and wear clothing like a man instead of a beast (1964). Consequently, the missing Mom of Genesis may, in fact, be related to the goddess figures who for millennia throughout the Middle East were associated with gardens, sacred trees, oracular snakes, and sexual awakening. Certainly, in *The Creation of Adam* Rembrandt sees her presence in the shape of a snake at the creation of humankind, and Rembrandt's Deity looks none-too-pleased about it! The serpent seems to be *protecting* Adam from the Deity.

Although most artists and biblical commentators see the serpent as a less-than-admirable character, the biblical text itself describes the serpent merely as *ārûm* (translated by modern biblical scholars as "cunning," "crafty," "subtle," "astute," or "wily"), and there is no hint in Genesis 3 that the creature is the embodiment of evil. Indeed, an effort seems to be made throughout the narrative to maintain a neutral view of the animal. At the same time, the serpent *does* seem to possess supernatural knowledge and the power of speech, like that of the male deity. While the text states nothing of an evil principle, either inherent in or external to the serpent, the biblical writer certainly projects the serpent as ready, willing, and able to circumvent God's command (as might a displaced goddess?). Thus, I see a strong intertextuality between the chaos/cosmos conflict presented as the defeat of the *goddess* in the *Enuma Elish* and the defeat of the *goddess mother-figure* in Genesis 1–3.

It became quite common in medieval art for the serpent appear as a female or for Satan to be portrayed as a mirror image of Eve. Indeed, there are numerous examples of this. For example, Michelangelo's serpent on the ceiling of the Sistine Chapel in Rome is unmistakably female, as is the one that tempts Adam and Eve on the façade of Notre Dame Cathedral in Paris. In one of the most famous versions of the Book of Hours, that of Duc de Berry, Adam and Eve are confronted by a flaxen-haired serpent who is the mirror image of Eve. The Dutch painter Hendrik Goltzius in his 1616 painting *The Fall of Man,* presents a reading of the garden scene that would seem to agree with mine. In Goltzius's painting, the serpent is particularly benign, indeed, almost charming, as in Duc de Berry's Book of Hours. In fact, the animal not only appears to be female, but once again, her features resemble those of Eve!

But why get rid of Mom? A partial answer may be found in Freud's theory that the primal bond to the mother foreshadows and over-shadows later ties to the father. As Freud states, "We knew, of course, that there had been a preliminary stage of attachment to the mother, but we did not know that it could be so rich in content and so long-lasting" (1916–17:583).[8] I suggest that this primal bond is present also in Hebrew Scriptures: before the figure of the Father-God may stand the Mother-Goddess.

"The Baby Has Daddy's Eyes and Mommy's Nose"

The creation of humankind (*'ādām*) begins with a declaration by God: "And God said: 'We shall make Humankind in our image, after our likeness; and they will rule over the fish of the sea, and over the birds of the heavens, and over the beast, and over all the earth, and over all creeping things that creep on the earth'" (Gen 1:26). The use of first-person plural verbs in Gen 1:26 (*na'aseh*—"we shall make") is distinctive and rhetorically difficult to reconcile since the antecedent seems to be God. That is, the sentence contains a singular subject and plural verb. As many commentators have noted, the use of a plural verb when God speaks occurs only two other times in the entire Hebrew Bible: Gen 11:7 (the Tower of Babel incident) and Isa 6:8 (where it is not problematic since the context makes it clear that God is speaking to, or at least in the presence of, seraphim). Many (traditional) inter-pretations have been offered regarding the use of the plural in this verse. Rabbinic commentators, for example, explain that the use of the plural connotes that God took counsel with someone or something. As to whom or what he consulted, there are divergent opinions. The most prevalent rabbinic view is that God is including himself with his entire celestial court, and consulting with them before creating the highest of his works; on the other hand, the dissenting rabbinic opinion is that if the intention *were* to tell the reader that God took counsel, the narra-tor would have explicitly stated whom he consulted, as in 1 Kgs 22:19; Isa 6:2-8; and Job 1–2.[9] Instead, these rabbis read *na'aseh* as the "plural of majesty": "let us make," similar to "let us go," "let us rise," "let us sit." In any event, the text does not seem to provide a clear answer to this use of the plural. But I would argue here that there may be an answer lying just below the surface of the narrative—Mom.

In the second part of the verse, the Deity states that humankind will be both "in *our* image" and "as *our* likeness." The narrator confirms that Adam was created "in *his* image" and reinforces that by repeating "in the image of God he created *him*." However, the narrator omits the further description of humankind as having been created in God's likeness. Is it possible, therefore, that the "we shall make" refers to God speaking to Mom when he declares his desire for paternity? If so, it could be that the narrator is telling us that humankind resembles and shares attributes of *both* parents, that is, *both* deities.

But which child has the attributes of which parent? In the Hebrew Bible, *ṣelem* refers predominantly to an actual plastic work (as in the images of rats in 1 Sam 6:5 and the molten images of false gods in Num 33:52 and 2 Kgs 11:18) or sometimes an idealized recreation (as in the paintings in Ezek 23:14). Occasionally it means a duplicate, but in a *diminished* sense when compared with the original (Ps 39:7). On the other hand, *dᵉmût* is generally used to signify the "appearance," "similarity," or "analogy" of nonphysical traits (in Ezek 1:28, for example, brightness is compared to the appearance of a rainbow). God says that his intention is to make Adam both "in our image" (that is, physically similar, whatever that may mean), and "in our likeness" (having the same abstract characteristics). The narrator, on the other hand, only says that Adam is in God's *image* and repeats it as a reinforcement. If Adam, the male-child, is created in the *paternal* parent's *ṣelem,* his image is in a diminished sense, while Eve, the female-child, seems to share her *mother's* abstract characteristics, having been created in her *dᵉmût,* her likeness, as her actions in Genesis 3 indicate. If this is the case, then Adam (the male) is, in effect, a diminished god while Eve, on the other hand, has the attributes of her fertility-goddess mother (in an undiminished form?). Interestingly, in a wordplay, *Genesis Rabbah* 18.1 connects the use of *b-n-h* ("build") with *b-y-n* ("discern"): "woman was endowed with intelligence *surpassing* that of man [emphasis added]." Is it possible that the rabbis noticed that there was a female present at the creation, and that Eve takes after her mother?

Joel Weinsheimer states that "the proper name is a sufficient (*but not necessary*) [emphasis supplied] pre-condition of creating a character" and that certainly applies to Eve (1979:1). Although Eve is not mentioned by name until chapter 3 of Genesis, her presence is obvious and her characterization is developed beginning with Genesis 2, where she is created/separated and differentiated from Adam. From this point forward, she seems to be the very personification of her goddess/mother.

After having rejected all that existed on the earth as his equal, finally Adam is presented with someone with whom he can identify. In *God Presenting Eve to Adam in Paradise,* the artist Francesco Villamenaengraver sees a rather voluptuous daughter being presented to Adam by her/their father. Although her hands are covering her breasts and her eyes are cast down, her leg position does not seem at all shy. In fact, her hip seems thrust almost invitingly toward Adam.

Once Adam sees Eve, he responds with apparent pleasure. Indeed, Villamenaengraver's Adam seems almost lascivious! As Umberto Cassuto notes, the sense of Gen 2:23 is "this creature, this time (that is, at last), is in truth someone corresponding to me" (1978:135). Indeed, Adam identifies with Eve so closely that *he* uses a word that corresponds to his own identity. Until now only the generic term *Adam* (humankind) has been employed by God who refers to and calls "Adam." But once this female has been created, the sociosexual terms of *'iš* (Man) and *'iššâ* (Woman) are used and used first by the male. It is he who recognizes that no word yet exists that fully signifies the equality implicit in their relationship, and Man picks a twinlike name to express his affinity for and kinship with Woman. Significantly, he abandons the word that resembles "earth" and that unites him more closely with the other animals. Just as *'ādām* and *'ādāmāh* are linked linguistically and function as parallels to describe Adam's relation with the earth, *'iš* and *'iššâ* function as parallels to signify their similarity. Son and daughter are separate and identifiable—and they behave accordingly: Eve acts; Adam does not.

Biblical commentators all agree that a conversation takes place in Eden. Most read the narrative as indicating that the serpent converses only with Eve and not with Adam. Read from that perspective, sinless Adam is tempted and seduced by temptress Eve (perhaps she was wearing a black negligée at the time?). I see the text differently, in a way that validates both the "nephew's reading" of this narrative as well as that of the scholars who see at least a remnant of (if not reference to) a goddess-figure in the serpent.

A reader discerns a story line (at least) two ways: what the narrator tells us and what the characters themselves say and/or do. In this narrative, both the narrator's report and the actions/words of Adam and Eve support my thesis that the goddess-figure is present and in the shape of the serpent. First, from the moment Eve and Adam are separated/differentiated in Gen 2:22, the narrator never mentions the primeval couple being apart from one another, never mentions the son doing one thing and the daughter another. Second, in the dialogue of vv. 1-6, the serpent speaks about "you" in the plural, and Eve answers in terms of "we." (For example, v. 5 states: "For God knows that on the day that you [plural] eat of it [*'ākāl^ekem*], your eyes [*'ênêkem*] shall be opened, and you [plural] shall be [*wihyîtem*] as gods.") As a result, it is likely that Adam is standing there with her, also being addressed. Third, when Eve eats of the fruit of the forbidden tree in the second half of Gen 3:6, she also gives some to Adam, and the text adds the phrase "to her husband *with her*" (*'immāh*). This grammatical construction is generally viewed as a prepositional phrase used as the attribute of a noun (Joüon 1923:132a). Therefore, this part of the verse should properly be read as "to her husband (*who was*) with her." Finally, the narrator reports in Gen 3:7 that "and the eyes of *both of them* [*š^enêhem*] were opened." Since Eve's eyes were to have been opened at the moment "she took of its fruit and she ate" (Gen 3:6), this verse seems to say that son and daughter *both* converse with the serpent; *neither* seems afraid of the creature; and they eat *simultaneously*.

If Adam is present, and there seems to be no textual evidence to the contrary, then Adam is silent and passive. That is to say, the Deity's son (like his daughter) is not reluctant to eat of the fruit, or even hesitant. Thus, since we know that Adam heard the prohibition (in Gen 2:17), and there is some doubt as to whether or not Eve actually heard the ban directly from God or merely from Adam, perhaps he too recognized the serpent as the goddess and, like the little boy on the farm, had no fear of his Momma.

Having eaten of the fruit that was forbidden to them, Adam and Eve (brother/sister, now husband/wife) flee from the sound of God in the garden.

God first questions his son regarding responsibility (Gen 3:9, 11). Faced with God's anger over the transgression, Adam states, "The woman whom you gave [to be] with me, she gave to me from the tree and I ate" (Gen 3:12). Interestingly, Adam uses *'immādi* (*with* me) rather than *lî* (*to* me) when describing his relationship to Eve, just as the narrator reports the actual eating of the fruit when reporting that Woman gave some to her husband who was "*with* her" (*'immāh*). The son does not call the serpent/mother *ārûmāh* ("cunning," "crafty," "subtle," "astute," or "wily") as the narrator had described her. If Adam viewed this creature as dangerous, here was the opportune occasion for him to speak. But he does not. *Why* not? Was the little boy on the farm correct? Does Adam recognize that "The Daddy sent her away because the children loved her and the Daddy wanted them to love only him"?

Of All Things upon Earth That Bleed and Grow, an Herb Most Bruised Is Woman (Euripides)

The fact that father and son are homologous needs little illustration: it is the central presumption upon which the Hebrew Bible depends, and it constitutes the basis for patrilineage. (Crucial to this book, it is also the central metaphor upon which psychoanalytic theory is grounded.) Throughout the biblical text, a son is regarded as a special blessing, more often than not the direct result of God's divine intervention in a couple's life. The birth of a daughter, on the other hand, by no means creates such positive attention. Why? As I stated earlier, beneath the surface of this Genesis narrative lie two interwoven subtexts: a father-daughter narrative in which the Adam material appears merely as a re-narration, and a story of a repressed fear of emasculation. Just as the father on the farm was threatened by his children's love of/by Momma ("The Daddy sent her away because the children loved her and the Daddy wanted them to love only him. But first she baked the cookies"), the biblical father (like the Greek gods of Hesiod) fears that the relationship of his son and wife, goddess and son, will cause his downfall; God, the male Deity, banishes his wife, the goddess; he is attracted to his daughter; and what makes the nearly absent mother and daughter so central in this otherwise emphatically masculine epic is *their* potential to threaten patriarchal power and rule, like that of their Greek counterparts.

Psychoanalysis, we have known for a long time, is about human sexuality. It is also, as any reading of Freud confirms, about the possibilities and limits of narrative. One great virtue of the Hebrew Bible, which may explain its apparently endless capacity to generate commentaries, is that it too combines these elements (see chap. 2). Read from the perspective of psychoanalytic literary theory, I find that as in (classic) psychoanalytic literary theory, the mother/goddess of Genesis 1–3 is the sexual female at the center of a battle between father and child, a catalyst initiating rivalry and hostility. Female sexuality is seen as potentially menacing and therefore is deconstructed. In the case of the mother/goddess, she is banished from the text; in the case of the daughter, the father's hostility toward his wife is displaced onto his female offspring daughter, and she, too, is controlled.

The Oedipal Conflict

Why is biblical female sexuality so problematic (as discussed on p. 32 and following)? As mentioned earlier, in psychoanalytic theory, "mother" as a sexual female is at the center of a battle between father and son, a catalyst initiating rivalry and hostility. So too in the Hebrew Bible as I discuss more fully in chapter 6.

According to Freud's famous Oedipus theory (based on the play[10] by Sophocles and viewed, of course, from the perspective of the male child rather than that of the mother, father, or female child), the male child first loves his mother, and his attachment to her becomes charged with phallic/sexual overtones. The boy views his father as a rival for his mother's love and wishes to replace him. Fearing retaliation (specifically, castration) by his father for these wishes, the male child experiences a conflict: love for his mother and fear of his father's power. The son's ego is transformed through the incorporation of paternal prohibitions to form his superego; and eventually he gives up his affinity for his mother, radically repressing and denying his feelings toward her while simultaneously identifying with his father. But these feelings are not repressed fully; they are expressed in sublimated activities, and the maternal shadow continues to be present. "The precursor of the mirror," writes Winnicott, "is the mother's face" (1971:117). Every step of the way, as the analysts describe it, a child "develops a relationship to father while looking back at mother" (Chodorow 1978:126). "Mother" becomes an internalized imago with two competing images. On the one hand, she is idealized, the womb being a protecting originator and sustainer of life. On the other hand, the boy links her sexuality with slaughter, since his desire for mother potentially castrates and kills (Freud 1916–17:488).

Freud's description of the family constellation and the role of the Oedipal conflict in sexual development (1925) is strikingly similar to the family construct in Genesis 1–3: God as father, Adam and Eve as his offspring,[11] and the shadowy, repudiated goddess as mother. Read within this framework, God-as-Father prohibits his offspring from desiring the goddess/mother. But the pre-Oedipal, prepatriarchal earliest love object, the mother, still lurks. This leads to a conflict.

On the one hand, biblical motherhood is construed as the ultimate destiny of essential womanhood. Narrative accounts amplify and clarify the importance of (male) offspring to a woman. "Give me children or I shall die," cries Rachel to Jacob (Gen 30:1), a plea repeated over and over throughout the biblical text. And although women appear in many roles in Hebrew Scriptures, it is a very rare positive image of a woman who is not identified as the mother of a son, reinforcing the position that the best thing that can happen to a young woman (the passive is significant here) is to have lots of (male) children.

Since the fertility *goddess* has been banned from the narrative, this *male* Deity now controls reproduction. That is, throughout Genesis, indeed throughout the entire Hebrew Bible, the wombs of women belong to God. Eve, for example, the first to give birth, triumphantly declares, "I have gotten a man *with the help of the Lord*" (Gen 4:1); in Genesis 16, Sarah tells Abraham that *YHWH* has kept her from having children; Abraham, convinced of Sarah's sterility, is informed by God: "*I* will bless her, and moreover *I* will give you a son of her" (Gen 17:15). Rachel is so desirous of children that she uses a surrogate mother (Gen 30:3) and then the narrator reports that "*God* remembered Rachel and *God* hearkened to her and opened her womb . . . she conceived and bore a son" (Gen 30:21-24). The passage ends with Rachel's plea for more sons: "And she called his name Joseph, saying 'The *Lord add to me* another son.'"

This male deity, however, seems insecure. While the concept of motherhood is exalted, at the same time it is potentially menacing since human female procreative power (and its inevitable link to fertility goddesses) rivals the authority of the male Deity. As I discuss in chapter 4, to countermand perceived female fecundity, God establishes a covenant with the *male* Israelites, a contract that makes Abraham and his male offspring "exceedingly fruitful" (Gen 17:6) and thereby repudiates goddesses and their female devotees.

While almost all interpretations of this text acknowledge its sexual nature, traditional exegesis has concentrated on Adam's Fall. However, I see this narrative highlighting God's fear of emasculation surfacing as a result of Eve's rebellion, a rebellion that reminds the Deity of the fecundity of goddess/mother.

It is along these lines that I would like to examine the prohibition forbidding the eating of fruit from the tree of knowledge of good and evil with its accompanying threat ("you shall surely die," Gen 2:16-17) and the serpent's reaction to the prohibition. "Now the serpent . . . said to the woman, 'Did God say, "You shall not eat of any tree of the garden'? . . . You will not die; for God knows that when you eat of it your eyes will be opened, and you will be like God, knowing good and evil" (3:1-5). The Deity/father has planted an invitation to transgress accompanied by a prohibition against doing so. Why did God prohibit the eating of the fruit? Was God or the serpent/mother/goddess telling the truth about the consequences of disobedience? These questions have been debated by many traditional exegetes, and the only point on which virtually all agree is that there are unresolved difficulties.

Many theologians write that God was correct in his determination to preserve the distance between himself and humanity, and that he acted throughout the creation narrative, as well as throughout the entire Hebrew Bible, with humanity's good in mind. Thus Skinner argues that the fruit was forbidden because God knew that it was not good for humanity and, specifically, that immortality "would have been unbearable for man in his present condition" (1930:97). In other words, God was being "merciful."

I disagree. I see a broader issue. The father/Deity gave freedom, but it was a limited freedom: Adam and Eve were free to live their lives in the garden that he had planted, but it was not *their* garden. Adam was to be God's gardener (this was, it may be supposed, a condition of his so-called freedom). Further, Adam and Eve were free to eat the fruit of all the trees in the garden *except* the one that seemed especially desirable to eat (Gen 3:6). As a result, they were to be deprived of the possibility of "knowing good and evil." But this concept would have had no meaning for them had not God introduced them to it: he specifically *forbade* them to eat the fruit that would give them that knowledge (2:17) but made it desirable for them to do so. That is to say, it appears that God, and not the snake, first put the possibility of disobedience into the minds of Adam and Eve; the only additional information that they learn from the snake is that God's threat of punishment by death for disobedience is empty.

Adam and Eve visually perceive that the fruit is good *(ṭôb)*: Eve sees that it is attractive *(neḥmād)* and deduces (no dummy, she!) that it would be "good to eat" *(tôh hā'ēṣ lᵉmaʾakāl)*. Since God already put temptation in the way of the two *before* the intervention of the snake, is it possible that God suggests the possibility of disobedience *in order* to expel them from the garden? Is God afraid of the loss of his power? Is God afraid that Adam and Eve might join forces with their mother/goddess and usurp his authority? The end of the narrative seems to point in that direction. In Gen 3:22 God "shows his hand": "Then YHWH said, 'Behold, the man has become like one of us, knowing good and evil; and now, *lest he should put forth his hand and take also of the tree of life, and eat, and live for ever*'" (emphasis added). As in the ancient Near Eastern legend of Adapa, which describes a mortal tricked into refusing the bread and water of eternal life by the god Ea, God too is determined to prevent humanity from obtaining eternal life. Although the sentence is incomplete, presumably a conclusion such as "I must take the necessary steps to prevent this" is to be understood.

Like Mother, Like Daughter: Eve's Rebellion

The old expression "The apple doesn't fall far from the tree" certainly seems to apply in this instance! Eve appropriates the forbidden fruit and in effect seizes her father's fruitfulness. That is, I see the seed-bearing fruit on the father's tree as a symbol of the Deity's sexual power, the "father's Phallus" in both its Lacanian meaning as a symbol of paternal authority and its Freudian significance as the physical sign of presence.[12]

Why "phallus"? As I discuss throughout this book, for humans, the phallus sits as an answer to two riddles, one of having and one of being. Do I have the phallus or not? Am I the phallus? Of course no one "has" it; no one "is" it, yet these are categories of experience within which humans represent themselves *to* themselves. This is the register through which differences are experienced. Having and not having bring together the question of the phallus and castration (discussed above and in chapters 4 and 6). Castration and the threat of castration are the imaginary form of the experience of difference. That is to say, the experience of having it or being it is a defense against castration. Significantly, it is fruit that represents God's potency.

As I discuss elsewhere, this symbolism becomes clearer if we follow the time-honored exegetical practice of reading the Bible intertextually (1993:78–79). Just before the children of Israel are to enter the promised land, a recapitulation of "the Father's original garden" (Frye 1982:72), the fruit taboo resurfaces and with it, its phallic significance: "When you enter the land and plant all [manner of] trees for food, you will regard its fruits as *uncircumcised*. For three years it will be to you a thing *uncircumcised*, and it *will not be eaten*" (Lev 19:23). Placed into this context, Eve desires her father's sexual power (symbolized by the [phallic] sign, the fruit that has been denied her). By asserting her desire to determine her *own* sexuality, she challenges God's usurpation of procreative power from the female fertility goddess(es) to himself (as I discuss on p. 66, it is God who consistently "opens the womb" of barren women). Read from this perspective, the iconographical moments of the garden and the Fall sequentially recapitulate the story of the pre-Oedipal state of ignorance and the knowledge obtained by psychosexual development.

By eating the fruit offered by her fertility-goddess mother, Eve obtains some of the inherent fertility of Momma, and she herself is now fruitful. Furthermore, by giving the "seed-bearing fruit" to Adam, Eve becomes the medium through which this symbol of potency (the Phallus in both Freudian and Lacanian meanings) is passed. Thus, Eve reminds the male Deity of the potential danger of female sexuality, a danger represented by the fruit. Eve's choice to give fruit, the conventional symbol of female sexuality, to a male represents the ultimate dispossession of her father and her sway over reproductive control. The daughter's act is a violation cursed by the father, and, like her mother before her, she is subject to a permanent barrier of separation. At the *daughter's* instigation, the son has cast aside his obedience and perpetual security, an action viewed by the Deity as an outright rejection. Thus, *because of* the sins of the daughter, sons leave their father's control ("This is why a man leaves his father" [Gen 2:24]).[13] Having effectively banished Momma and her fecundity from the garden, God, perceiving Eve's newfound fruitfulness, expels Adam and Eve from the vicinity of the tree of life as well (thus assuring himself of being the sole immortal).

This banishment of Adam and Eve from Eden has been a favorite topic of many artists. Indeed, Benjamin West tells the story quite dramatically in *The Expulsion of Adam and Eve from Paradise*. He uses theatrical gestures, rich paint textures, and clashes of blinding light and shadowy darkness. Although Genesis does not state how Adam and Eve were expelled from Eden, artists often portray the (male) archangel Michael as the agent of God's wrath. In Benjamin West's painting, an angry looking Michael is directed by a sharp beam of light overhead, perhaps referring to the flaming sword or perhaps a reference to God's rage.

Although God gave Adam and Eve the commandment to be fruitful and multiply, the couple remains childless while in the Garden of Eden, and until their rebellious act, Adam and Eve are not even aware of their nakedness.[14] The commandment to be fruitful and multiply is now transformed into the structures of taboo, transgression, and punishment. Adam becomes a laborer, and West portrays him as quite unhappy about the prospect. Along these lines, the punishments meted out to Eve and the serpent are particularly interesting. West sees Eve as practically pleading for a stay of execution. But the text is not quite that clear. "To the woman he [God] said: 'I will greatly multiply your pain in childbearing: in pain you will bring forth children, and your desire shall be for your husband and he shall rule over you'" (Gen 3:16). In the structure of Hebrew poetry, the second half of a line is closely related in content to the first half: it carries the thought further, either repeating, clarifying, restating, or contrasting (Berlin 1985; Kugel 1981). This part of the verse could then be read as:

> I will greatly multiply:
> your-pain-in-childbearing/in-pain-you-will-bring-forth-children
> your-desire-shall-be-for-your-husband/and-he-shall-rule-over-you.

In other words, "In pain you shall bring forth children" duplicates "your pain in childbearing." Likewise, "he shall rule over you" parallels "your desire shall be for your husband." Therefore, the husband's rule lies in the wife's need for her husband because of her sexual desire. And it is the result of this female sexual desire that childbirth is to be painful.[15]

In light of the missing Mom, the curse upon the serpent is equally significant. Although West portrays the serpent slinking away, totally vanquished, textually there is some ambiguity. "I shall put enmity between you and the woman, and between your seed and her seed; he will bruise your head, and you will bruise his heel" (Gen 3:15). It is difficult to determine the precise meaning of the second part of this verse in the Hebrew text because of the unspecified pronouns and the inexplicit subject-verb agreement. Literally, the second part of the verse reads, "He will bruise the head of you [masculine], and you [mas-

culine] will bruise the heel of him." One way of interpreting this verse
is by referring to the nouns in the first half of the sentence. Thus, the
meaning of this half of the sentence may be construed as: "He [that is,
the seed of Woman] will bruise the head of you [the seed of the ser-
pent], and you [the seed of the serpent] will bruise the heel of him [the
seed of Woman]." All of the masculine pronouns refer to "seed," a
word that is masculine in Hebrew but does not necessarily refer to
males. If this reading is correct, from the perspective of psychoanalytic
literary theory, the curse that the Deity inflicts upon mother(s) and
son(s) is perpetual tension (could Freud have been right after all?)!

At the same time, the Deity punishes mother(s) and daughter(s):
beginning with Eve, there is no clear license for female sexuality in the
Hebrew Bible despite—or perhaps *because of*—her desire for her husband. Indeed, the taboo the Deity establishes immediately before creating Eve, and the admonition given to Adam, imply a deconstruction
of female sexuality *before* it is even constructed. That is to say, when
Eve is created, she is not authorized as Adam's sexual partner, but as his
asexual "helper who is his counterpart." But Eve rebels. Although
Woman may not have been *created* as a sexual being, having eaten of
the forbidden fruit, Eve sexualizes the garden and thereby challenges
the Deity's power. As a result, throughout Genesis 1–3, Eve's role as
Woman is under constant negotiation. Until her position in the family is fixed as the "Mother of All the Living" (which occurs only after
the expulsion, see note 14), Eve is the crucial character. Yet her narrative centrality is in conflict with the repeated ways she is shifted from
margin to margin. That is, until Eve has been evicted from her father's
garden into motherhood, Eve as a sexual female is a problem. And the
story of Eve is at the heart of the concept of Woman throughout the
Hebrew Bible. Eve is Everywoman, the prototypical woman, all of her
sex who are yet to come: "[the childless woman is viewed] as intrinsically evil; a foreign object, a sexual object, dirty. But in due course she
becomes the mother of new members of the lineage. In the second
capacity she is intrinsically good, the very criterion of virtue and cleanliness, the antithesis of a sexual object" (Leach 1983:74–75).

Conclusion: The First Father–Daughter "Seduction"[16]
But where is the incest (aside from the obvious brother-sister/spousal
relationship of Adam and Eve)? The ambivalence of the father's part in

the Fall that I discuss as being the focus of considerable theological commentary, perhaps can be seen also as Freud's "catastrophe" (discussed below), with its dangerous potential inherent in the daughter's "transition to the father object" (Freud 1925:241). Significant for purposes of this chapter, the catastrophe Freud describes is a sublimated father-daughter incest. If read from that perspective, a father-daughter incest motif can be seen as the second subtext of the Genesis narrative. The father/deity is locked into a conflicted text of desire and prohibition. That is, he desires Eve, yet forbids Eve's sexuality; he simultaneously wants but does not want the transgression he has provoked, a transgression he will deny and punish. This ambivalence is textually revealed by its most psychologically accurate defense. Using Freud's concepts of "*psychic* reality" and "*primal* fantasy" (seduction can be a *representation* of the father's repressed and deflected sexual desires, or even a metaphor for power, a "primal fantasy"), *actual* incest need not occur. The gap between a reality orientation and the subjugation of the "imaginary" or the realization of the actual situation, the very structure of fantasy, is thus bridged. Freud observed among his patients that the father often deflected his guilt from himself to (variously) the nurse, the mother,[17] and by way of the Oedipus complex, to the child herself. So too in this narrative. The father/deity projects his unfulfilled and repressed desire onto others and thus is able to deny paternal complicity.

The seduction is displaced first onto the (phallic) serpent, the rejected fertility goddess. But how can a goddess be a *phallic* symbol? As I have discussed earlier, a phallic signifier does not denote any sexual gender; it is a sexually neutral representation of power. Thus, from the perspective of the father, the serpent/goddess is a phallic symbol. There are other indicators for the serpent's phallic symbolism as well. The first is the obvious Freudian association of shape. Second, since Hebrew has no neuter gender, nouns must be either masculine or feminine, and the word for serpent (*nāḥāš*) is, indeed, masculine.

The serpent as seducer thus established, blame is then displaced onto the daughter herself in her seduction of Adam. The chain of deflections to protect the father begins. It is not the father but the serpent who seduces the daughter and, by the end of this narrative, it is the daughter who seduces Adam, her "father"! Paradigmatically, the "shamed shames the shamer."[18]

Ironically, however, rather than masking the threat of deflected desire, the text reconstitutes it. Because of the emphasis placed on Eve's derivation from Adam's side, and therefore Adam's implied paternity, the narrative reinforces the paradigm of a tacitly condoned but overtly disclaimed act between father and daughter. The original father-daughter story, which has been so problematic, is repressed but remains visible in Adam. Adam, the acknowledged son, becomes the father, making father and son analogous (and as Boose points out, this relationship is then changed in Christianity to synonymous [1989:48]).

Genesis 1–3 begins a long tradition of paternal displacement and attributing the origin of evil: here, as elsewhere, the problem revolves around women. Significantly, from now on (with the exception of the anomalous story of Ibzan in Judg 12:9), biblical fathers assiduously avoid ever giving daughters away. In fact, the Hebrew Bible avoids daughters almost altogether[19] once the collective catastrophe of Gen 6:4, brought about by the generic "*daughters* of men" occurs. Read from the perspective of Freud, perhaps the garden should be avoided rather than revisited!

Chapter 4

Oedipus Wrecks: The Covenant of Circumcision

Cut or Be Cut Off (בְּרִית מִילָה)

As discussed throughout this book, the culture reflected in the Hebrew Bible is particularly and vigorously dedicated to protecting the human penis and its physical environs. This zealous protection is extended by the language or rather, I should say, by the *lack* of specific relevant terminology for designating the penis as well as by the scanty usage of the few, euphemistic, recorded terms (see p. 77).

This state of affairs is paradoxical because the society that created biblical literature is undoubtedly phallic and phallocentric. Characterizing biblical/ancient Israel as a phallocentric society is by no means an empty generalization. The Hebrew Bible posits the human penis as the explicit, emblematic, and exclusive symbol of religious identity and membership of the communal order. Thus, the penis symbolizes the special link between this society's God and the (male) members of the community. It serves as a physical reminder both of inclusion *in* the community and exclusion *from* it. Circumcision, taken over from other cultures and reinterpreted, defines males and males only as the full members of the covenant community.

Circumcision and Paternal Identification

The sexual symbolism of circumcision is powerful in its reverberations. *Berît mîlah* (the covenant of circumcision) is with Abraham alone. Sarah is not included. Instead, Sarah is mentioned only as the bearer of Abraham's seed, blessed by God as though the patriarch's sperm were self-generating: *nātattî mimmennāh lekā bēn*—"I will give to you *through her* a son" (Gen 17:16). In other words, although both Abraham *and* Sarah are to be the bearers of kings and nations, the covenantal relationship is with males only, first with Abraham, then with Abraham's son, Isaac. Sarah is identified through the filter of Abraham's experience. Clearly, the covenant community is the community of males (Gen 17:10), and the essence of the arrangement is the multiplication of men. (And by head count, Abraham's grandson Jacob plays a prodigious role in the "multiplication of men," since he sires twelve sons [and only one daughter]; by the time he goes to Egypt he has accumulated sixty six bloodline descendants, sixty-four of them male!)[1]

Since there is an implicit male erasure of the female role in procreation, the covenant of circumcision signifies that procreativity lodges in the relationship between God and human males. Male sexuality forms the nucleus of filiation (see Eilberg-Schwartz 1990), a common bonding, and the penis is the focus of the holy covenant. As Sarna states, the "thigh is symbolic of the reproductive organs, the seat of pro-creative powers" (1966:170–71). In Genesis 24, for example, when Abraham wants his slave to fetch a wife for Isaac, he commands the slave to "put your hand under my thigh and I will make you swear by the LORD . . . to go to my country, to my kindred to take a wife for my son." Similarly, in Genesis 32, when Jacob is finished fathering, he wrestles with an angel who touches the hollow of his thigh and puts it out of joint (discussed further in chap. 5).[2]

Displacement in literature can reflect the unconscious symbolic relationships between parts of the body. Such displacements are familiar in popular language. The riddle that asks, "Why do men think so much and women talk so much," with the answer, "Because men have two heads and women have four lips," expresses the respective upward and downward displacement of genitals and face. Similarly, Roman masks whose tongues are phalli illustrate the unconscious equation of tongue and phallus. A related metaphorical expression of this equation informs the Christian characterization of Christ as "God's word made flesh." The fecundating power of the "word of God" explicit in certain annunciation scenes also seems to equate tongue and phallus. Based on the number of literary examples of linguistic displacement, it seems rather likely that in both of the Genesis examples cited above, the testicles rather than the thighs are being touched, reinforcing the ultimate symbol (and reality) of male procreative powers.

The male organ is thus linked with power, and female sexuality is deconstructed. Sarah apparently supplies nothing of her essential being to her son Isaac and is merely the vehicle through which this covenantal relationship is established and maintained. Woman is the soil in which male seed is planted.

> Semen as seed, the child in essence, the part for the whole . . . the child
> is fashioned solely by the impregnating principle provided by the father.
> . . . [As such] Abraham is the symbol of a change in a world view pre-

cipitated by the idea that men had come to view their role in conception as primary . . . the shift from the knowledge of participation to the assumption that it was the primary role. (Mace 1953:206)

Of course, this idea of conception is not unique to the Hebrew Bible. Aeschylus expresses the Greek view: "The mother is no parent of that which is called her child, but only the nurse of the new-planted seed that grows. The parent is he who mounts" (in Lattimore translation, 1967).

Circumcision and Castration

Interestingly, however, this link with power, the penis, is to be circumcised. Not surprisingly, the *'ār'lah* (foreskin), designating the part removed from the penis and dedicated to the divine, is a specific term mentioned sixteen times in contexts of circumcision (the other contexts in which it is mentioned are either agricultural or martial). What is surprising, however, is that the penis itself is called "flesh" (a word that has many other connotations) or "meat" rather than "penis." Indeed, the original commandment given to Abraham regarding the covenantal circumcision combines the terms "foreskin" and "meat": "You shall be circumcised in the meat of your foreskins, and it shall be a sign of the covenant between me and you" (Gen 17:11). There are other euphemisms for male genitals that seem to highlight a preoccupation simultaneously to privilege the organ(s) and yet deflect its/their importance. The specific term *'āšek* (testicle) occurs only once in Leviticus, where it is decreed that a man with a ruptured testicle (among other physical defects) cannot officiate as an Aaronite priest before God. There is a single occurrence of "shameful parts" in Deuteronomy:

. . . or a hunchback, or a dwarf, or a man with a defect in his sight or an itching disease or scabs or crushed testicles [shall not come near to offer the Aaronite offerings]. (Lev 21:20)

When men fight with one another, and the wife of the one draws near to rescue her husband from the hand of him who is beating him, and puts out her hand and seizes him by the private parts, then you shall cut off her hand; your eye shall have no pity. (Deut 25:11-12)

Another euphemism for male genitalia is *marg'lōtāyw* (literally "the place of the legs/feet"),[3] which probably derives from *regel* (foot), a common enough biblical euphemism for penis (see, for example, Exod 4:25; Judg 3:24; 1 Sam 24:4). A crude reference to penis is that of 1 Kgs 12:10, where Rehoboam's advisors counsel him to refuse the populace's request that the oppressive measures instituted by King Solomon, his father, be lifted and reply instead "*qāṭānnî 'ābāh mimmāt^enê 'ābî*" (literally, "my small finger is thicker than my father's waist"). Although the word *māt^enāyim* often signifies "waist" or "hips," here, as elsewhere in the Hebrew Bible, it is probably a reference to "penis." In Exod 28:22, for example, the priests are ordered to wear pants "from waist to thigh" while officiating at the altar, and Jeremiah wears a "linen girdle" on his "waist." Thus, it makes more sense to translate the advice given to Rehoboam that his response be "my small finger is thicker than my father's penis."

I find it somewhat perplexing, however, that a text that valorizes the circumcised human penis as a symbolic marker of the [male] link with the divine and frequently designates the foreskin does not mention the penis itself. Why not?

Fear. Although YHWH promises to bless Abraham's seed, he immediately establishes the vulnerability of Abraham's organ and Abraham's dependence upon God for fertility. Certainly, no other part of the body would emphasize as effectively the connection between Abraham's reproductive capacity and the Deity's ultimate potency, particularly since Abraham and the men of his household are circumcised as adults, an obviously memorable procedure.

Since the covenant endows the male with the ability to engender life, and then extends this ability from father to son, by implication Abraham now possesses God's procreative powers. The narrative account of the covenantal relationship is therefore a paradigm of the Freudian male-child's Oedipus conflict, the lure of which is affiliation with the father, the superiority of masculine identification and masculine prerogatives over feminine. As such, there is a potential threat to paternal authority, and struggle is inevitable. In fact, many scholars suggest that this motif is an important aspect of continuity between the books of the Hebrew Bible. David Jobling, for example, identifies antagonistic aspects of heredity in Judges and Samuel (1986:53), as does Alice Bach, who writes: "Beginning with the birth of Samuel, spiritual father to both Saul and David, and ending with the death of Saul and his sons, . . . coming of age . . . can be read as a record of war games of slaughter and betrayal" (1990:37).[4]

Circumcision can thus be seen as a partial castration, the price God-as-father exacts from Abraham-as-son (and his sons) to be in the analogous paternal position.

Oedipus Wrecks: Moses and God's Rod

Of course, the identification of, or link between, the human circumcised penis and the divine phallus is far from theologically unproblematic. It relates to questions about the Hebrew God's gender and to the general problem of humanity's [dis]similarities to that God. To be sure, it has been argued that the deity in the Hebrew Bible is not male and has no sex, as I discuss on p. 58. Yet, as pointed out in chap. 3, male designations for the divine qualities and modes of action predominate in Hebrew Scriptures and as many scholars have noted,[5] one of the most distinctive features of Genesis is the frequent use of a variation on the divine epithet "God of your/his/their *father*[s]," with "Abraham" and/or "Isaac" added in apposition to "father" (for example, Gen 24:12; 28:13; 31:5, 29; 32:10; 46:1, 3). This appellation is particularly appropriate in the patriarchal narratives, since they revolve around the lives of fathers. Indeed, according to Peter Miscall, the text *is* the chronicle of the fathers: "that is the core, the essential meaning" (1983:4). Even when the epithet is not used, however, it is clear that Hebrew Scriptures describe the special, personal relationship of a particular male deity and a particular male community in terms of father and son.

A significant link between psychoanalytic literary theory and biblical scholarship lies in the privilege that both accord the language of images and symbols. For Freud, phallic symbols were particularly significant. One phallic image that seems to connect the two disciplines is God's rod, mentioned first in Exod 4:1-5 and later in 7:8-12, an object that changes its form into a serpent and then back again into a rod. Since the language of images and symbols is equally important in mythology,[6] a discipline that bridges psychoanalytic literary theory and biblical scholarship, I would like to continue this discussion of circumcision and paternal identification by returning *to* Egypt, instead of *leaving* it as Moses did.[7] I read the Egyptian myth of Isis and Osiris as a lens through which I view the symbolism and hence significance of the Oedipal construct and biblical father-son relationships as highlighted in the narrative of Moses and God's rod. Unfortunately, no complete account of the myth of Isis and Osiris has been preserved in an Egyptian text, although several references and additional and varying details are found in Egyptian religious writings and monumental inscriptions. The only extant text of the whole legend is Plutarch's *De Iside et Osiride,* a late form of the myth with several Greek influences.

However, Plutarch does provide a very useful story outline. In depicting this myth I have relied on Griffiths, Parkinson, and Ochshorn.

Briefly summarized, Osiris, the great grandson of Re, grandson of Shu, and first son of Geb and Nut, succeeding his father as king in Egypt, married his sister, Isis. Osiris, widely regarded as a just and wise king, organized the agricultural, religious, and secular life of his people and, assisted by Isis, acquired additional territory through many peaceful foreign conquests. This happy state of affairs was soon destroyed, however, by Seth, the younger brother of Osiris. Jealous of his older brother's power and prestige, Seth wanted the throne and accolades for himself. When Osiris returned to Egypt from travels abroad, Seth invited him to a banquet at which seventy-two accomplices were present also. During the festivities a beautifully decorated casket specifically built to the measurements of Osiris was brought into the hall. Seth promised that the much-admired casket would be given to the person who fitted inside it perfectly. Of course, when it was Osiris's turn to try it out for size, it was just right! Seizing the opportunity to usurp his brother's position, Seth and his followers closed the lid, fastened it securely, and threw the casket into the river Nile in the hope that it would be carried out to the Mediterranean Sea and lost forever. Unfortunately for Seth, the casket washed ashore near the city of Byblos on the Syrian coast, close to the base of a young tamarisk tree, which quickly grew to enclose the casket inside its trunk. The King of Byblos noticed the tree, ordered it to be cut down, and had it made into a column to support the hall roof in his palace.

Meanwhile, back in Egypt, Isis had heard what Seth had done to Osiris, and in great distress she set out to find her husband/brother. Eventually she came to Byblos, succeeded in having the palace column removed, retrieved the casket, and took it back to Egypt, where she hid it in the marshes of the Delta. Although Osiris was dead, Isis at least had the body of her late husband/brother.

One night Isis left the casket unattended and Seth discovered it. Determined to destroy his brother's body permanently, he cut it up into fourteen pieces and distributed them over all of Egypt. When Isis became aware of this outrage, she traveled throughout the country searching for the various body parts, assisted by her sister, Nephthys (who also happened to be the wife of Seth). Gradually, they found thirteen of the fourteen pieces, reassembled them, and reanimated them. The only part of Osiris's body she could not find was his penis, which had been eaten by a Nile fish. To replace this irretrievably lost member, Isis created a simulacrum—the Phallus. The resurrected Osiris had no further part to play on earth. Thus, he became the ruler of the dead, and Isis superseded Osiris as the fertility deity in Egypt. The simulacrum of Osiris's penis was now an object of veneration, and in honor of this Phallus, according to Plutarch, "the Egyptians even at the present day celebrate a fertility festival" (Plutarch 1936:47). Herodotus, in Book 2 of *The Histories,* graphically describes the celebration:

> The Egyptians . . . have . . . eighteen-inch-high images, controlled by strings, which the women carry round the villages; these images have a penis that nods and in size is not much less than all the rest of the body. Ahead there goes a flute-player, and the women follow, singing in honor of Osiris. Now why the penis is so much bigger and is the only movable thing in the body—about this there is a sacred story told. (Herodotus 1987:152)

Neither Plutarch nor Herodotus says anything further about the excessive dimensions of the Phallus or its movement. Indeed, Herodotus seems bound to silence. Apparently, it is a secret that had to be guarded —religiously. Indeed, Isis is depicted time and again in Egyptian monumental art hovering over the dead, penis-less body of her late husband/brother while holding a large simulacrum; the religious aspects of this cult apparently included hymns of praise dedicated to Isis as the new fertility goddess.[8] In more modern times, the religious practices of this cult so astonished Voltaire that he used it as an illustration of relativism: "The Egyptians were so far from attaching any disgrace to what we are desirous as much as possible to conceal and avoid the mention of, that they bore in procession a large and characteristic image, called Phallus, in order to thank the gods for making the human frame so instrumental in the perpetuation of the human species" (Voltaire 1906:309).

A long and tedious commentary would be necessary to give all of the details of this myth's wealth. In political terms, for example, the myth has been described as preserving dim historical elements of a time during the Predynastic Period when Egypt was divided into the two kingdoms of Upper and Lower Egypt, each with its own ruler. According to Parkinson (1991), Osiris represents an early king whose death led to war between the two kingdoms. In agricultural terms, the death and resurrection of Osiris as a very early nature god apparently were celebrated each year in ceremonies at the time of the Nile flood when the crop was sown and when the harvest was gathered (Sarna 1991:39). In ritual terms, the old agricultural ceremonies were joined with the cult of the dead to form the official Osirian rites and festivals, performed at the places where parts of the body of Osiris were reputed to be found, such as Athribis (heart), Busiris (backbone), Memphis (head), and so on. The festivals included "mysteries," dramatic performances of episodes relating to the life, death, and resurrection of Osiris, and often involved the planting of seed in Osiris-shaped molds to germinate and grow by the end of the festival (Griffiths 1980). But what is particularly striking from a psychoanalytic literary perspective is that the myth of Isis and Osiris interprets the dramatic relationship between the castrated real penis of Osiris, the onetime fertility god, and the oversized Phallus—now a fertility symbol—carried by the female devotees of the new fertility *goddess.*

What is the relationship between the spectacular simulacrum of the displayed, fully erect, sacred Phallus of Osiris carried in procession during religious ceremonies and God's rod? Ilana Pardes writes that since Near Eastern myths and rituals often involve goddesses who resurrect dying gods emblematic of the cycles of agrarian fertility, there is a goddess, possibly Isis, "behind" all of the women of the Exodus narrative (1992:93). I see this text somewhat differently. Rather than focusing on the women, as does Pardes, I am more interested in the power struggle between the father-figure (God) and the male-child-figure (Moses and ultimately all the Israelite males). That is to say, I would like to posit the question, "Who has the Phallus?"

As I discuss throughout this book, while the term *phallus* is interchangeable with *penis* in ordinary usage, in psychoanalytic literary theory Phallus does not denote the anatomical organ; rather, Lacan (1977b) associates Phallus with the concept of power. The Phallus is emblematic of that which we want but cannot or do not have, irrespective of which sex we happen to be. As Lacan describes it, the Phallus is "a term which, having no value itself . . . can represent that to which value accrues" (1977b:43), and Ragland-Sullivan adds that "the phallic signifier does not denote any sexual gender [or] superiority" (1986:271). For the cult of Osiris, the Phallus comes "in place of" Osiris's penis. It is a fabrication, a constructed model, an artifact that simulates what is missing and, simultaneously, renders it sacred and larger than life to make it a goddess-cult fertility object. Indeed, Lacan uses this very myth when he distinguishes between the penis as *organ* and the Phallus as "the simulacrum that it represented for the Ancients" (1977b:285). I read this Exodus narrative in a similar way: like Osiris's simulacrum, God's rod represents the ultimate power of a sacred Phallus.

When God first identifies himself to Moses, it is as "the God of your *father,* the God of Abraham, the God of Isaac, and the God of Jacob," reminding Moses (who had been reared by Pharaoh's daughter) of the covenant made with the patriarchs (his biological father's ancestors)— a covenant that in no way includes the fertility goddess, Isis! Moses, perhaps remembering the parades of women carrying the immense Phallus so graphically described by Herodotus, or perhaps anticipating skepticism by his fellow Israelites still in Egypt (who, for 430 years have been witnessing these fertility rites of Isis), says in effect, "Okay. I'll tell them 'the God of your *fathers* has sent me,' but what good will that do? They're going to need proof." Thereupon, God gives Moses instructions. First, Moses is to tell all the "*sons* of Israel" that "the Lord God of your *fathers,* the God of Abraham, the God of Isaac, and the God of Jacob has sent me." This simple statement establishes opposition between "the *sons* of Israel" and the *women* of the Egyptian villages, women who "religiously" parade with an oversized fertility symbol and worship a *female* fertility deity. God reinforces this schism linguistically by saying "this is my *zikrî* (memorial)," a word etymologically related to the word *zākar* (male).

Next, Moses is told to gather the elders of Israel and, using the same formulaic language ("the God of your *fathers,* the God of Abraham, of Isaac, and of Jacob"), to remind them of the covenant, a covenant made only with the *male* members of the community. The centerpiece of this covenant is God's promise that Abraham will have vast numbers of descendants, but only because of the intervention of the Israelite deity: "I shall establish my covenant between me and you, and I shall make you exceedingly numerous . . . this is my covenant with you: You shall be the father of a multitude of nations. . . . I shall make you the father of a multitude of nations. I shall make you exceedingly fertile, and make nations of you; and kings shall come forth from you" (Gen 17:2; 17:4-6). By these two acts, Moses subliminally associates God (the Israelite *male* deity) with Abraham's fertility, thus diminishing the role of Isis (the Egyptian female fertility deity) in procreation. Moses, however, still is not convinced completely. As a result, God draws upon the authority of his "rod."

In the Hebrew Bible, four words are commonly translated as rod, all of which refer to an elongated object. While the distinctions in English are not particularly pronounced, in Hebrew the words are used for quite different purposes. The *maqqel,* for example, is a rod in the sense of a "walking stick" or "hand-staff"; the *shevet* is a rod used for punishing; and the *ḥoter* is used generally to denote a "twig." A *matteh,* the term used in reference to God's rod, denotes a leader's staff and carries the Lacanian weight of power in both positive and negative contexts. In Ps 110:2, for example, the psalmist sings that "YHWH will send *maṭṭēh ʿuzzʿkā* (your strong rod) out of Zion," while Ezekiel (7:11) uses the term negatively: "violence has risen to a *maṭṭēh-rešaʿ* (wicked rod)." Indeed, the only place where *matteh* is used to refer to a shepherd's rod is here in the Exodus narrative, where the Deity proves his might to Moses (the hesitating future leader) by changing his *matteh* into a . . . *naḥaš* (snake)! Snakes and rods, two time-honored phallic symbols, represent both Freudian sexual symbolism (the two phases of the male organ in its active and quiescent states) and Lacanian Phallic/power symbolism. By juxtaposing a snake and his rod, God establishes *his matteh* as *the* signifier of ultimate authority, a simulacrum of even greater proportions than those that the devotees of Isis carried, a signification that continues throughout the confrontation with Pharaoh.[9] Thus, like Sarna (1991:38–39), I see the interactions between God, Moses, Pharaoh, and the magicians as attempts to discredit Egyptian polytheism in general, and worship of the Egyptian fertility goddess Isis in particular.

When Moses returns to Egypt, he presents himself before Pharaoh but wields God's rod, and this time it turns into a serpent (*tannim*) rather than a snake. Pharaoh's magicians, wielding their *own* rods, apparently possess the same power. Thus, at first it seems that the emissaries of the Egyptian fertility goddess[10] carry phallic symbols as potent as God's rod: both sides can transform their elongated objects into serpents. However, the change in reptile from *naḥaš* to *tannim,* snake to serpent, is significant from the perspective of traditional biblical scholarship and psychoanalytic literary theory since both disciplines rely on the same strategy: being open to the sudden switches and rearrangements that reveal alternate messages and expose the dynamic play of meaning behind what may seem to be a simple statement.

In the case of specific word choice, repetitions and shifts represent the basis for a wealth of scholarly material among biblical scholars and psychoanalytic literary critics alike. The study of lexical similarities and differences is a mainstay, since words can mean more than they seem to mean and do more than they seem to do. Among biblical scholars, Berlin (1989), for example, explores how "lexical cohesion" (the ways in which words are linguistically connected within a sequence) plays a role in interpretation, and how awareness of this relationship can lead to better readings. In a very different kind of criticism, Bloom (1976) examines "poetic crossings," the ways in which a text can destroy its own integrity if examined within the framework of lexical similarities and differences. This particular change in word choice (from *nahaš* to *tannim*—snake to serpent) has been commented upon by biblical scholars. Cassuto (1983:95), for example, attributes the change to geographical factors: the snake, he claims, is more suited to the desert, where the sign was given to Moses, than the serpent of the Egyptian setting. Sarna, in a more literary vein, notes the "special relevance to Pharaoh, who is addressed as follows in Ezekiel 29:3: 'Thus says the Lord God: "I am going to deal with you, O Pharaoh, king of Egypt, the *hattanim haggadol* (Mighty Serpent)"'" (1991:21).

I prefer to examine the change from snake to serpent from the perspective of both traditional biblical exegesis and psychoanalytic literary theory. In biblical Hebrew, *nahaš* ("snake") derives from the verb "to hiss." It is used literally to signify the actual creature and figuratively for enemies or oppressors (see, for example, Jer 8:17; Isa 14:29). The term *tannim* ("serpent") is an *intensive* noun that derives from the verb "to elongate." It is used in more dramatic and dangerous circumstances, for example, a "*venomous* serpent," "*devouring* dragon," "sea- (or river) monster" (as in Deut 32:33; Jer 51:34; Gen 1:21). Used in the figurative sense, it refers to enemies, and again, the metaphoric usage is intensified, that is, it refers to *particularly* dangerous enemies such as the Egyptians (Ps 74:13) or, more commonly, to the personification of chaos (Isa 27:1; 51:9).

Here in the Exodus narrative, Moses is first introduced to God's power by a *nahaš*, a "hiss." When Moses does the wand-into-serpent trick before Pharaoh, God's rod becomes the more dramatic *tannim* (serpent), intensifying the strength of God's authority in the eyes of Moses who, faced with the magicians of Isis, still may need encouragement. When the magicians of the fertility goddess, Isis, perform the same act, it appears that God's rod, in the hand of Moses, is no greater than that of Isis in the hands of her magicians. The more God's rod is wielded, however, the greater the significance of *tannim* and its derivation from the root verb "to elongate." As God's rod becomes longer, it becomes more potent, more able to wreak destruction upon the Egyptians. Finally, God's rod swallows up the sorcerers' rods. Most important, since by metathesis *bala'* ("swallow") suggests *ba'al* ("possess"), by "swallowing" the rods of Pharaoh's magicians, God's rod now possesses the symbolic procreative power and authority of Isis. At this point, God's rod, *the* most elongated, and thus ultimate Lacanian Phallus, becomes the simulacrum that firmly identifies this Deity as the most powerful. In the Lacanian sense, the symbolic and functional value of God's rod highlights God's desire—and ability—to vanquish Pharaoh's magicians, and stands for the ultimate symbolic authority that it carries and that Pharaoh and the magicians of Isis lack. Due to God's "elongated" rod, Pharaoh and his magicians symbolically have been castrated. Equally significant, the fertility goddess, Isis, has been dethroned. The Israelites' fertility Deity, God, is one, and he is Male. Parenthetically, it should be noted that metathesis allows a more Freudian interpretation as well: *bala'* (swallow) also suggests *be'ilah* (sexual intercourse). Perhaps it is in this context that Sarna describes the book of Exodus as "the greatest *seminal* text of biblical literature" (1991:xii; emphasis added).

As the myth of Isis and Osiris highlights, although the Phallus is a symbol and not an organ, it undeniably derives a part of its signifying attributes from what the real penis can evoke. Indeed, Freud proposed that symbolization works by pictorial analogy. Long, thin objects regularly represent the phallus, and concave objects, vessels, and containers represent the vagina.[11] As a result, it may not always be easy or even productive to differentiate sharply between penis and Phallus. Indeed, although psychoanalytic literary theory has benefited enormously from Lacan's distinction between the two, the metaphors of veiling and unveiling deployed by Lacan himself emphasize the difficulty of differentiating between them (1977b:281–91). As Lacan writes (1977b:287), the Phallus, "by virtue of its turgidity . . . is the image of the vital flow as it is transmitted in generation," emphasizing its irreducible anchorage in the function of reproduction. Thus, Silverman (1992:89) notes that "to veil the Phallus in this way is to permit it to function as a privileged signifier, as Lacan himself acknowledges. It is also to conceal the part that gender plays within many important Lacanian texts." In the Exodus narrative, the association of penis and Phallus is particularly strong. As if to highlight this relationship, the narrator reports an otherwise irrelevant episode: on the trip back to Egypt, Zipporah, Moses' wife, *circumcises* their firstborn son while Moses carries—the rod of God![12]

How do snakes, serpents, penis, Phallus, and Isis relate to the construct of God-as-father–Israelite-(male)-as-son relationship in the Hebrew Bible? When Moses threatened Pharaoh with the eighth plague, locusts, he warned that it would be "something that neither your *fathers nor fathers' fathers* have seen." Later, in the desert God explains to Moses that the purpose for the entire conflict with Pharaoh is "that you may recount in the hearing of your *sons* and of your *sons' sons* how I made a mockery of the Egyptians and how I displayed my . . . *signs* among them." I see these two simple statements linking the snakes, serpents, penis, Phallus, and Isis to form a construct that locks God and Moses, and ultimately God and the male Israelites, into a classic, Oedipal conflict. Let me explain.

According to Freud's famous Oedipal theory (based on Sophocles's play; see chap. 3, note 10), the male child first loves his mother and his attachment to her becomes charged with sexual overtones. In the world of the son's unconscious fantasy, Mother is the object of incestuous desire. At this stage, the son's ego identity focuses on the active, masculine genital organ—the penis. Father, who also possesses a penis, becomes a model. Simultaneously, however, the boy views his father as a rival for his mother's love, an adversary who must be destroyed or removed for gratification to be achieved. But the boy recognizes that Father is the *legitimate* owner of Mother, and as a result, the son views his desire as a transgression that produces anxiety, guilt, and renunciation. Fearing retaliation (specifically, castration) by his father for his incestuous wishes, the boy experiences a conflict: love for his mother and fear of his father's power. In Lacanian terms, Father's penis, the anatomical organ, becomes Father's Phallus—the symbol of Father's power. The only way the male child can keep his penis and masculine identity is by transcending the familial Oedipal triangle and replacing it with the father-dominated superego, a process that for Freud is "designed to make the individual find a place in the cultural commu nity" (1931:229). "The father is the oldest, first, and . . . only author- ity" (1900:293).

According to Freud, the Oedipal conflict, although universal in structure, undergoes transformations and is subject to cross-cultural variability. As Spiro (1961:486–87) notes, this is particularly true in societies in which the conflict is not successfully resolved and thus necessitates constant repression. With Freud and Lacan as the basis, I read this narrative in the following way: God is the father-image, Moses is the son, and the entire panoply of Egyptian gods and goddesses (the fertility cult of Isis in particular) is a *composite* mother-image.

Moses (the male-child figure) first loves his "mother" (Isis) and has the unconscious desires that Freud describes. (It is important to remember that for Freud, the reality reference of the Oedipus story is to the inner psychic reality of latent desire [1914:16–18]. That is, the events of the story constitute unrecognized wishes; they are products of fantasy rather than actual reproductions of memory. In fact, in the historical formation of psychoanalysis, Freud replaced the fairy tale of infantile parental seduction, in which the reality reference of the story was to *actual,* external, objective events [1896:203], with the Oedipus myth.) Consistent with Freud's theory, the son's ego identity (in this narrative, Moses) focuses on his active, masculine genital organ (remember Zipporah and the strange circumcision scene?). When Moses sees God's rod symbolically rendering the simulacrum wielded by Isis's magicians impotent, in effect he hears the father's voice, what Lacan calls "*le Nom-du-Père*" ("the Name-of-the-Father," the verbal expression of the father's function as a disciplinarian, see p. 6). Thus, as in Lacan's paradigm, Moses, fearing retaliation for his wishes, expe- riences a conflict: love for his mother (polytheism in general and Isis in particular) and fear of his father's power (in other words, if the oversized Phallus of Osiris can be destroyed, what about Moses' penis?). Consequently, Moses sublimates his desire for the Egyptian goddess/mother whose fertility rites he had observed for most of his life, identifies with his father-image, Israel's male Deity, and renounces his affinity with and worship of Isis. By accepting YHWH as *the* supreme Law (the will of the Father), Moses and his offspring, the "sons of Israel," become a "kingdom of priests" (Exod 19:6). By reminding Moses of the covenant made with the *fathers,* the power of God's rod thereby is linked to the male organ, as male sexuality replaces and sublimates the procreative power of Isis; and for Moses and the "sons of Israel," the penis, and not the simulacrum of Osiris, is the focus of the holy covenant.

Once in the wilderness, however, God reminds Moses that this link with power, the penis, is to be circumcised. In fact, only those who *are* circumcised can commemorate their deliverance from Egypt. While biblical scholars have discussed the political and religious implications of this covenant,[13] they have not paid much attention to the token that seals the arrangement. Why the penis? Certainly, if the purpose was to distinguish this band of wanderers from all other people, a more obvious part of the body might have been chosen, for example, piercing the ear or the nose. Indeed, there are some interesting resonances in the terms of a relationship that stipulates that those who do not *cut* will be *cut off.*[14] "And the uncircumcised male who does not circumcise the 'meat' of his foreskin, that person shall be cut off from the people; he has broken my covenant" (Gen 17:14).

Significant for the purposes of this chapter, for Freud (1916–17:165; 1937:122), circumcision is the "symbolic substitute" for castration, for what is no longer there. Since the circumcised penis both asserts the possible threat of castration (the foreskin has been removed) and denies it (the head of the penis is prominent as in an erection), from this perspective, the covenant between God, Abraham, and subsequent male offspring established in Genesis 17 reflects a chain of fathers and sons, and thereby the tensions of male power. As a result, the sexual symbolism in the relationship between Moses and God is powerful in its reverberations. The original covenant was with males only, and the essence of the arrangement was the multiplication of men. However, offspring are possible only with the assistance of *this* male god ("*I* shall make you exceedingly numerous. . . . *I* shall make you the father of a multitude of nations. . . . *I* shall make you exceedingly fertile, and make nations of you").[15] Of course, not only psychoanalytic literary theorists have reached this conclusion. Indeed, relying heavily on ethnographic literature, Eilberg-Schwartz argues that "the practice of circumcision, despite its role in symbolizing the covenant . . . nonetheless symbolized the fertility of the initiate . . . and ability to perpetuate a lineage of male descendants" (1990:142).

Repeating the terms of the covenant to Moses has two results first, God implicitly erases the female fertility rites of the followers of Isis. Since the covenant of circumcision signifies that procreativity now lodges in the relationship between God and human *males,* Isis, the Egyptian fertility goddess/mother, is displaced by the fertility God/father. Male sexuality forms the nucleus of filiation, a common bonding, and the Israelite penis, rather than the Egyptian god Osiris's simulacrum, is once again the focus of the holy covenant. The male organ is linked with power (in the sense of both Eilberg-Schwartz's comparative fertility thesis and the one I am developing here), and goddess/mother-worship is rechanneled.

Since the covenant endows the male with the ability to engender life, and then extends this ability from father to son, by implication Moses would *seem* to possess both God's procreative powers and the authority to wield God's rod, a paradigmatic representation of the Freudian male child's Oedipus construct. However, the second consequence of reminding Moses of the terms of the covenant is that God immediately establishes the vulnerability of the human anatomical organ, the penis. Although once again God promises to bless Israel's seed, Moses must depend upon *this deity* for fertility. Certainly, no other part of the body would emphasize as effectively the connection between male reproductive capacity and the Deity's ultimate potency. The lure for Moses is affiliation with the father/God and the power inherent in his rod, the superiority of masculine identification and masculine prerogatives over the feminine influence of Isis. Freud writes that "whosoever accepted this symbol (circumcision) showed by so doing that he was ready to submit to the father's will, although it was at the cost of a painful sacrifice" (1939:1561.) However, as in Freud's Oedipal construct, the potential threat of castration is always there and struggle is inevitable. Oedipus wrecks!

Curiously, the Freudian account of the Oedipus story reveals a peculiarly selective reading of Sophocles's *Oedipus Rex.* Laius, who is rife with anxieties, is absolved by Freud of his crime, and his sins and fears have been displaced by the guilt of his son, Oedipus. In the biblical narrative, the relationship between Moses and God exposes similar displacements. Circumcision, seen as a partial castration, is the price God-as-father exacts from Moses-as-son to be in a somewhat, but not quite, analogous paternal position vis-à-vis the "sons of Israel." That is, only the Deity has a thoroughly intact organ, and thus only the Deity can provide offspring.

Circumcision as Feminizing

The midrash asks: "Why is it written, 'And the LORD will pass over the door' [Exod 12:23]? . . . Read it [door] literally as 'opening!' . . . the opening of the body. And what is the opening of the body? That is the circumcision" (*Zohar* 2:36a; in Wolfson 1987:204). In Freudian analysis (as elsewhere), of course, the door or gate is a symbol of the female genital orifice (Freud 1916–17:156). Thus, this sexual displacement, read from a psychoanalytic perspective, allows Israel to be portrayed as a female with respect to God, despite the fact that the covenant is made only with males. Ezekiel 16:6 is a graphic example: "I passed by you [feminine] and saw you [feminine] weltering in your blood, and I said to you [feminine] 'Live in your blood.'" By reminding Moses that he and his offspring, the sons of Israel, are to be circumcised, God displaces his own anxieties and views Moses, as well as the "sons of Israel" as female. Hence, there is no threat to his power.[16]

Circumcision, therefore, has at least two ramifications in the Hebrew Bible. First, it enables the son to emulate the father. That is, in place of specific priests and priestesses of Ishtar dedicating their sexuality to the *goddesses* by engaging in ritual sexual intercourse in the *goddesses'* honor in order to celebrate and enhance the fertility of the goddesses, Abraham and his sons celebrate the fertility of a *male* Deity and *male* procreativity. From this perspective, Moses' relationship to God's rod reads almost like a Freudian case-study: Moses-as-son emulates the father; in place of the women of Egypt dedicating their sexuality to the goddess Isis by engaging in a ritual parade while carrying Osiris's oversized phallic simulacrum, Moses will now celebrate the fertility (and virility) of a *male* Deity and *male* procreativity. Implied within this construct, however, is a warning by the father/God: "If you worship women, and specifically, Egyptian goddesses (that is, if you continue to desire Mama/Isis), I'll finish the job started by circumcision, and fully castrate you to make you a woman." This implied threat symbolically ensures that the son never can be as powerful as the father.

The Deity's warning leads to the second ramification of circumcision: it metaphorically transforms male Israelites into females in their relationship to God. In other words, the circumcised men of Israel, the male "nation of priests" become "Daughters of Zion" (Boyarin 1992:475). In Lacanian terms, Abraham and his offspring may possess the penis but never the Phallus, the ultimate symbol of paternal authority and the privilege it signifies. As a result, only the Deity can provide a thoroughly intact opener of a womb. Thus, as many commentators have noted, the stories about Moses in Exodus through Deuteronomy are not really about the man, but rather the God who stands behind the man. Despite Moses' seeming power, he does nothing except in response to the Deity's commands. Indeed, Schnutenhaus describes Moses as a "Jahvemarionette" (quoted in Coats 1988:33).

This construct of the relationship of Moses and God and the heavy emphasis on God's rod lasts beyond Egypt. In Num 21:4-9, for example, "venomous snakes" attack the Israelites because of their rebellion against both God and Moses, their bites causing the death of many of the people. The remaining Israelites confess their sins, and Moses, interceding for them, receives instruction for the remedy: a bronze *snake* on a *pole* that will reverse the fatal quality of the bites. Those stricken need only see this double phallic symbol in order to survive the fate inflicted by the snakes. Although there is no explicit connection between God's rod and the bronze snake, in Exodus and Numbers, serpents, rods, and God's power merge. As in the myth of Isis and Osiris, a sacred phallus has been invested with power—this time, God's. Rabbinic legends reinforce the phallic symbolism of God's rod in Midrash *Exodus Rabbah,* which relate the history of God's *matteh* (how it was handed down from Adam, generation by generation, until it came into the possession of Moses); the tetragrammaton (YHWH), which was inscribed upon it; the mnemonics of the Ten Plagues, which were also engraved on it; and other similar details (*Exodus Rabbah,* 8.2).

The fundamental themes of psychoanalytic literary theory—desire, the meaning of the father-figure, law, and guilt—characterize the relationship of the deity and the sons of Israel. God's rod has displaced Isis; Israelite male sexuality has displaced Egyptian sacralization of female sexuality; and Egyptian women carrying eighteen-inch-high images with nodding penises have been displaced by the *circumcised* penis of the Israelites, the manifest symbol of the relationship of the male Israelite and God. For Freud, Oedipus wrecks. So too for Israel.

Chapter 5 ———————————————

Daddy-Dearest and the "Invisible Spirit of Wine"[1]: Theme and Variations

Theme

Genesis relates two episodes of a father drinking wine to excess, having a sexual encounter with his offspring, and subsequently condemning not his offspring but his grandchildren. Genesis 9:18-27 narrates the tale of an inebriated Noah, and Genesis 19 relates the story of Lot. As discussed below, most commentators have excused the fathers' behavior and censured the children. This chapter presents an alternative reading—one in which neither father is blameless. According to my reading, under the influence of alcohol, Lot and Noah acted upon repressed desires or frustrations.

The Lot story exemplifies the most common type of incest and has many similarities to clinical reports of father-daughter incestuous relationships: the disintegrated family, the father who has lost his patriarchal role, the abuse of alcohol, the mother who looks away, and the involvement of more than one daughter. The usually unconscious desire of the father (see chap. 3) toward the daughter is, in this instance, consciously acted out. Similarly, psychoanalytic literary theory, other literary representations of the incest motif, and clinical situations involving father-son incest allow the Noah narrative to be read as involving either Noah's *fantasizing* about a homosexual activity or, possibly, even actually *initiating* such a liaison with his son, Ham.

As I discuss more fully in chapter 4, Freud refers to the sexual nature of the child's relationship to his or her parents as an Oedipal construct or Oedipal relationship based on Sophocles's play (Freud 1909).[2] Briefly, the young child has an unconscious, erotic affection for the parent of the opposite sex and, as a result, a jealous aversion to the same-sex parent. Freud claims further that parents unintentionally actually encourage their children in this Oedipal relationship. Of course, it is natural for fathers to be affectionate toward their daughters and for mothers to have a similar relationship with their sons. But, according to Freud, the child notices this preferential treatment and bears a grudge against the parent who seems to interfere. Thus the child follows his or her own sexual drive by choosing between the two parents accordingly. As a result, the same-sex parent develops an unconscious hostility toward the child who is attempting to "steal" the other parent's love. Freudian theorists write that the primary incest scene (that is, the Oedipal relationship) must be successfully resolved for the healthy mental development of every individual. *"If not, the desire may be repressed or sublimated and return in another, less appropriate, setting such as an incestuous relationship with one's son or daughter"* (my emphasis; Freud 1905:68; 1909:132).

Literary representations of this primary incest scene abound. For example, as a by-product of incest with the mother, many myths contain a theme of jealous hatred toward the father that stems from sexual rivalry (as in Hesiod's *Theogony*, discussed in chap. 3). Often, however, the son's hatred is focused only indirectly toward the father's life. Instead, the son's animosity is directed toward his father's genitals. In addition, there are many myths in which the father attempts to castrate his son (again, as in Hesiod's *Theogony*). In many cases, the theme of actual castration, sometimes carried out upon the father by the jealous son and sometimes carried out upon the son by the jealous father, is replaced either by the substitution of other body parts for dismemberment of genitalia (blinding, for example) or by a symbolic castration, that is, the loss of power. The story of Samson is particularly interesting in this regard, since the cutting of his hair is both a *symbol* of castration and simultaneously an explicit loss of Samson's physical prowess. Further, from the perspective of psychoanalytic literary theory, the Oedipal significance of Samson's blindness as upwardly displaced castration can be associated to Icarus's fall, since hubris requires a failure to "see" intelligently and in*sight*fully and therefore is punished accordingly. In other words, it is as grandiose for a blind man to lead others as for Icarus to disobey Daedalus and for the citizens of Babel to build a tower reaching to the heavens.

Significantly, there are many myths in which the symbolic castration of the son by the father is an incestuous homosexual relationship (Rank [1912] 1992). That is to say, from a psychoanalytic perspective, this homosexual incest in effect "feminizes" the son (Freud 1909:138), and thereby the father diminishes his son's status and power (see p.

103). Generally speaking, in these myths the father's actions occur either because the father wants to prevent his son's attack on him or because the father has not successfully resolved his own homosexual fantasies/desires (Freud 1909:139).

Just as the Oedipal relationship is represented frequently in general literature and is particularly prevalent in mythology, so too is the analogous relationship of fathers and daughters. One difference, however, is the *perspective* of the narrative. The mother/son relationship is generally presented from the son's point of view. On the other hand, the father-daughter relationship is rarely presented from the point of view of the child but mainly from the *father's* perspective (as in the Lot narrative, discussed below). Often, the father having had an incestuous relationship with his daughter(s) condemns the offspring (again, as in Lot's case).

Noah and Ham

Genesis 9:18-27 narrates the unconventional behavior of an inebriated Noah and his sons Shem, Ham, and Japheth:

> The sons of Noah who went forth from the ark were Shem, Ham, and Japheth. Ham was the father of Canaan. These three were the sons of Noah; and from these the whole earth was peopled. Noah was the first tiller of the soil. He planted a vineyard; and he drank of the wine, and became drunk, and lay uncovered in his tent. And Ham, the father of Canaan, saw the nakedness of his father, and told his two brothers outside. Then Shem and Japheth took a garment, laid it upon both their shoulders, and walked backward and covered the nakedness of their father; their faces were turned away, and they did not see their father's nakedness. When Noah awoke from his wine and knew what his youngest son had done to him, he said, "Cursed be Canaan; a slave of slaves shall he be to his brothers." He also said, "Blessed by the LORD my God be Shem; and let Canaan be his slave. God enlarge Japheth, and let him dwell in the tents of Shem; and let Canaan be his slave."

This short episode, which constitutes a link between the story of the Flood and the table of nations, is puzzling. Because of its brevity and textual inconsistencies, a number of scholars have suggested that this narrative is merely a "splinter from a more substantial tale" (Speiser 1964:62). If so, it might account for some of the many unanswered questions. A fuller account, for example, might address why Ham is spoken of as the youngest son in v. 24 and listed as the second of three sons in v. 18; or exactly what Ham "had done to" Noah that incurred such wrath; or how Noah "learned" what occurred; or why, if it was Ham who was guilty of some significant misdeed, Noah's curse is directed at Canaan; or why this particular punishment was selected; or why Japheth is allied with Shem; or why a threefold emphasis on Ham's paternity of Canaan; or, or, or . . . many obvious elements of critical importance that need clarification. Have two different stories been merged? Is a part of the text missing? Although text critics (scholars who "correct" one text in light of another) and source critics (scholars who do not view the Masoretic Text as a unified entity, but rather examine narratives as disparate units) have much to say about the linguistic and literary development of the Hebrew Bible, I prefer the approach of literary scholars who view this text as a puzzling but unified whole. As such, I assume that even *this* narrative in its present state is intended to make sense. That is, there is a coherence in the narrative that various readings help explicate.

The narrator of this enigmatic tale begins with a seemingly inconsequential piece of information in presenting the genealogy of Noah: Genesis 9:18 tells us the names of Noah's sons, reasonably enough, and then casually mentions that Ham is the father of Canaan. Typical of biblical narrative, this offhand comment is an example of a frequently used literary technique of the biblical writer—introducing information presumably irrelevant to the immediate context yet crucial to the understanding of subsequent developments. Without it, we would be as ignorant of the identity of the *object* of Noah's curse as we are of its *cause*.

Then the story begins. After the Deluge, Noah was "the" tiller of the soil. (According to *Tanḥuma* Genesis 11, Noah invented the plow; that is, Noah was the initiator of true agriculture as opposed to hoe agriculture or horticulture.) The article *the* implies something well known about Noah, possibly a tradition as a folk hero—or perhaps by initiating viticulture, Noah was the first to discover the soothing, consoling, and enlivening effects of wine! Indeed, many commentators who discuss this passage excuse Noah's excessive drinking exactly because he *was* the first wine-drinker. For example, John Chrysostom, a church father, writes that Noah's behavior is defensible: as the first human being to taste wine, he would not know its aftereffects. According to Chrysostom, Noah "through ignorance and inexperience of the proper amount to drink, fell into a drunken stupor" (Hamilton 1990:202–3). Philo, a Hellenistic Jewish philosopher, goes even further in exonerating Noah. He notes that one can drink in two different manners:

> For there is a twofold and double way of becoming drunken: one is to drink wine to excess, which is a sin peculiar to the vicious and evil man; the other is to partake of wine, which always happens to the wise man. Accordingly, it is in the second signification that the virtuous and wise man is said to be drunken, not by drinking wine to excess, but merely by partaking of wine. (Philo 1971:160)

Philo goes on to explain that Noah was not "drinking to excess" but "merely . . . partaking of wine."

The rabbis place Noah in a somewhat more ambiguous light:

> Satan thereupon slaughtered a lamb, and then, in succession, a lion, a pig and a monkey. The blood of each as it was killed he made to flow under the vine. Thus he conveyed to Noah what the qualities of wine are: before a man drinks of it, he is innocent as a lamb; if he drinks of it moderately, he feels as strong as a lion; if he drinks more of it than he can bear, he resembles a pig; and if he drinks to the point of intoxication, then he behaves like a monkey, he dances around, sings, talks obscenely, and knows not what he is doing. (*Genesis Rabbah* 36:3)

It was not only the ancients who felt it necessary to exonerate Noah, at least partially. Indeed, this kind of apologetic permeates the work of most contemporary scholars. For example, when Nahum Sarna discusses Noah's drinking, he says that "no blame attaches to Noah since he was oblivious to the intoxicating effects of his discovery" (Sarna 1989:65). Similarly, George Knight writes:

> Under no circumstances are we to bring a moral judgment to bear upon Noah as he falls drunken in his tent. Man learns only from experience. In our day, every material discovery brings its compensatory disadvantages, road deaths from the development of the internal combustion engine, unspeakable devastation from the discovery of nuclear fission. Noah is the "guinea-pig," so to speak, from whom all mankind has been able to learn that along with drunkenness goes moral laxity, and that the drugging of the higher powers of human consciousness leads to sexual license. (Knight 1981:105)

Back to the story. The narrator relates two facts: first, having become inebriated, Noah "uncovered himself within his tent" and second, Ham "saw his father's nakedness." At this point, the text takes on several additional layers of ambiguity, all of which revolve around sexuality.

There appears to be little doubt that Noah's "uncovering himself" means exposure of his genitalia. In fact, both Habakkuk and Lamentations mention such exposure by the inebriated and associate it with shame and loss of human dignity:

> Woe to him who makes his neighbors drink of the cup of his wrath, and makes them drunk, to gaze on their shame! (Hab. 2:15)

Rejoice and be glad, O daughter of Edom, dweller in the land of Uz; but to you also the cup shall pass; you shall become drunk and strip yourself bare. (Lam. 4:21)

Further, there is little doubt that Ham saw his father's exposed geni talia. Not surprisingly, there have been several interpretations of this anecdote. However, there has been little unanimity as to what actually occurred within the confines of Noah's tent. For example, the Babylonian Talmud, tractate *Sanhedrin,* has an interesting dialogue on the episode, and rabbinic sources are divided on whether Ham castrated his father or engaged in a homosexual act, the former interpretation relying upon the fact Noah has no children after the Flood. Rav maintains that Ham castrated his father, while Samuel claims that he sexually abused him:

> [With respect to the last verse] Rav and Samuel [differ,] one maintaining that he castrated him, whilst the other says that he sexually abused him. He who maintains that he castrated him, [reasons thus:] Since he cursed him by his fourth son, he must have injured him with respect to his fourth son. But he who says that he sexually abused him, draws an analogy between *"and he saw"* written twice. Here it is written, *And Ham the father of Canaan saw the nakedness of his father,* whilst elsewhere it is written, *And when Shechem the son of Hamor saw her [he took her and lay with her and defiled her].* Now, on the view that he emasculated him, it is right that he curse him by his fourth son; but on the view that he abused him, why did he curse his fourth son: he should have cursed him himself?—Both indignities were perpetrated. (*Sanhedrin* 70a)

More recently, W. G. Cole suggests that although Gen 9:22 cites "looking" as Ham's only crime,[3] Ham did more than mere looking and thinks the words "what his younger son had done to him" reveals a sexual attack on the father (Cole 1959:43). Along these lines, J. M. Robertson draws attention to the similarity of this story to that of the castration of Uranus by Kronos (1900:44). F. W. Bassett suggests that the idiomatic expression "saw his father's nakedness" could mean that Ham "had sexual intercourse with his father's *wife* [my emphasis]" (Bassett 1971:235). However, other scholars disagree. E. A. Speiser notes that while the term "saw his father's nakedness" relates to genital exposure (contrast Gen 42:9 and 12), it does not necessarily imply sexual offenses (cf. Gen 2:25 and Exod 20:26; Speiser 1964:61). Similarly, Calum Carmichael writes: "For those who think the incident between Ham and Noah involved a homosexual act . . . they speculate—wrongly, I think—that because the act was so abhorrent the biblical author did not spell it out. My view is that a lawgiver found the narrative *suggestive* of the topic of sexual encroachment on a father" (1997:99).

And Nahum Sarna takes Ham's actions quite literally, that is, Ham is guilty of having seen Noah's genitalia and then compounds his crime (lack of modesty and filial respect) by leaving his father uncovered and "shamelessly bruiting about what he had seen" (Sarna 1989:66). Sarna seems to backtrack, however, by adding that v.24 ("Noah knew what his younger son *had done to him*" [my emphasis]) and the severity of Noah's reaction suggest that the Torah has "suppressed the sordid details of some repugnant act" (Sarna 1989:66).[4]

But whose "repugnant act"? As I stated earlier, based on psychoanalytic literary theory, other literary representations of the incest motif, and clinical situations involving father-son incest, the act could have been either Noah *fantasizing* about the homosexual activity or possibly actually *initiating* such a liaison with his son Ham.

While the narrator is silent as to what actually occurred between Noah and Ham, the text does report that Ham told his brothers about the encounter. Having "learned what[?] his youngest son had 'done to him,'" Noah curses Canaan, condemning him to *'ebed 'ābādîm* (literally, "slave of slaves," a grammatical construction that expresses the extreme degree of servitude) and blesses Shem and Japheth.[5] The text is silent as to how Noah became aware of the situation and why Canaan, not Ham, is cursed. Saadia and Ibn Janah construe the curse to mean "Cursed be [the father of] Canaan," a phrase that has already appeared twice in this brief narrative. Ibn Ezra has an interesting reading of this verse. He claims that "his youngest son" does not refer to Ham as *Noah's* youngest son but rather to Canaan as *Ham's* youngest son (quoted in Sarna 1989:66). Thus, Ham is the offended party, and *his* son Canaan the perpetrator of some base deed. Accordingly, Noah, as grandfather, blames Canaan for "defiling" Ham. All that can be said with any surety about Ibn Ezra's reading is that Noah remains "pure," the righteous man saved from the Deluge by the Deity and from condemnation by most commentators.

Although source critics might argue that in the fuller story Canaan, son of Ham, was a participant in the offense against Noah, there are so many questions and ambiguities relating to this narrative in general that perhaps we can look for explanations within the text itself by using the approach of psychoanalytic literary theory. As in the psycho-analytic process, one way to arrive at possible answers is to raise (per-haps obvious) questions.

Question one: How did Noah "uncover himself within his tent"? (Did he intentionally remove his clothing and *then* lie down, or did he accidentally expose himself while sleeping?)

Question two: If Noah intentionally removed his clothing (rather than accidentally kicking off his garment while asleep), can we assume that he was relatively sober (as Philo maintains above), at least sober enough to disrobe? (Or, in the words of *Genesis Rabbah,* was Noah a lamb, lion, bear, pig, or monkey?)

Question three: When did Ham enter the tent? (That is, was Ham *already* in the tent when Noah arrived, or did Ham wander in some-time later?)

While these questions might seem meaningless, they will become more relevant and ultimately lead to the most germane question: If Ham entered the tent first and Noah intentionally removed his cloth-ing in Ham's presence, was Noah initiating (either consciously or unconsciously) an incestuous encounter?

Since the text does not state explicitly that Noah lost consciousness, and because it requires at least some coordination to remove clothing, I am assuming that Noah was probably not drunk enough to pass out. If Noah disrobed *aware* that Ham was in the tent, again, there are (at least) three possible scenarios, each of which could be said to rely upon Noah's reduced inhibitions due to the effects of the wine. All three of these readings are based on the premise that under the influence of alcohol, Noah was more likely to act upon repressed desires or frustra-tions. (Or, as Joseph Conrad wrote, "It is a maudlin and indecent ver-ity that comes out through the strength of wine" [Conrad 1912:194].)

Option one: Noah undressed before his son arrived, and when Ham arrived, Noah initiated a forbidden fantasy—an incestuous liaison with his son.

Option two: Noah disrobed in his son's presence, and by doing so, Noah's heretofore repressed fantasy of an incestuous, homosexual encounter with his son was brought to the surface of his consciousness but *not* acted upon.

Option three: Ham, seeing his father naked, is the one who initiated a sexual encounter (as most commentators suggest).

The third scenario, one that most rabbinic authorities seem to favor, appears to be the *least* reasonable. If Ham had either castrated his father or initiated a homosexual act, it seems rather unlikely that he would then run outside looking for his brothers Shem and Japheth as witnesses. Indeed, clinicians report that in most cases, children who have had incestuous homosexual relations do not report the incident until many years later (Medlicott 1967:135). More likely, therefore, are either of the first two readings, options that help explain the extreme nature of Noah's curse: his guilt and his shame.

While many elements of the conventional vocabulary of moral deliberation (words such as *ethical, virtuous, righteous,* and their opposites) are largely alien to the psychoanalytic lexicon, the concepts of guilt and shame do appear, albeit in technical (and essentially non-moral) contexts (Smith 1986:52). Guilt and shame are described as different emotional responses stemming from different stimuli, reflecting different patterns of behavior, and functioning in different social constructions (although the two are often related). Their primary distinction lies in the norm that is violated and the expected consequences.

Guilt relates to internalized societal and parental *prohibitions,* the transgression of which creates feelings of wrongdoing and the fear of punishment (Piers and Singer 1953). Shame, on the other hand, relates to the anxiety caused by inadequacy or failure to live up to internalized societal and parental *goals and ideals* (as opposed to internalized prohibitions), expectations of what a person should supposedly do, be, know, or feel. These feelings of failure often lead to a fear of psychological or physical rejection, abandonment, expulsion (separation anxiety), or loss of social position (Alexander 1948:43). The person shamed often feels the need to take revenge for his or her humiliation, to save face. By "shaming the shamer," the shamed person reverses the situation and feels triumphant (Horney 1950:103).

One might correctly apply to this narrative the Freudian theory that the primary incest scene (the Oedipal relationship) must be successfully resolved for the healthy mental development of every individual or the repressed desire may return in another setting. When Noah "awoke from his wine," apparently either he realized that an *actual* incestuous, homosexual encounter with his son Ham had occurred, or he recognized his *repressed* desire for such a relationship. Presumably as

a result, Noah understandably felt guilt (for having violated the societal norms that prohibit homosexuality) and shame, hence, Noah's
need for revenge in order to maintain his dignity and self-esteem. In
other words, Noah "shamed the shamer." Using what reads anachro-
nistically like classical Freudian defense mechanisms, Noah attempted
to alleviate his own anxiety by using methods that would deny, falsify,
or otherwise distort his heretofore repressed fantasy. First, Noah sublimated the obviously dangerous memory or idea—his desire for Ham.
Next, Noah rejected *himself* as the source of his uncomfortable feelings
and attributed the origin of these emotions to Ham. That is, instead of
saying "I wanted Ham," Noah said "Ham wanted me." Essential here
is that by displacing his emotions, Noah, the *subject* of unresolved
incestuous, homosexual desires changes himself into the *object* of these
desires. By doing so, Noah is able to provide a rationalization for his
curse. As a result, Ham is forced into the position of shouldering
Noah's displaced guilt and shame.

But why curse Canaan and not Ham? Looking at artistic and literary representations of this narrative in light of psychoanalytic literary
theory might provide a different insight into Noah's actions than that
of traditional biblical scholars. Renaissance painters appear to display
a rather playful approach to this biblical episode, one that seems also
to echo Freudian thought and recent clinical data. Generally speaking,
the pictures portray the obviously masculine naked patriarchal figure
lying in a drunken state. However, significant from the perspective of
psychoanalytic literary theory and actual reported incest cases, there is
considerable sexual confusion in the representation of the three brothers, Japheth, Shem, and Ham. A twelfth-century mosaic, for example,
shows Ham without a beard beside his two bearded brothers, perhaps
suggesting the oft-used theme that beards and masculinity are equated,
as in the well-known Samson narrative of Judges 13–16. The artist
Jacopo de'la Quercia (c. 1430) shows only two brothers, one carrying
a cloak with averted eyes and behind him Ham (presumably) with his
garments drawn up to expose his own genitalia. Hiding in the vines is
a mysterious feminine figure. (Might she represent a feminized por-
trayal of Ham?) Giovanni Bellini (fifteenth century) portrays a nude,
heavily bearded Noah cavorting about. Ham, smooth-skinned, is pic-
tured in the middle of the scene.

For purposes of this chapter, I am most interested in Michelangelo's
reading of the text in his Noah panel in the Sistine Chapel. Michelangelo

shows all three brothers with feminine hair arrangements. However, the brother nearest to Noah is the most masculine, with clearly identifiable male genitalia, the second brother has male genitalia but a rather protuberant feminine-like abdomen and is being embraced from behind by a dark Ham without any male genitals to clearly identify his sex.

The decreasingly masculine representations of each of the brothers suggests that Michelangelo's reading of the narrative portrays the first brother as sufficiently secure in his own masculinity not to hurry to look at his father's genitals, the second brother as confused, and Ham *as* a female. *Why* would Ham be portrayed in such a feminized style? Significant for purposes of my reading, clinically it has been generally accepted that homosexual seduction by the father threatens the son's masculinity and overwhelms him with a passive feminine identification (Medlicott 1967). That is, the father who makes sexual approaches to his son symbolically castrates him by "making a woman" of him, which is consistent with my interpretation of the representations of Michelangelo and other Renaissance artists. In other words, these painters are portraying Ham from *Noah's* perspective—as feminized.

Surprisingly, there has not been much of a literary influence of the Noah narrative, perhaps because we know so little of the family dynamics. Notwithstanding, the few instances of the Noah motif could also be said to support Noah, rather than Ham, as the initiator of the sexual encounter. For example, English mystery-play pageants[6] generally portray Noah as the convivial drunkard and his wife as an ill-tempered shrew who makes his life on the ark quite intolerable. Similarly, Clifford Odets's 1954 play *The Flowering Peach*[7] turns the story of Noah and the Flood into a Jewish family sitcom. Noah tipples, calls his wife, Esther, "girlie," and says things like, "What am I, a loaf of bread? Don't bitter me," whenever someone tries to flatter him. Esther complains, weeps, and complains some more. Sibling rivalries divide their grown sons: Shem, the wheeler-dealer; Ham, the rake; and Japheth, the misfit and mother's favorite, affectionately known as "Jafey." Again, of interest because of their Freudian nature, both of these literary representations portray Noah as feeling inadequate in his masculinity, having difficulty in mastering women and thus vulnerable to engage in a homosexual relationship, as well as emasculating his male partner (in this case, Ham) in the process.

But this still does not explain fully why Canaan, and not Ham, is cursed. Psychoanalytic literary theory suggests that by consigning Ham's son and further progeny into abject slavery, Noah symbolically castrates Ham. As I discuss throughout this book, although the word *phallus* is interchangeable with *penis* in ordinary usage, this is not the case in that branch of psychoanalysis that concerns itself with psychosexual development. In the discourse of psychoanalysis, the word *Phallus* does not denote the anatomical organ but rather the signifier or symbol of what we desire but lack, and is most often associated with the concept of *power*. By making Canaan the "slave of slaves," Noah makes Canaan powerless, lacking a Phallus, in effect having the same standing as females. Ham, while not physically castrated, is symbolically castrated by the enslaving of Canaan and his progeny. Noah, on the other hand, is exonerated and can maintain his status as "righteous."

Lot and His Daughters

But Noah is not the only father who imbibes with tragic results. The story of Lot and his two daughters is disturbing, complicated, and (probably, therefore) one of the most oft-discussed incestuous relationships in the Hebrew Bible. Genesis 19 relates that two angels in (male) human form come as visitors to Lot's house in Sodom to warn him of its impending destruction. Lot makes a lavish drinking feast[8] for them and invites them to stay overnight. All of the men of Sodom, young and old, surround the house and demand that he surrender the "men" to them. The details of this scene are chilling and the narrator emphatically emphasizes the number and strength of the mob: "Before they lay down, the men of the city, the men of Sodom, surrounded the house—from young to old, *all the people, entirely*" (Gen 19:4, my emphasis). Lot's response is strange and shrouded in secrecy: "Lot went out of the entrance-way to the men, and shut the door after him" (Gen 19:6). This narrative, like that of Noah, practically begs for questions to be asked. The most obvious are: Why does Lot deliberately depart from the protection of his house in order to present his alternative in secret? Why doesn't Lot elicit the assistance of the angels to thwart the plan of the townsmen? I have seen few answers that satisfy me.

Lack of explanations not withstanding, for whatever reasons, Lot becomes a procurer rather than protector: "Please, my brothers, do not so wickedly. Look, I have two daughters who have not known man. Please, I shall bring them out to you. Do to them as is good in your eyes. Only to these men do nothing because they came under the shadow of my roof" (Gen 19:7-8). Lot speaks to the men of the town as though they were comrades. Indeed, he even addresses them as "brothers" (Gen 19:7). Inexplicably, even though Lot recognizes that their proposal is evil, he tries to substitute an equally abhorrent act. The men of Sodom want the angels, but Lot offers his daughters who, he stresses, have not "known man," their virginity being a necessary aspect to the last part of the narrative. Indeed, Lot *volunteers* to hand them over to be abused by the crowd. Further, since the daughters are betrothed (Gen 19:14), and since the rape of a betrothed woman is a crime punishable by death (Deut 22:23-27), Lot's actions could have implicated him as an accomplice.

Lot's offer to the mob is incredible! The willingness of a father to hand over his own daughters to be raped rather than allow the homosexual rape of a stranger who happens to be a guest in his home is baffling; more remarkable still, the narrator's views about the potential violence to the daughters is not revealed directly. Nevertheless, the narrative presents a powerful portrait of the effects of threatened sexual violence. Most curious of all, however, is that although commentators recognize that the proposed sodomy against the (male) angels is portrayed as reprehensible, they have been rather *sympathetic* to Lot's actions toward his daughters. Instead of condemning the offer of his daughters as rape victims, they point to the "mitigating circumstances," the demands of "hospitality" that excuse his behavior. For example, as Leah Bronner has observed, nowhere in classical rabbinic literature is there a discussion of the daughters' feelings about the matter, nor is there a condemnation of Lot (Bronner 1994:113–14). This is unusual since classical rabbinic literature tends to discuss all aspects of life and normally is not reticent regarding sexual matters. Yet it remains silent on this important issue.[9] Reformer John Calvin writes that "Lot's great virtue was sprinkled with some imperfection. . . . Although he does not hesitate to prostitute his daughters. . . . Lot, indeed is urged by extreme necessity" (quoted in Lerner 1986:172). And modern commentators have essentially followed this line of reasoning. Their pro-Lot position is illustrated by this statement of Bruce Vawter:

> Certainly to our tastes he [Lot] proves himself to be more sensitive to the duties of hospitality than those of fatherhood. . . . The spectacle of a father offering his virgin daughters to the will and pleasure of a mob that was seeking to despoil his household would not have seemed as

> shocking to the ancient sense of proprieties as it may seem to us. . . .
> Really, there is no need to make excuses for him, as far as the biblical
> perspective is concerned. In all the stories about him the soundness of
> Lot's judgment is never the point at issue. . . . He is a good and not a
> bad man. (1977:235–36; see also Skinner 1930:307; Sarna 1989:135;
> Speiser 1964:123)

John Skinner's assessment of Lot's character is similar. He states, "Lot's
readiness to sacrifice the honor of his daughters . . . shows him as the
courageous champion of the obligations of hospitality in a situation of
extreme embarrassment, and in recorded to his credit" (1930:307).
Nahum Sarna agrees, commenting that "Lot is true to his code of
honor. Hospitality was a sacred duty, according the guest the right of
asylum" (1989:135).

Surprisingly, E. A. Speiser, who otherwise annotates Genesis line by
line, has no comment here. His only hint of a gloss on the incident
with the daughters is this sentence: "True to the unwritten code, Lot
will stop at nothing in his effort to protect his guests" (1964:123). Lest
I be accused of viewing these readings as cases of exegetical mal[e]-
practice, Nehama Leibowitz's comments are as favorable towards Lot
as the male scholars quoted above: "Lot tried to maintain Abraham's
way of life, even in the heart of Sodom striving to preserve, at the risk
to his life, the elementary obligations of hospitality to strangers . . .
resulting in his throwing his daughters to the mercy of the populace,
in exchange for his guests" (Leibowitz 1981:176).

Although Susan Niditch correctly points out that the potential rape
of the divine messengers is "a doubly potent symbol of a cultural, non-
civilized behavior from the Israelite point of view" (Niditch 1982:369),
she ignores the threat of sexual brutality to the daughters. Why would
this not be equally reprehensible in the Israelite perspective? Could it
be possible that Freud's theory with regard to the role of mythology is
tacitly expressed by the *narrator?* That is, as I discuss in chapter 3, this
myth serves the same function for an entire *people* that dreams and literature provide for the *individual*—psychological release for the
impulses repressed in the course of development, impulses that have
become unconscious and brought to the surface only in narrative
form. To phrase it differently: Were Lot's actions a simple strategy to
protect the visitors, or were they an accurate precursor to the incest
both Lot and the narrator (acting as a substitute for entire *people*)
unconsciously desire, incest that Lot actually commits at the end of the

chapter? At the very least, I read this incident as Lot's repressing his own desire to "know" his daughters and displacing this desire upon the townsmen.

In any event, having offered to have his daughters gang-raped, in an interesting reversal, Lot is saved by the angels and almost as an after-thought, the two daughters are saved from a brutal crime. The mob storms the house and is about to break the door when the angels strike blind all the men of Sodom, warn Lot of the imminent destruction of the city, and prophetically tell him that he and his family will be saved.

At this point, the narrative needs an available Eve to pluck fruit and offer it to the father. Conveniently, the only other survivors of Sodom are Lot's two daughters with whom he escapes to the city of Zoar, Lot's wife having been turned into a pillar of salt (discussed on p. 110). But Lot is afraid to stay there and flees once more *with his daughters,* this time to the rocky hill-country above the Dead Sea plain. And where do they take refuge? In a *meʿārāh* (cave).

The image of the cave is quite potent: generally speaking, it signifies movements of descent to a lower world. The cave is referred to as "Sheol" in various places in the Hebrew Bible: it is where the spirit of Samuel is conjured by the Witch of Endor; it is the belly of Jonah's whale; and it is the pit into which the speaker of the penitential psalms has been cast. The cave/underworld is generally dark and its inhabitants stripped of all clothing by death the leveler (in contrast to the garden of sexuality directed toward fertility, discussed in chap. 3). On the other hand, the cave is also a place where lost treasure is found, threatening monsters are confronted, and help is enlisted for the accomplishment of a goal. Psychologically, the underworld of the cave is synonymous with the subconscious, from which we wake "up" every morning. It is the home of dreams, intuitions, hidden desires, and suppressed energies. Most important, however, is that the sexual connotation of the cave is obvious both psychoanalytically (Freud 1916–17:156) and linguistically. To quote David Gunn, "[*Cave*] associates easily with words such as a bare place, to be naked, exposed, to strip oneself, and nakedness, genitals" (1980:94).

Once in the cave, the despairing daughters, who were betrothed in Sodom, conclude that not just Sodom but the whole earth has been laid waste, and that there are no men left. On two successive nights they give Lot wine, "lie with" him in a cave (the place where one "sleeps" [in death] with one's father) and "seduce" him into impregnating them. The narrative suggests that the father did not knowingly participate in this incestuous act. Although it is unclear just who he thought had stopped by the cave on the two sequential nights of his seduction, twice we are told that "he knew not when *she* lay down and got up." Unlike Noah who could at least plead ignorance of the effects of wine, Lot becomes inebriated on two successive evenings with the result that the man who offered his betrothed daughters to gang-rape deflowers them himself.

It is significant that when Freud writes about female virginity, he does not consider the young woman's position, but that of the man. Indeed, the value Freud attaches to virginity is phrased in a discourse of scientific logic and subjective justification: "The demand that a girl shall not bring to her marriage with a particular man any memory of sexual relations with another is, indeed, nothing other than the logical continuation of the right to exclusive possession of a woman, which forms the essence of monogamy, the extension of the monopoly over the past" (1905:136).[10] Freud's logic presents a mixture of legal monopoly, right, and cognitive concerns (memory). The crux of his essay is a circular argument that moves from the woman's feeling via the male act to the male feeling that inspires his guilt, its projection on the woman, and thus, ultimately, her hostility. As Mieke Bal notes, from a value, virginity becomes a danger (Bal 1994:15). Certainly this is the case with Lot and his daughters.

Patriarchal law decrees that the "product" of sexual union, the child, belongs exclusively to the father (Gallop 1989:109). In the case of Lot and his daughters, it would appear that this maxim is followed to the extreme. Describing his daughters as virgins, Lot tells the Sodomites that they "had not known man" (Gen 19:8). These daughters "belong" exclusively to Lot. At the end of the narrative, the wombs that bear Lot's sons *mo'āb* (literally, "from my father") and *ben-'ammi* (literally, "son of my kinsman"!) are those of his two daughters, repossessed by Lot as a means of reproduction.

As in the case of Noah, Lot's offer to sacrifice his daughters incestuous relationship with them is not treated in the text as wrong. Indeed, it goes unpunished and without further narrative comment.[11] There has been considerable clinical psychiatric interest in the Lot narrative since it seems to be the prototype of parent-child incest, in part because it is more directly related to actual clinical incest than the Oedipus story.[12] When clinical practitioners examine parent-child incest, the questions frequently considered include, among others: What was the setting and family structure in which it occurred? What was the frequency of the behavior in question? What were the respective personalities and roles of the parent and the child-victim? What was the personality and role of the other parent in the incest case? What was the effect on the participants? These are the questions asked by psychoanalytic literary theorists as well.

With regard to the questions of setting and family structure, the setting is a catastrophic situation wherein the daughters believe the world was destroyed. Medlicott notes that the lack of privacy of the cave is quite similar to the primitive housing situation in many cases of clinical incest (1967:135). And although the daughters in this instance appear to be the active initiators of the incestuous behavior, the fact that more than one daughter is involved brings the story closer into line with clinical incest in which the incestuous father commonly moves from older to younger daughters.

The personalities and roles of the parents and victims also seem to fall into the classical incestuous paradigm. Lot, the incestuous father, has lost his status as the all-powerful patriarchal father who holds his family together. Indeed, Lot is saved from the mad[dening] crowd by the very visitors whom he felt it necessary to protect! By blinding the would-be attackers, the visitors in effect symbolically castrate both Lot and the townsmen. That is to say, by blinding the townsmen, the narrator uses the frequent substitution of eyes for the dismemberment of genitalia (discussed on p.94). And like many incestuous fathers, Lot appears to have had a problem with alcohol, allowing himself to become inebriated on two consecutive nights.

In addition, the role of Lot's wife is not out of keeping with clinical incest stories. Ernest Jones writes of the remarkably close association between the ideas of salt and fecundity and points out that salt, both in absence and excess, prevents fruitfulness and sexuality (1938:72). Therefore, from a psychoanalytic perspective, it is particularly appropriate that Lot's wife was turned into a pillar of salt.

Once again artists seem to have interesting readings of Mrs. Lot. For example, Albrecht Dürer's *Lot and His Daughters* seems almost clinical. This scene (painted on the reverse side of his *Madonna and Child—*

anything Freudian there, do you suppose?) portrays Lot and his two children fleeing from the destruction of Sodom and Gomorrah, which erupt in blinding explosions of fire in the background. Significantly for purposes of this chapter, Lot's wife, visible but clearly from a distance, is on the path at the upper left. By looking back, Mrs. Lot could be viewed, in effect, as having looked away from what was going on between father and daughters, a behavior common in clinical incest. The only information we have as to the last question, the general effect of the incestuous behavior on the victims, Lot's daughters, is that they both became pregnant and their sons fathered two tribes who were persistently thorns in Israel's flesh. In other words, Lot's grandsons, like Noah's, are damned because of Grandpa's actions.

Interestingly, various paintings on this theme are less forgiving of Lot than biblical commentators. Lodovico Carraci (1555–1619), for example, portrays an unrestrained and erotic Lot, significantly portrayed as the *aggressor*. Here, a sexually aroused Lot grasps a voluptuous daughter while the other daughter waits in the background. Noteworthy from a clinical perspective, the figure of Mrs. Lot is seen in the distance, as in Dürer painting. In Bonifazio de'Pitati's colorful painting *Lot and His Daughters,* one of the women is seen plying Lot with wine, a beverage he is obviously enjoying. Her bright red dress is disheveled and she is barefoot as she apparently tries to excite her father. Two *putti,*[13] one of them wearing a mask, appear behind the other daughter, who is fully dressed and holding a mirror. Since in Renaissance iconography the mirror was a symbol of prudence, wisdom, and ideas of truth, while falsehood was alluded to by the mask, the daughters of Lot could be viewed as acting out the struggle between *voluptas* (carnal pleasures) and *virtus* (goodness and virtue). But perhaps the mirror and mask had an additional meaning to Bonifazio's fellow Venetians, who were accustomed to donning elaborate facial ornamentation during their annual *carnevale* festivities, events that were known for their license and *drunkenness!*

Most damning to Lot's reputation, however, is Albrecht Altdorfer's *Lot and His Daughters* (1537). In his depiction of the story Altdorfer shows clearly that he does not accept the totally passive role supposedly played by Lot. For some reason, it seems as if these artists may be more Freudian readers of the biblical text than biblical commentators, and perhaps at least as creditable. It would appear that based on clinical reports and the readings of Renaissance artists, the unconscious desires of Lot have surfaced!

Variations

Although the following biblical examples are not actual cases of true father-daughter incest, I would like to mention them briefly. The first case, that of Judah and Tamar, involves an equally forbidden father-in-law/daughter incestuous relationship. The second incident, Boaz and Ruth, consists of a father-figure/daughter-figure liaison. I have included these two narratives in this chapter because the three stories of Lot's daughters, Tamar, and Ruth have been read as installments in a series that supplies King David with a genealogy. That is, the first story narrates the birth of the maternal forefather, Moab; the second narrates the birth of the paternal forefather, Perez; and the third story brings together Ruth the Moabite and Boaz of Perez's lineage.

In the first story, Tamar, like Lot's daughters, uses incest to solve a serious domestic problem (Genesis 38). At the beginning of the story, Tamar is married to Er,[14] one of Judah's sons. The death of Er without a son made Onan subject to the levirate law. Although marriage between a man and his brother's wife is strictly forbidden in the Pentateuchal legislation of Leviticus (18:16 and 20:21, discussed in chap. 2), the only exception to the prohibition occurs when the brother dies without a son. According to Deut 25:5, a man has an *obligation* to marry his widowed sister-in-law: "When brothers dwell together and one of them dies and leaves no son, the wife of the deceased shall not be married to a stranger, outside the family. Her husband's brother shall unite with her [literally "go in to her"], take her as his wife and perform the levir's duty."

This institution is known in Hebrew as *yibbum* or "levirate marriage."[15] The second son, Onan, refusing to follow the laws of the levirate marriage, lets his seed "go to spoil" on the ground. (Although Targum Jonathan and *Genesis Rabbah* 8:5 connect the name with the Hebrew *'on* ["grief"], it could also be understood to mean "vigorous," perhaps a piece of biblical humor! How this contraceptive device of coitus interruptus evolved into a synonym for masturbation— onanism—is a semantic enigma.)[16] What he did was "displeasing to YHWH" and God slays him as well. Although the text does not make clear specifically why Onan incurs divine wrath, the development of the narrative seems to indicate that Onan's failure to impregnate Tamar is considered an unpardonable crime, since the provision for voluntary renunciation of the levirate duty found in Deut 25:7-9 did not apply at this time. However, it could also be argued that by frustrating the purpose of the levirate marriage, that is to say, perpetuating the line of his brother for purposes of inheritance, Onan has placed his sexual relationship with Tamar in the category of incest.

Judah, fearful that his youngest son upon whom the levirate responsibility now lies might follow in the ill-fated footsteps of his two older brothers, banishes his daughter-in-law, Tamar, to widowhood in her father's house. In this state, she is not free to remarry; she is still subject to the authority of her father-in-law; and she now must live with and be provided for by her parents. Tamar, in effect, has been purchased through marriage by Judah, the head of the family, and thereby is part of the estate of her dead husband, Er. As such, she remains the property of the clan after his death.

When the widowed Tamar realizes that her claim for a husband is unlikely to be satisfied even through the third son of Judah and that she will remain childless, relegated to live in her father's house, she becomes desperate. She deceives her father-in-law by disguising herself as a prostitute. Oblivious to her identity (see p. 39), Judah has intercourse with her (the incestuous relationship forbidden in Lev 18:15). The text does not tell us why Tamar felt she had to keep this matter within the family nor why she felt that, disguised as a harlot, she would have a better chance at Judah, but the ruse works: she conceives, the problem is solved, and David's lineage is further established.

In the second narrative, Ruth, a daughter-figure, delivers a demand for marriage to a father-figure related to her by marriage.[17] Indeed, Boaz addresses Ruth as "my daughter" (Ruth 2:8, 3:10); as Athalya Brenner notes, even if this address implies a recognition of her inferior social status or younger age (most readers tend to read Boaz as older; see Ruth 3:10), the similarity of this story to the other two is striking (1997b:103 n.36). The motifs of wine and drinking, fatherly cooperation, family survival, and the daughter's desire for a son are present in various measures in all three stories.

Conclusion: The "Righteous Father" Syndrome

It is not entirely unreasonable to wonder if there are more correspondences between the Noah narrative and the well-known stories of Lot,

Judah, and Boaz than first appear. The stories of Noah and Lot are, of course, in many ways similar: both Lot and Noah are saved as righteous men from destruction and the seed of Judah and the seed of Boaz are saved from destruction as well. However, all *four* are involved in creation myths, and all *four* are sexually involved with their children.

More importantly, the patriarchs Noah, Lot, Judah, and Boaz are absolved from any culpability and free to maintain their status as righteous—in their own minds, in the viewpoint of the narrator, as well as in the writings of most commentators. Accordingly, perhaps the most significant similarity between the stories of Lot's incestuous relationship(s) and Noah's is that within the patriarchal world of the Hebrew Bible, fathers commit incest with their children and remain unpunished while the children and grandchildren involved are damned forever.

Chapter 6 ——————————————

Boys Will Be Boys:
Sibling Rivalry and the Fear of Castration

"The most dangerous word in any human tongue is the word for brother.
It's inflammatory."—Tennessee Williams, *Camino Real*

Background

Many ancient mythologies contain tales of two brothers, one of whom
is killed or defeated by the other in some way. Often, one of the brothers is of heroic character, sometimes immortal, while the other is of
human origin, weaker, and *very* mortal. Fated to perish young, the
weaker brother leads a diminished existence beside his heroic brother,
as in the relationships of Heracles and Iphicles, of Agamemnon and
Menelaus, and of Hector and Paris. Certainly, the tragic theme of
feuding brothers is one of the most frequent conflicts in biblical literature. The first murder in the Bible is fratricide, and the subsequent
relationships of Esau and Jacob, Joseph and his brothers, Jehoram and
his brothers, and Absalom and Amnon are far from harmonious.
Freud relates the frequency and powerful elemental effect of the sibling
conflict to our first impressions of childhood: siblings are our first
potentially *conquerable* rivals.

The explosive emotions of sibling rivalry are almost commonplace.
As pre-Freudian Saint Augustine commented: "I have seen with my
own eyes and know very well an infant in the grip of jealousy: he could
not yet speak, and already he observed his foster-brother, pale and with
an envenomed stare" (quoted in Lacan 1977b:20). Like other inimical
brothers, many of the biblical brothers are *bound* by familial ties yet
separated by hatred. The "envenomed stare" that Augustine describes
permeates their narratives and as a result, their stories read like prototypical Freudian case studies of the sibling construct.

This chapter examines the sibling relationship of Jacob and Esau in
light of Freud's theory of brother/brother conflicts. In chapter 7 I continue the discussion of sibling rivalry but extend the sibling construct

from two brothers to brother/brother/sister. Sadly, in all the narratives I examine, initial love turns to hatred.

As in the preceding chapters, I have included several artistic and literary representations of the narratives that I read in light of psychoanalytic literary theory in an attempt to provide another insight into these texts, an insight other than that of traditional biblical scholars.

There are several theories as to the early sources of sibling rivalry. The most prevalent revolve around three emotions: envy, jealousy, and competition. Generally speaking, *envy* is the term used when one person wants what another person has. It could be looks, clothing, a job, or a friendly disposition; whatever it is, one is desirous of another's achievements or possessions. *Jealousy* is the term used when a person perceives someone else as a threat to a meaningful relationship. We often associate jealousy with romantic or sexual interactions, but the term can be applied to family, business, or friendship triangles as well. *Competition* is the action resulting from envy or jealousy, one's reaction to feeling lesser than someone else, or one's attempts to gain what another person has. We compete covertly when we do not express our desire to do as well as or better than another person, but we feel the pain of inferiority or rejection intensely and we act out accordingly. External competition is when we express or act out our needs openly. Either way, good or bad, external or covert, competition results from envy or jealousy, although the source of our envy or jealousy may change or be sublimated over time.

According to Freud's well-known theory, the sibling relationship is quite similar to that of the Oedipal conflict discussed in chapter 4: jealous rivalry and the attendant fear of castration. Indeed for Freud (and other psychoanalytic theorists), it is only through the primary parent complex that the significance of the sibling complex can be correctly appreciated or understood. To summarize Freud's writings on the subject (1905a), one's relationship with siblings is a "second edition" of the etiologically earlier relationship with one's parents, less intense but basically unchanged in content. That is, a child's relationship with his or her parents corresponds, with modifications, to his or her relationship with siblings. Since the original Oedipal complex is repressed, the impulses associated with the parents but rejected by the child are associated instead with the siblings. Once the siblings are substituted for the parents, these impulses are able to develop in a less impeded and more lasting manner.

The displacement of the Oedipal feelings to the siblings is determined by the family structure. If both children are boys, the older child perceives his younger brother as preferred and begins to associate his younger sibling in his father's position as competitor for the mother's affections. Being in a weaker position, the younger child makes a better enemy than the more powerful and feared father. That is, the older brother believes he will have more success against his younger brother than against his father. Unfortunately for the older brother, however, the younger son is often favored and protected by the mother. Freud sees another scenario in the case of an older brother/younger sister. I shall discuss this theory in chapter 7.

Jacob and Esau and Momma: Freud's Unholy Trinity

Jacob, son of Isaac and Rebecca and younger brother of Esau, has a dream in which he is attacked by a mysterious assailant who wrestles with him until daybreak (Gen 32:25-31). Reading this narrative and the account of the relationship of Jacob and Esau in light of psychoanalytic literary theory, Wilhelm Müller's striking comment, although dated, is still relevant: "Often, to understand the significance of an entire myth, one must assume that what seems about to occur, but is *prevented,* really *does* occur" (1856:422, emphasis added). From this perspective, I see Jacob's struggle with the mysterious assailant who wrestles with him until daybreak as an anxiety-filled nightmare, basically libidinous and suggesting a fear of castration. Although the sexual content of this dream appears in the repressed form of anxiety, an earlier dream of his, dreamed while fleeing from his home to the household of his future father-in-law, Laban (Gen 28:12-15), is its counterpart.

Dream Theory

In *The Interpretation of Dreams* (1900), Freud explains that dreams fulfill repressed desires by allowing the unconscious to communicate to the conscious. The unconscious sends overwhelming urges upon the sleeper's mind, "condensing" a set of images into a single picture and "displacing" the meaning of one object onto another. Freud describes these dream images as "primitive hieroglyphics," the signs of which are to be individually "translated" into a creative story, or what is remembered as a "dream," by the preconscious or conscious mind. These raw materials are context-bound and cannot be analyzed in isolation

(1900:132). As Freud observes, "the same piece of content may conceal a different meaning when it occurs in various people or in various contexts" (1900:137) and must be "inserted into the psychical chain that has to be traced backwards" (1900:133). That is, the meaning of a dream, like that of a literary text, varies according to the language and culture of the dreamer or reader and can be understood only retrospectively. The dreamer must decipher symbols that have no fixed meaning just as a reader must interpret signifiers that are indeterminate.

This primary process of dream-work, with its characteristic turns analogous to figures of speech, simultaneously presents and distorts, represents and misrepresents, opposing dream images and concealed meanings.

In Freudian theory, dreams result from an unconscious impulse seeking fulfillment—that is, a desire not actually fulfilled in waking life.[1] But the "forbidden" dream thoughts (the figurative activity of a dream, or what analysts call the "latent" content) do not stand for the dream stories that the dreamer remembers (referred to as its literal or "manifest contents"). Instead, the dream is a symbolic fulfillment of unconscious wishes, a transformation of a dreamer's forbidden desires or residue from the previous day. In other words, an unconscious wish meets up with a censoring thought at the unconscious level, at the preconscious level, or even at a dim, conscious level, and strives for an illusory satisfaction. But why are these unconscious wishes distorted in dream images?

According to Freud, it is due to "censorship," the force of repression that exists at the edge between the unconscious and the preconscious and that will not allow these powerfully charged thoughts to surface in their original form. Part of a dreamer's reaction to censorship derives from sleep's paralyzing effect on the motor end of psychic apparatus, and a "forbidden" idea is stripped somewhat of its dangerous capacity to influence action. As Donald Moss writes,

> Detached from an active, erotic, body, the dreamer is also detached from that active body's linguistic proxy, syntax. Syntax mediates the formal demands of time, place and person. Such demands turn superfluous as the erotic body, paralyzed with sleep, turns superfluous. Sentence, unobliged to that body's spatial/temporal coordinates, unravels into rebus. (1989:357)

So under the influence of censorship, the "subversive" material is transformed into a series of images, and that series of images is what the dreamer remembers. Hence Freud's dictum: "A dream is a [disguised] fulfillment of a [suppressed or repressed] wish" (1900:160). What Jacob "remembers" is described in Genesis 28 and 32; but what are the "subversive" or "latent" contents of Jacob's dream(s)?

Wrestling with Wrestling: Jacob's Dream

As stated above, Jacob, son of Isaac and Rebecca and younger brother of Esau, has a dream in which he is attacked by a mysterious assailant who wrestles with him until daybreak:

> Jacob was left alone. A man wrestled with him there until break of day. He saw that he did not prevail against him and he touched the hollow of his thigh, and the hollow of Jacob's thigh was put out of joint as he wrestled with him. He said, "Let me go, for the day breaks." He said, "I shall not let you go unless you bless me." He said to him, "What is your name?" He said, "Jacob." He said, "Your name will no longer be called 'Jacob' but 'Israel' for you have contended with God and with humans and have prevailed." Jacob asked him and said, "Tell me, I pray you, your name." He said, "What is this that you ask my name?" And he blessed him there. Jacob called the name of the place "Peniel": "for I have seen God face to face and my life is preserved." (Gen 32:25-31)

This theme as an art motif received a considerable and bewildering variety of symbolic interpretations in the Middle Ages, and one of the most common was that it represented each person's fight against the forces of evil. In early Christian art it is God who is shown struggling with Jacob, a theme I discuss more fully below. In fact, Jacob's struggle is so popular with early Christian artists that its representation is found in the Vienna Genesis, a sixth-century illuminated manuscript housed in the Nationalbibliothek, Vienna; in an eighth-century fresco in Santa Maria Antica, Rome; in an eleventh-century fresco in the cathedral of Hagia Sophia, Kiev; and in many medieval sculptures and in manuscripts such as the St. Louis Psalter. In the Stanza d'Eliodoro in the Vatican there is a painting of the subject by Raphael and a fresco by Baldassore Peruzzi. Rembrandt produced a painting of Jacob and the angel that is in the Berlin Museum, and Claude Lorrain used it in a night landscape, displayed now in the Hermitage. Delacroix depicted the struggle in a fresco in the church of Saint Sulpice, Paris, where it represents the struggle with nature in order to wrest her secrets. In the twentieth century, the sculptor Sir Jacob Epstein showed Jacob and the angel locked in a passionate embrace. Of all of these artistic representations, however, it is Bruno Goldschmitt's contemporary artistic reading in *Jacob's Struggle with the Angel* that seems to portray most fully the angst that I discuss below.

Jacob's dream, like most night dreams, contain peculiar images and bizarre language that need to be interpreted.[2] The way we interpret dreams can be an effective tool for understanding the way certain literary texts work, particularly narratives *about* dreams. And tales of dreamers abound in ancient Near Eastern literature. Indeed, the importance and frequency of biblical dreams are well recognized.[3]

In the dream that Jacob remembers (and the narrator relates), Jacob and a "man" wrestle until the break of dawn. The fight comes seemingly out of nowhere. We are never told why they are struggling. What we are told, remarkably, is that Jacob's adversary "saw that he did not prevail against him," and as the dawn approaches, the assailant becomes desperate to disengage himself. Unable to overcome Jacob by sheer force, the unnamed wrestler delivers a sudden, powerful blow to the "hollow of Jacob's thigh"[4] and tells Jacob to release him. Jacob responds, "I will not let you go, unless you bless me." Immediately, the unknown assailant changes Jacob's name to Israel, explaining, "You have wrestled with God and with humans, and have prevailed." Refusing to reveal his own name, the mysterious stranger vanishes and Jacob is left limping.

Everything about this story is extraordinary: that God in some form fights with Jacob, that Jacob prevails, that he then demands to be blessed, and that the unnamed wrestler acquiesces. In addition to its obvious meaning that promises Jacob divine blessings, this dream, if read from the perspective of psychoanalytic literary theory, is a reenactment of Jacob's relationship with Esau and is a replica, in highly condensed form, of all of the preceding Jacob/Esau narratives.

Let me explain. Jacob's dream is a prime example of the Freudian model of all three dream stages: the very primitive, fantasy-based primary-process of dream-work called "condensation" and "displacement"; that confusing stage of dream-work called "secondary-process" in which generic opposites such as fantasy/reality, abstinence/lust, punishment/reward mingle; and the later process of dream-work, waking, the stage during which Jacob himself translates his dream images into a coherent narrative, in effect interpreting his own dream.

What are Jacob's unconscious wishes? How does Jacob's dreamwork work? In order to understand Jacob's dream, it is necessary to look at his earlier relationship with his brother.

Jacob and Esau—Phase I

The relationship of Jacob and Esau has been the focus of a great deal of commentary, both exegetical and literary. Most of the nonbiblical/nonrabbinical literary versions of the animosity of Jacob and Esau are allegorical. One of the earliest of these is the twelfth-century *Ordo de Ysaac et Rebecca et Filiis Eorum* in which Esau represents the "pharisaical Jews" and Jacob the "faithful Christians." Literary interest in the subject was particularly strong in sixteenth-century England and Germany, where it inspired numerous stage productions including Hans Sachs's *Comedia: Jacob mit seinem bruder Esaw* (1550) and a Styrian church drama by Thomas Brunner; *A newe mery . . . Comedie or Enterlude . . . treating upon the Historie of Jacob and Esau* (1568), all of which depicted Jacob in a positive way and Esau quite negatively and used the Reformation as the vehicle for a diatribe. For example, *The Historie of Jacob and Esau* (1557–58), a comedy attributed to Nicholas Udall, depicts Jacob as the "true Protestant" while Esau is represented the "Catholic Antichrist." From the opposite perspective, a seventeenth-century treatment of the relationship of Jacob and his brother is the anonymous *Comedia famosa dos successos de Iahacob e Esau* (1699), a Spanish verse play that portrays Jacob as the "true Christian" (that is, "faithful Catholic") and Esau is the "heretic" (that is, "rebellious Protestant").

In the late nineteenth century, the German Protestant playwright Wilhelm Schaefer wrote the drama *Jakob und Esau* (1896), and there has been a significant revival of interest in the subject during the twentieth century, again presenting the conflict of the brothers in allegory. For example, in the first part of his unfinished David trilogy, *Jaakobs Traum; ein Vorspiel* (1918; *Jacob's Dream,* 1947), Richard Beer-Hofmann uses the text to justify Israel's universal mission. On the other hand, Laurence Housman's *Jacob's Ladder,* one of his *Old Testament Plays* (1950), denigrates both Jacob and Esau in virulent anti-Semitic language.

At this point, however, I am most interested in the biblical narrative itself. According to the Hebrew Bible, the primary characteristic of Jacob seems to be his sibling rivalry with Esau, which begins quite early—in fact, while still in the womb! Rebecca's unusually difficult pregnancy is particularly significant: not only is the report of it unique in biblical literature, but the Hebrew text uses an unusual verb *wayyitrōṣāṣû*, which means literally "they crushed" or "they thrust" one another. This early fighting foreshadows the future hostile relationship between the siblings. Because of the level of the uterine warfare, the formerly barren matriarch even curses the fact that she is pregnant. Indeed, the Hebrew, which is an incomplete sentence, literally reads "If so, why then am/do I . . . ?" the sense being something like, "Why then did I yearn and pray to become pregnant?" or "Why do I go on living?"[5]

Greatly perplexed and anguished, Rebecca seeks divine guidance.[6] Like Hagar before her (as told in Gen 16:7-14), Rebecca goes to Beer-lahai-roi, and again, like Hagar before her, Rebecca receives an oracle concerning the birth and destiny of her sons: "The LORD answered her, 'Two nations are in your belly and two peoples will be separated from your bowels; one people will be stronger than the other, and the elder—the younger will serve'" (Gen 25:23; see comment below on this translation). As is the case throughout the Hebrew Bible, the exact wording the Deity uses is significant. In the first part of his speech, he uses words that are not normally used in reference to reproductive organs (*beḇiṭnēk*—"in your belly" and *mimmē 'ayik*[7]—"from your innards"); the Deity, in effect, is acknowledging the extreme nature of Rebecca's suffering and emphasizing her bitterness and pain.

The second part of God's oracle is equally important and again, not surprisingly, the ambiguity of biblical Hebrew muddies the waters. The phrase in Gen 25:23, *rab ya'ăḇōd ṣā'îr* usually is translated as "the elder will serve the younger" (with no marks of punctuation). That is, Rebecca's younger son, Jacob, will dominate her older son, Esau. However, due to the peculiarities of the language, technically this translation is not the only correct possibility. Briefly, in English (and most other European and Near Eastern languages) the subject of a sentence usually *precedes* the verb and the direct object usually *follows* the verb, as in "the elder [subject] will serve [verb] the younger [direct object]." In biblical Hebrew, however, the subject may come either before or after the verb. In other words, sometimes it is impossible to tell which word in a biblical verse is the subject and which is the direct object, particularly if the verse is in poetry (as in this case). So, while this verse *may* mean "the elder will serve the younger" (the usual translation), it is equally valid to translate it as "the elder [direct object]—the younger [subject] will serve [verb]." As a result, this verse can be understood to mean *either* that Jacob will serve Esau *or* that Esau will serve Jacob!

God's message is unclear. And since this prediction contains two *opposite* meanings Rebecca can hear it to mean whichever she chooses. Fortunately for Jacob (but not for Esau), she chooses to reverse the law of primogeniture.

Jacob's feelings toward Esau do not improve upon birth. Instead, Jacob tries to thwart his brother right from the beginning: "When her days to be delivered were fulfilled, behold, there were twins in her belly. The first came out red, all over, like a hairy garment, and they called his name Esau. After that, came out his brother, and his hand took hold of Esau's heel, and his name was called Jacob. Isaac was sixty years old when she bore them" (Gen 25:24-26). The narrator's physical description of Esau is somewhat paradoxical: Esau is "red, all over." On the one hand, *'admôni*—"red"—is used *admiringly* in the Hebrew Bible. For example, David is described as "ruddy" in a positive context: "He was ruddy, and had beautiful eyes, and was handsome" (1 Sam 16:12). In addition, contemporaneous Egyptian and Cretan art as well as Ugaritic texts equate "red skin" with *heroic* stature. And, of course, there is the *pārāh 'ădummāh*—"red heifer"—the animal whose ashes were used in the ritual purification of persons and objects defiled by a corpse (Num 19:2). Since the Bible prescribes that the red cow be without blemish and have no defect, almost by definition the term *red* is not used pejoratively. On the other hand, the report of Esau's "hairy garment" is reminiscent of the account of the boorishly uncouth Enkidu in the Epic of Gilgamesh (see chap. 3, note 7) whose entire body was covered with hair ("His body was covered with matted hair like Samuwan's, the god of cattle" [Sanders 1984:63]). All we can say for sure about Esau at this point in the story is that he has a ruddy complexion and a lot of hair.

Surprisingly, the narrator does not describe Jacob's looks, but *does* describe his first act upon being born: Jacob holds on to the heel of his older brother and attempts to forestall Esau's birth. But Jacob is unsuccessful.

The Feud Continues

As the story progresses, the contrasts between the two brothers become more pronounced: "The boys grew. Esau was a skillful hunter, a man of the outdoors; Jacob was a simple man, dwelling in tents. Isaac loved Esau because he relished his venison; and Rebecca loved

Jacob" (Gen 25:27-28). This contrast, Esau the outdoorsman versus Jacob the homebody who dwells in tents (the hallmark of a pastoralist, according to Gen 4:20),[8] provides all the necessary background for Jacob's next act of vengeance against his older brother, one that eventually results in Jacob's usurpation of the blessing intended by Isaac for Esau. That is, Jacob is able to fool his father precisely because he *is* at home while Esau is off hunting.

It is at this point in the narrative that the family constellation of preferences becomes particularly significant. Despite the fact that Isaac prefers Esau for culinary reasons, no reason is given for Rebecca's preference (although it may have been based upon her understanding of God's pronouncement).[9]

Jacob's rivalry with Esau intensifies with the passing of time. Having been thwarted in his earlier attempts to be the eldest *legitimately*, Jacob finagles Esau into bartering his rights as firstborn for a meal of boiled pottage:[10]

> Jacob cooked pottage. Esau came from the field, and he was faint. Esau said to Jacob, "Give me to swallow, I pray you, of that red pottage, for I am faint"—therefore was his name called Edom [red]. Jacob said, "Sell me this day your birthright." Esau said, "Behold, I am at the point of death. What profit will this birthright do to me?" Jacob said, "Swear to me this day." And he swore to him, and sold his birthright to Jacob. Jacob gave Esau bread and pottage of lentils. He ate and drank, and he rose and went away. Thus Esau despised his birthright. (Gen 25:29-34)

Let's examine this situation. Jacob is home cooking. Esau, returning from the fields, is famished. Indeed, *ʿāyēp* (often translated as "faint") is used in contexts where there is dire need of food and drink. In this case, Esau is *so* hungry that he tells his younger brother (and where was Mom when *Esau* needed her?) "I am at the point of death!" Whether Esau is referring generally to his perilous life as a hunter or describing his present condition, Jacob takes the occasion to exploit his brother's misery—he demands Esau's birthright as a quid pro quo. And although Esau agrees to the transaction, Jacob wants more: he wants an oath, an unqualifiedly sacred act that—given the self-imprecations against the violator that *all* biblical oaths contain—is a potent means of reinforcing Esau's verbal commitment. Esau, the hungry, hairy hunter, swears to the sale and loses his inheritance to Jacob, a mama's boy with smooth skin who does not venture far from home, preferring instead to cook stew with Rebecca. Jacob's plan has worked—Esau's oath makes the transaction irrevocable.

Getting Esau to sell his birthright for food seems to contextualize Augustine's observation of a child's "grip of jealousy" (quoted on p. 115), and the way in which Jacob later tricks Isaac into bestowing Esau's blessing on him confirms Augustine's description. Jacob knows precisely what he wants—all of the rights and privileges that belong rightfully to his older brother, Esau. Why? Not only was being the firstborn son worth a larger share of the patrimony (according to the birthright law of Deut 21:7, the firstborn brother was to receive a double share of his father's estate), but also more importantly, the firstborn son was considered to be possessed of a unique sanctity. Since he belonged to God, he was accorded a privileged position: "I have hallowed to me all the firstborn in Israel, both man and beast" (Num 3:13).

Being the primary guarantor of the future of the family line and of the preservation of the ancestral heritage, the firstborn son ranked second only to the head of the family, the paterfamilias, whose successor he would automatically become (as Isaac's blessing in Gen 27:29 makes quite clear).[11] In effect, the firstborn son *becomes* his father and upon the father's death assumes all of his rights. In the Lacanian sense, the son ultimately overtakes his father and gains his father's Phallus (used in the sense as I have discussed throughout this book). At this point, then, Jacob, desiring all of these perquisites, yet physically unable to prevent Esau from being born first, Jacob takes the more devious means of exploiting his brother's misery in order to eliminate his brother's birth-advantage and guarantee his own ultimate status.

But Jacob still is not satisfied! Apparently, having obtained Esau's birthright is not enough—Jacob's ultimate goal is to vanquish his brother completely by diverting his blind father's blessing, intended for Esau, toward himself. And not only is Jacob encouraged by Mommy-Dearest, he accomplishes his goal through her machinations. With Rebecca's help, Jacob, having bought Esau's birthright for a bowl of lentil stew, will now deprive his brother of a final paternal blessing, sacred words intended to seal Esau's destiny as patriarch.

The Coup de Grâce

The story unfolds dramatically and continues to emphasize the family dynamics. As if on a stage, the narrative develops through a series of conversations in which all four members of the nuclear family participate, but only in pairs and never as an entire family unit. Highlighting their sibling rivalry, Jacob and Esau never appear together. Equally significant is the fact that Rebecca never speaks with Esau, her eldest child, and has only one brief conversation with Isaac, again underscoring the overarching relationship between mother and younger son. Perhaps due to feelings of guilt, neither of the co-conspirators confronts the wronged Esau.

While Rebecca hovers in the background manipulating the situation, the entire focus is on Jacob's final act of sibling-rivalry: securing for himself the blessing intended for his older brother. Indeed, the Hebrew noun *berākāh* ("blessing") occurs seven times and its verbal form twenty-one times. Since the birthright is no longer the issue, nothing is said about the disposition of property. Surprisingly, however (and possibly due to wishful-thinking), Esau still hopes to receive his father's blessing even though he knows he has lost his birthright.

The family drama opens with the first conversation—that of Isaac and his favorite son, Esau. The dialogue creates an impression of impending death:[12]

> When Isaac was old and his eyes were dim so that he could not see, he called Esau, his eldest son, and said to him, "My son." He said to him, "Here I am." He said, "Behold, now, I am old and I know not the day of my death. Now therefore take, I pray you, your weapons, your quiver and bow, and go out to the field and catch me some venison and make me savory food, such as I love, and bring it to me that I may eat, that my soul may bless you before I die." (Gen 27:1-4)

Isaac's total blindness, or perhaps some illness, prompts him to name his successor. Consistent with the patriarch's penchant for a good piece of game, Isaac repeatedly emphasizes the meal (vv. 19, 25, 31, 33), a hint, perhaps, that this feast is not just a means of inducing gastronomic well-being, but also a ceremonial precursor to the ritual act of blessing. The words Isaac uses stress the ritual setting: "that my soul may bless you," which appears here, is repeated three times later in this sad episode (Gen 27:19, 25, 31). Clearly, these precise words are of great importance to both the father's and the son's understanding of the coveted blessing. Isaac can bless *his* offspring by virtue of the power and authority vested in him, having received a similar blessing himself.

The plot thickens during the second conversation that takes place between Rebecca and *her* favorite, Jacob:

> Rebecca heard when Isaac spoke to Esau his son. Esau went to the field to hunt for venison, and to bring it. Rebecca spoke to Jacob, her son, saying, "Behold, I heard your father speak to Esau your brother, saying, 'Bring me venison and make me savory food, that I may eat, and bless

you before the LORD before my death.' Now, therefore, my son, hear my voice according to that which I command you. Go now to the flock and fetch me from there two good kids of the goats, and I will make them into savory food for your father, that he may eat, and that he may bless you before his death." Jacob said to Rebecca, his mother, "Behold, Esau, my brother, is a hairy man and I am a smooth man. My father perhaps will feel me and I shall seem to him a deceiver, and I shall bring a curse upon me, not a blessing!" His mother said to him, "Upon me be your curse, my son! Only hear my voice and go fetch me them." He went, and he fetched, and brought them to his mother, and his mother made savory food such as his father loved. Rebecca took the best clothes of her eldest son Esau, which were with her in the house, and put them on Jacob, her younger son; and she put the skins of the kids of the goats on his hands and on the smooth of his neck with the skins of the kids. She gave the savory food and the bread which she had prepared into the hand of her son Jacob. (Gen 27:5-17)

Once again, the narrator reinforces the parental preferences by telling us that Isaac spoke to "his" son, Esau, and Rebecca spoke to "her" son, Jacob. Thus, alert to the interests of her preferred child, Rebecca makes it her business to know what is going on when Isaac summons Esau.[13] Rebecca provides the vehicle by which Jacob can receive the coveted blessing—she even offers to prepare the meal of deception herself. In order to impress upon Jacob the importance and solemnity of the forthcoming occasion, Rebecca adds the phrase "in the presence of the LORD" to Isaac's words that had outlined the patriarch's plans for the blessing ritual.[14] Jacob, more concerned with the consequences of detection than with the morality of his actions, hesitates. But true to character, Rebecca confidently brushes aside Jacob's fears.

Aided and abetted by Momma, Jacob proceeds with his deception.

He came to his father and said, "Father." And he said, "Here I am. Who are you, my son?" Jacob said to his father, "I am Esau, your first-born; I have done according as you did tell me. Arise, I pray you, sit up and eat of my venison, that your soul may bless me." Isaac said to his son, "How is it that you have found it so quickly, my son?" and he said, "Because the LORD your God sent me good speed." Isaac said to Jacob, "Come near, I pray you, that I may feel you, my son, whether you are really my son Esau or not." Jacob went near to Isaac, his father. He felt him and said, "The voice is Jacob's voice, but the hands are the hands of Esau." He did not recognize him because his hands were hairy like his brother Esau's hands; So he blessed him. He asked, "Are you really my son Esau?" He said, "I am." He said, "Bring it near to me and I shall eat of

my son's venison that my soul may bless you." He brought it near to him
and he ate, and he brought him wine and he drank. His father Isaac said
to him, "Come near now and kiss me, my son." He came near and
kissed him. And he smelled the smell of his garments and blessed him
and said, "See, the smell of my son is like the smell of the field that the
Lord has blessed. Therefore, God give you of the dew of heaven and the
fatness of the earth, plenty of corn and wine. Let peoples serve you, and
nations bow to you; be lord over your brothers, and let your mother's
sons bow down to you. Cursed be those who curse you, blessed be those
who bless you." (Gen 27:18-30)

Upon approaching Isaac, in obvious trepidation, Jacob can utter only
a single word, "Father." When questioned by Isaac about his identity,
it appears for a moment that Jacob might not be able to continue his
scheme, but he rallies and rises to the challenge by invoking God's
name—in an outright lie. Although visually impaired, Isaac draws
upon his remaining senses of hearing, touch, taste, and smell. While
the distinctive quality and inflection of Jacob's voice puts his imper-
sonation of Esau in jeopardy, the skin disguise is so effective that it
saves the day. But Isaac, ready to bless his son, is vaguely disquieted
and renews his probing, asking "Are you really my son Esau?" Jacob
can no do more than utter a single word: "Yes," he lies (again). At the
moment of crisis, Jacob almost freezes.

For some reason, Isaac still is not convinced completely and imposes
the test of taste by demanding his meal. Isaac's repeated emphasis on
the meat being prepared Esau's special way accentuates what endeared
Esau to his father in the first place—Esau's cooking skills. In fact, the
text emphasizes Isaac's craving for Esau's delicacies (Genesis 27), thereby retrospectively making sense of the unique expression *kî-ṣayid
bᵉpîw*—literally "for [there was] hunt in his mouth" (Gen 25:28). Jux-
taposed with its closest analogue, the description of Noah's dove
returning to the ark, *zayit ṭārāp bᵉpîha*—literally "and an olive leaf
plucked in her mouth" (Gen 8:11), Isaac's relationship with Esau
highlights the connections of hunt/prey/food/nourishment and seems
to conjure a reversal of the parental animal or bird of prey feeding its
young. Fortunately for Jacob, Rebecca's catering service enables him to
face successfully the final challenge: Isaac's discerning sense of smell.

Since the clothes of a shepherd emit the rather unpleasant odor of
the flock and the herd (unlike those of the hunter, which give off the
more palatable scent of the fields), it is not surprising that Isaac could

believe that Esau was standing in front of him. Fully convinced that his favorite son, Esau, is his chef and waiter, Isaac mistakenly blesses Jacob. The blessing is complex and comprehensive: it assures fertility of the soil, political and military preeminence, and God's consummate protection—everything Jacob wanted! Jacob had performed the final coup de grâce with nervous haste: as the narrator reports, "he went, he took, he brought."

But then disaster strikes! Dinner is served:

> As soon as Isaac had made an end of blessing Jacob, and Jacob was scarcely gone from the presence of Isaac, his father, Esau, his brother, came in from his hunting. He also had made savory food and brought it to his father and he said to his father, "Let my father arise and eat of his son's venison, that your soul may bless me." Isaac, his father, said to him, "Who are you?" And he said, "I am your son, your first-born, Esau." Isaac trembled very much and said, "Who then was he that took venison and brought it to me and I have eaten of all and have blessed him? Moreover, he will be blessed!" When Esau heard the words of his father, he cried with a great and exceedingly bitter cry and said to his father, "Bless me, me also, Oh, my Father!" He said, "Your brother came with cunning and took away your blessing." He said, "Is he not rightly named Jacob? He has supplanted me these two times: he took away my birthright and behold, now he has taken away my blessing." He said, "Have you not reserved a blessing for me?" Isaac answered and said to Esau, "Behold, I have made him your lord, and all his brothers I have given to him for servants. With corn and wine have I sustained him. What shall I do now for you, my son?" Esau said to his father, "Have you but one blessing, my Father? Bless me, even me also, Oh my Father!" Esau raised his voice and wept.
>
> Isaac, his father, answered and said to him, "Behold, your dwelling will be of the fatness of the earth and of the dew of heaven from above. By your sword you will live, and you will serve your brother; and it will come to pass when you will have the dominion, you will break his yoke from off your neck."
>
> Esau hated Jacob because of the blessing with which his father blessed him. Esau said in his heart, "When the days of mourning for my father are at hand, then will I slay my brother, Jacob." (Gen 27:30-41; *N.B. I have intentionally left all of the pronouns, confusing as they may be, rather than providing the antecedents.*)

A little too slow at the hunt, Esau returns with Daddy's dinner. Esau, twice victimized by his younger brother, is devastated when he discovers what has happened. His lengthy conversation with Isaac stands in contrast to Jacob's monosyllabic discourse. And, despite

Isaac's closeness to Esau, Isaac no longer calls him "my son." Since biblical blessings and curses had a potency and dynamism all their own, the destiny that was solemnly conferred upon his younger son is irreversible (Gen 27:37), and Isaac seems overwhelmed with the horror he has inflicted on his favorite child.

Although Esau now despises Jacob, he defers any plans of retribution against the brother who has defeated him twice and asks his father for only one thing—to be blessed by him with however small a blessing. Esau resorts to bitter sarcasm— he puns on *bekhorah* ("birthright") and *berakhah* ("blessing," that which his brother had stolen from him) and reminds his father (and reader) that indeed Jacob had been named aptly (Jacob had been named for his grasping of Esau's heel while emerging from the womb (*'āqab*—a play on the name *Jacob*).

Momma Saves the Day!

By now, Rebecca realizes that Jacob is in danger and, still protective of her favorite son, acts decisively once again.

> The words of Esau, her older son, were told to Rebecca, and she sent and called Jacob, her younger son, and said to him, "Behold, your brother Esau comforts himself, planning to kill you. Now, therefore, my son, obey my voice. Arise, flee to Laban, my brother, to Haran. Dwell with him a few days, until your brother's fury turns away from you and he forgets that which you have done to him. Then I will send and fetch you from there. Why should I be bereaved of you both in one day?" (Gen 27:42-45)

Rebecca, who earlier seems to have misjudged the depth of her older son's outrage and the intensity of his vindictive reaction, clearly is alarmed and sends for Jacob, who may well have been in hiding. Both Jacob and Rebecca are now in precarious positions. If Esau carries out his threat, Jacob will be killed when Isaac dies.[15] Once again, the resourceful Rebecca has a plan: "Rebecca said to Isaac, 'I am weary of my life because of the daughters of the Hittites. If Jacob takes a wife of the daughters of the Hittites, such as these of the daughters of the land, from among the native women, what good will life be to me?'" (Gen 27:46). Rebecca realizes that, for his own safety, Jacob must be sent away at once. But this is no small task. Rebecca needs her husband's agreement, yet she cannot possibly divulge the true reason for Jacob's sudden departure lest her own involvement in the deception be exposed. Eureka!—she hits upon the perfect solution—Jacob needs a wife! And this scheme works because Esau's marriages to local women has become an intolerable torment to his parents: "When Esau was forty years old, he took to wife Judith the daughter of Beeri the Hittite, and Basemath the daughter of Elon the Hittite; and they made life bitter for Isaac and Rebekah" (Gen 26:34-35). Using guilt as the ultimate tool, Rebecca's words contain an implicit rebuke to Isaac for his favoritism of Esau, a rebuke that guarantees to assuage any lingering uneasiness Isaac might feel for having blessed the wrong son.

The last bit of this family saga is the final conversation between Isaac and Jacob, and once again revolves around insuring Jacob's good fortune.

> Isaac called Jacob and blessed him and charged him, and said to him, "You shall not take a wife of the daughters of Canaan. Arise, go to Paddam-Aram, to the house of Bethuel, your mother's father, and take you a wife from there from the daughters of Laban, your mother's brother. El Shaddai bless you, make you fruitful, and multiply you, that you may be a multitude of people, and give the blessing of Abraham to you and to your seed with you, that you may inherit the land in which you are a sojourner, which God gave to Abraham." Isaac sent away Jacob. He went to Paddam-Aram, to Laban, the son of Bethuel the Aramean, the brother of Rebecca, mother of Jacob and Esau. (Gen 28:1-5)

Isaac's final blessing of Jacob upon sending him to sanctuary with his uncle confirms the younger son's title to the birthright.[16] Rebecca has urged Jacob to flee, and Isaac, who knows nothing of the *real* reason for Jacob's journey, urges him to go.

Not surprisingly, the rabbis had several commentaries on the relationship of Jacob and Esau prior to Jacob's leaving home. However, while the biblical account treats Esau with a certain degree of understanding,[17] in the aggadah[18] the story is reinterpreted to discredit Esau thoroughly and glorify Jacob completely. For example, according to *Genesis Rabbah,* Rebecca, while pregnant, passed a synagogue, and Jacob tried to "break forth"; but when she passed near a pagan house of worship, Esau struggled to be born (*Genesis Rabbah* 63:6). Further, Esau had threatened to kill his mother if he was not permitted to be born first, and it was to save Rebecca that Jacob had agreed to Esau's primogeniture (*Midrash Hagigah Genesis* 25:22; cf. *Pesiktha Rabbathi* 12:4).[19] The aggadic description of Jacob at birth is "clean, smooth, extraordinarily handsome, and born circumcised"; while poor Esau is described as "hairy and bearded, blood-red in color, and with all his teeth fully developed" (*Genesis Rabbah* 63:7–8). In addition, Esau's "ruddy" color is interpreted as signifying that he was "altogether a shedder of blood" (*Genesis Rabbah* 63:8). The rabbis describe the boys' religious education along similar lines: while both brothers attended school up to the age of thirteen (or according to one version, fifteen), they parted completely once they had reached their religious majority. Jacob studied at the schools of Shem and Eber, and spent all his life in the pursuit of learning while Esau became a dissipated idolator (*Genesis Rabbah* 63:10; *b. Yoma* 28b).

Not surprisingly, the rabbis write that Jacob's desire to have the birthright was not influenced by any selfish motives but by his wish to be privileged to offer the sacrifices, at that time the prerogative of the firstborn (*Genesis Rabbah* 63:13; *Numbers Rabbah* 4:8). Even so, it was only because of Esau's manifest unsuitability for a spiritual office that Jacob was willing to sacrifice his life for the spiritual privileges of the birthright (ibid.). As a result, God, of course, assisted him in obtaining the blessings (*Genesis Rabbah* 65:17–19). When Jacob went to see his father, "the Garden of Eden entered with him"; but when Esau came to Isaac "Gehenna went in with him" (*Genesis Rabbah* 65:22).[20]

Back to the text. . . .

Dream Number One: Jacob's "Ladder"

At this point in the narrative, Jacob, fleeing from his home after receiving Isaac's unwitting blessing, travels for a bit, lies down for the night, has a dream.

> He dreamed and behold! a ladder[21] set up on the earth, and the top of it reached to heaven; and behold, the angels of God ascending and descending on it! And behold, the LORD stood above it and said, "I am the LORD, the God of Abraham your father and the God of Isaac; the land on which you lie, to you will I give it and to your seed; and your seed shall be like the dust of the earth, and you shall spread abroad to the west and to the east and to the north and to the south; and in you and in your seed will all the families of the earth be blessed. Behold, I am with you and will keep you in all places to which you go, and will bring you back to this land; for I will not leave you until I have done that of which I have spoken to you." (Gen 28:12-15)

Jacob has been encouraged by his mother to leave home in order to find a wife. Just before setting out on this venture, Isaac had bestowed a fertility blessing upon him: "May El Shaddai bless you, make you fertile and numerous, so that you become an assembly of peoples." "El Shaddai" is usually explained as a cognate of the Akkadian *sadu*, "mountain" and as discussed on p. 56 and following, is associated with the Hebrew *šād*—"breast." Most linguists see a semantic development from rounded "breasts" to "hills" and "mountains," and certainly similarities exist between these "blessings of the breasts" and the fertility cults of the Israelites' Canaanite neighbors. Perhaps Isaac was remembering the Canaanite goddesses Ashcrah and Anat, whose iconography featured prominent breasts. Jacob, having received the blessing he extracted underhandedly from his father, approaches Paddam-Aram, the house of Bethuel, his mother's brother, to take a wife and dreams that angels of God are ascending and descending a stairway of some sort, a very strange image. Certainly Freud's explanation seems apt: ladders, steps, and staircases ". . . or more precisely, walking on them, are clear symbols of sexual intercourse. . . . The common element here is the rhythm . . . perhaps, too, the increasing excitement and breathlessness the higher one climbs" (1900:322).[22]

In search of a wife, Jacob dreams of potency; his dream reinforces Isaac's fertility blessing bestowed in the name of "god of the breasts." Freud would be pleased.

Intermission

The story of Jacob's sibling rivalry is interrupted by the narrative of Jacob in Haran: Rebecca sends Jacob to woo and wed one of his cousins, a daughter of his Uncle Laban. As soon as he arrives in Haran, he meets Rachel, the younger of his two cousins, who is bringing her father's sheep to water at the well. He wants to marry her, and to do so Jacob agrees to work for her for seven years. At the end of that time, however, Laban tricks him into marrying his eldest daughter, Leah, instead. Jacob must now work another seven years for Rachel.

Married to two sisters (any conflicts there, do you suppose?)[23] and in a concubinage arrangement with the sisters' maids, Jacob fathers twelve sons and a daughter. After a very complicated (and stormy) relationship with his uncle/father-in-law, Laban, Jacob decides to return home and slips away when the opportunity presents itself. The complications continue, and interesting as they are, they are not particularly significant for this reading (except perhaps to note Jacob's strained relationships with father figures).

Back to the Dream

Jacob and his entire entourage have now left Laban and are returning home. Understandably tense the night preceding his encounter with Esau, Jacob's wrestling-match dream can be viewed as an expression of his desire for Esau's forgiveness and reconciliation with his older brother. That is to say, the wrestling match with the strong stranger who does not reveal his name (but to whom the narrator merely refers as "a man") both replicates Jacob's struggles with Esau and anticipates future strife upon returning home. Although in Jacob's mind it is Esau who has the obstructionist interest, the wrestler is not represented as Esau himself, but rather, he represents Esau in some manner. He is, as it were, Esau's alter ego. Read this way, the dream represents Jacob's repressed and forbidden dream thoughts as modified by condensation and displacement—modified nearly beyond recognition.

The Primary Process of Jacob's Dream-Work: Condensation and Displacement. According to Freud, the first part of dream-work is condensation: the manifest dream (the story that a dreamer remembers) has a smaller content than the latent one (the "forbidden" dream thoughts). However, while the manifest dream is an "abbreviated translation" of the latent dream thoughts, condensation is far from being a simple process of merely omitting details. Instead, composite figures and structures are formed so that as little as possible is left out. As a result, dreams often superimpose various words and ideas. This is most clearly demonstrable in the way condensation treats words or names. A thing with one name may be associated in a dream with an event with a similar name, even though neither word occurred in the dream.[24]

The second activity in the primary process of dream-work is displacement, that which Freud regards as "the most powerful instrument of the dream-censorship" (1916–17:233). According to Freud, elements in the manifest dream (the literal contents of a dream as the dreamer remembers them) replace elements in the latent dream thoughts (the figurative activity of a dream, the forbidden dream thoughts) via a chain of associations in order to disguise these censored thoughts. As a result, the intensity of a repressed wish is detached from the wish itself and passes on to other thoughts that in themselves are of little value. Displacement in dreams is similar to the way jokes work in that a switch of context allows for a play on words. In both cases, however, the linkages may be forced and often far-fetched.

In Jacob's dream, condensation—the primary-process of dream-work—revolves around the words *wayyigga' bᵉkap-yᵉrēkô* ("touched the hollow of his thigh"). Jacob conflates three of his earlier struggles with Esau—the prenatal grabbing of Esau's heel, the birthright of the firstborn, and the subsequent sale of the birthright by Esau—into a single struggle with this unknown assailant, an assailant from whom he extracts a blessing.

Jacob's unconscious wish is not revealed by the manifest text of the dream as such, but rather by what Lacan calls "the lacunae latent within it" (1958:251). Jacob's dream is a product of his past and present that fantasizes his future, a regression in the service of an ego formation. That is to say, Jacob's dream is not his actual unconscious wish, but rather a distortion of it. The most condensed content of Jacob's dream goes piece by piece into his dream story via a string of associations. What is particularly interesting about Jacob's dream is that it is a mirror image of the physical interactions Jacob had with Esau before the dream.

Let me explain. In the first instance, Jacob had grabbed Esau by the ankle. In Jacob's dream, the stranger grasps *Jacob* by the hip to bring him down. The second struggle is particularly interesting since it crystallizes Jacob's ultimate desire to castrate his older brother, as well as Jacob's own fear of castration, typical of the paradigm of sibling jealousy.

As discussed throughout this book, within literature, the theme of actual castration often is replaced by either the substitution of other body parts for dismemberment of genitalia (blinding, for example) or by a symbolic castration, that is, the loss of power. In this case, as part of Esau's sale of his birthright to Jacob for the famous pottage dinner, Esau was forced to swear an oath to Jacob making the transaction irrevocable. In biblical narratives, swearing was accomplished generally by placing the hand on the partner's hip or thigh.[25] In linguistic terms, this type of an oath is an expression of a semantic universal that taboo body parts are subject to a spatial displacement by a more or less contiguous organ. That is, hips and thighs have been charged with genital meaning. In effect, Jacob is symbolically castrating Esau by stealing the rights of the firstborn (again, I am using Lacan's use of Phallus as power concept). In Jacob's dream, fearing his brother's retribution, the unknown assailant injures him by striking his *thigh!* By displacing his fear of Esau and the possibility of actual or symbolic castration onto the assailant, Jacob can be wounded but not vanquished. In other words, this dream is an echo of the castration *wished* upon

Esau but *feared by Jacob himself.* Indeed, the morning after the dream it is Jacob who is limping, Jacob who has come away wounded.

Jacob, of course, fears his brother both because of the sale of the birthright and the deception in connection with their father's blessing. Although in his dream Jacob wrestles all night and still can retain his animosity toward his brother, Jacob's own repentant feelings result in a self-punishment—limping. And the dream is completely successful in calming Jacob's conscience. Jacob does not let his brother/stranger go but insists on being blessed by the vanquished Esau-replacement.

The Secondary-Process of Jacob's Dream-Work. In vv. 27-29 the procedure is reversed during the secondary process of dream-work. It is at this stage that Jacob retraces his chain of associations in order to decode or interpret his dream. This phase of dream-work takes place while a dreamer is beginning to awaken and attempts to return from the pictorial language of dreams to ordinary waking expressions, from fantasy to the introduction of a reality. Since the conscious mind prefers to put the irrational dream sequence into a recognizable and familiar logical order, the sequence of events is often taken out of order. That is, during this stage, a dreamer reorganizes the hieroglyphics, the pictorial dream images, into a relatively consistent and comprehensible narrative, filling in its gaps, smoothing over its contradictions, and reordering its chaotic elements. The intelligible pattern that the conscious mind wants to impose on the dream images can ignore or falsify what is patently there (just like a reader Freud identifies who is so engaged in a text that he or she ignores the misprints [Freud 1900:499]). What was visible to the mind's eye in the dream remains unchanged, but the conscious perspective produces a revision of it. The dream that one recalls is a transformation of an original dream, never remembered exactly—only in *re*-vision. In this context, revision means to "see again" in two senses: to recall a dream and to generate a new narrative, to substitute a text for a text.

In a dream, raw materials are transformed in ways that must be analyzed, deciphered, and decomposed, and the focus is on symptomatic aspects (distortions, ambiguities, absences, and elisions). Dreamers continuously shift from metaphorical expressions to literal meanings, from repressed wishes to reality, and from indeterminate to determinate signifiers. When we dream, we confer meaning to textual elements by successively displacing them. In other words, we revise personal dramas into scenarios of remembering, repeating, and working through.

Dream images are rendered into texts and contexts by reordering seemingly arbitrary contiguity to meaningful contiguity, parataxis to syntaxis. Opposing two competing strategies, dreamers perceive symbols that enable an authentic image to be reconstructed from its distorting fragments. At the same time, dreaming gives meaning to textual elements by allowing them to be successively displaced. The dream and its interpretation form a mirror image: dreams transform concepts (wishes or ideas) into symbolic images; dream interpretation travels the same road in reverse, from the semantic (the concept or idea) to the semiotic (the symbolic image used to represent the abstract thought).[26]

Jacob's Repression. When Jacob recalls his dream, the rationality of his daytime experiences imposes a narrative sense and coherence on the apparent absurdity of his dream sequence. In other words, the ambiguity of the stranger's blessing may be explained by the Freudian concept of "repression."

Freud describes repression as the "preliminary stage of condemnation" (Freud 1915:148). Certainly, Jacob anticipates a condemnation by Esau that apparently he feels he deserves. In the dream, the nightlong wrestling is representative of Jacob's desire to castrate Esau and must be repressed since Jacob fears his older brother—for good reason!

"Sin" and "fear" are two words redolent of the vocabulary of guilt (see p. 101 and following). And for Jacob, as in Freudian theory, guilt anticipates his condemnation and punishment. Indeed, the sequence—the wrestling match, defensive words, threat of punishment, condemnation—fits Freud's paradigm discussed above (Freud 1905:175). Thus, in Jacob's dream of the struggle with the wrestler, the threat of retribution by Esau is repressed and replaced with a blessing by Esau's alter ego.

During the secondary process of dream-work, when Jacob is translating his dream into a coherent "scenario,"[27] he frees himself from the consequences of his repressed wishes by an almost classical example of the Freudian defense mechanism: rejection and disavowal. Freud's general description of this psychological process sounds as if it had been written specifically to describe Jacob: "He rejects the incompatible idea [that is, wrestling with Esau] together with its effects [possibly losing] and behaves as if the idea had never occurred to him at all [Jacob is blessed instead]" (1894:58)!

Conclusion

Typical of Freudian dream theory, the dream figure is more than merely a representative of Esau: the wrestler is a composite. In his dream, Jacob combines father and brother, Isaac and Esau, into a single entity, the dream opponent who before blessing Jacob, asks his name—a paraphrase of his father's earlier question. In his dream, however, Jacob answers truthfully, "Jacob." And Jacob's name is changed—again. In other words, the first time Jacob changes his name he does so deceitfully; now, Jacob's change of name is demanded by the assailant, a father-substitute: "No longer is your name to be called Jacob, but Israel."

The assailant then adds the otherwise-mysterious explanation as to the name-change: "for you have striven with God and with humans and have prevailed," an explanation that further extends the identity of the wrestler. For Jacob, this mysterious being, the celestial patron of Esau, now represents the psychological transformation of Isaac, his father, to God. Indeed, this transformation is so complete that after the struggle with the stranger Jacob states: "I have seen *God* face to face."

Ambiguity, another common aspect of dream-work is present in Jacob's combination of two vague expressions: "see the face" in biblical literature can describe an experience of either cordiality or hostility with a human or the divinity. Similarly, "face to face," which is used in the Hebrew Bible only of divine-human encounters, can be either an adversarial confrontation or an experience of extraordinary intimacy. In Jacob's dream, this ambiguity simultaneously portrays the perilous and auspicious nature of Jacob's furious struggle. Since the dream figure comprises ultimately brother, father, and God—all of whom are to forgive Jacob and sanction his deeds—the figure *cannot* give his name but instead blesses Jacob *in the name of these three feared opponents*— "you have striven with God and with humans."

And of course, consistent with Freudian theory, I see a sexual content repressed in Jacob's wrestling dream; it is repressed by a castration or Oedipal anxiety. The earlier dream of Jacob, dreamed while fleeing from his home after receiving Jacob's unwitting blessing, is this dream's counterpart.

In search of a wife, Jacob dreams of fertility and potency; in fear of his brother, Jacob dreams of castration—the sibling rivalry/inimical brothers motif carried to the extreme. Sound Freudian?

Chapter 7

My Sister, My—Hmmm . . . :
Brother-Sister Incest and Sibling Rivalry

"Indeed, it is said that we all descend from such relationships."
—Henrik Ibsen, *Ghosts*

As I discuss in chapter 6, according to Freudian thought, it is only through the primary parent complex that the significance of the sibling complex can be appreciated or understood. If both children are boys and there are no female siblings (as in the case of Esau and Jacob) the younger brother gradually assumes the father's position as competitor for the mother's affections—at least from the perspective of his older sibling. But Freud sees another scenario in the case of an older brother/younger sister. Just as the younger brother becomes a competitor in place of the father but reduced to childlike proportions, a younger sister becomes the substitute for the mother. In the fantasies of her brother, the girl takes on the image of the pure female ideal. Mother, because of her relationship with Father, becomes unworthy of this status in the young boy's eyes. This displacement is fostered, in great part, by the children's similarity in age, thought, and emotions. Almost by definition, they are closer to one another than to the adults.

This chapter examines the sibling relationships of three brothers in light of Freud's theories of the brother/brother/sister dynamics and conflicts. As in the brother/brother narrative of Jacob/Esau, the biblical examples I examine in this chapter ultimately have the same end result: love becomes hatred. And in this chapter as in the previous ones, I have included several artistic and literary representations of the narratives that I read in light of psychoanalytic literary theory in an attempt to provide another insight into these texts, an insight other than that of traditional biblical scholars.

Background
Throughout this book I explore some of the many mythological creations of the incest motif, particularly relating to parent-child incest.

Just as parent-child incest stories abound in various mythologies, sibling incest narratives exist in mythology as well as in the Hebrew Bible. For example, the Egyptian legend of Isis and Osiris, the Greek myth of Kronos and Zeus (who married their sisters), the Japanese legend of Izanami and Izanagi who procreated in "imitation of the birds," are just a few of the many examples.

Brother/Sister in Creation Myths

In creation myths, sibling incest is represented often as the relationship of the sun and the moon. Some North American tribes, for example, say that the moon is a young woman and that sun is her brother. According to one myth, the moon (sister) visits her brother (the sun) secretly during the night but finally is discovered since he has left a mark on her face with his hands, a telltale handprint. This same myth occurs in Panama, and in Oceania where "the moon is sometimes darkened by the hand of her brother Mani [the sun god]" (Rank 1932:365). In Cherokee mythology, the genders are reversed. According to one myth,

> The sun, a young woman, lived in the east and the moon, her brother, lived in the west. The young woman had a lover who always visited her in the dark. He came by night and departed before daybreak. She wondered who it could be. To find out, one night she rubbed his face with ashes (that handprint again!). When the moon rose the next evening, its face was smeared. Then the sister knew it was her brother who had visited her. She was so ashamed that in the future she kept as far away from her brother as possible. (Rank 1932:370)

Among the Chiglit Eskimos, the first two humans also were siblings: "By night the sister is seduced by her unrecognized brother. Finally, to determine who her nightly lover could be, she blackens her hands with soot and leaves marks on his face. The next morning she recognizes her brother and flees from him, but he pursues her passionately" (Rank 1932:371). It is almost impossible not to notice the obvious relation of these tales to the tales of pursuit of the daughter by the father discussed in chapter 3.

Indeed, the close relation of these tales of siblings to the father-daughter tales is highlighted by the Italian folktale "The Girl without Hands." Briefly:

> After the death of his wife, the king decides to marry his own sister, Penta, and tells her so. In her desperation, she severs both her hands and sends them to her brother with the comment that he should "gladly

enjoy that which he seemed to wish for more than anything in the world." The king orders her sealed into a chest and deposited into the sea. After many adventures, she is fished up in a foreign city. The country's widowed king falls in love with her and marries her. Their child is born during the king's absence and the mother informs him by letter. Unfortunately, the letter is falsified so that the mother and child will be sentenced to death; however, they are only exposed in the wilderness, where a sorcerer finally resolves everything happily and she regains her hands. (Rank 1932:370–72)

As in the related father myths, the incest fantasy asserts itself through doubling. The king who marries Penta, who has been fished from the water after his wife dies, can be seen as the doublet of the king who wishes to marry his sister Penta. The exposure (if we combine the two doublets) would thus have occurred when the king recognizes his disfigured sister as his spouse (perhaps from her hands). The father's severing of hands or breasts of the daughter who refuses to submit, however, is reported as punishment. In contrast, in the siblings myths the hands are the telltale sign leading to recognition. In a legend of the Indians of the lower Fraser River (American Pacific Coast) reported by Rank, the same tale appears:

One night a sister smears her lover with soot; then she recognizes him the next morning as her brother, who has led her to commit incest. On finding that she is pregnant, she is filled with intense shame and begs the brother to go far away with her. But when their son grows up, he notices their great resemblance to one another and discovers the whole truth. Brother and sister die willingly by fire. (Rank 1932:371–76)

Variations of this tale among Indo-Europeans are replete: Dianus and Diana, Phoebus and Phoebe, Iolaus and Ioleia, Pyrrhus and Pyrrha, Liber and Libera, Niödr and Nerthus, and many others.

Biblical Brother/Sister Relationships
Despite the numerous extra-biblical tales of brothers and sisters, brother/sister relationships in the Hebrew Bible are not particularly plentiful. This seems somewhat surprising since virtually all of the powerful male characters are married, and most probably they had opposite-sex siblings. Yet narratives that deal with brother-sister relations are few and far between. Indeed, the accounts of Abraham and Sarah (half-siblings), the sons-of-Jacob and Dinah, the Aaron/Moses/Miriam triad, the Amnon/Absalom/Tamar construct, and the brothers and the female "beloved" in Song of Songs are the only sustained narratives

concerning brothers and sisters. Other references to "sister" and/or "brother" are either a ruse manufactured by the literary characters (such as the Isaac and Rebecca narrative), metaphorical (Hosea's children), or lists of genealogies.

According to psychoanalytic literary theorists, under the pressure of moral defense, the undisguised element of the sibling incest fantasy in most literature (including biblical brother/sister tales) can be divided into two large groups. First, following the classical Oedipus schema, one literary form of brother/sister incest takes place through a lack of knowledge of the relationship. Since the kinship is discovered only after the acts have been committed (that is, the incest occurs naively—without awareness of the partner's identity), the reactions of repentance and defense appear only after the relationship is discovered. In his *Poetics,* Aristotle claims that it is a particularly effective literary device to have relatives, ignorant of their kinship and about to bring upon themselves the guilt of serious sin, experience an emotional scene of recognition.

Second, and more frequently, the lovers recognize each other as siblings before the longed-for but prohibited union can occur. In effect, this is the technique used by the narrator of the Abraham/Sarah relationship of Gen 12:10-20 and 20:1-18.[1]

What's Mine Is Mine and What's Yours Is Mine, Too!

One of the most tragic sibling relationships recorded in the Hebrew Bible results in rape, a case where an unfulfilled desire results in sexual violence. Of course, there are many stories of rape in the Hebrew Bible, indeed, too many: Shechem rapes Dinah in Genesis 34; the Levite's wife is gang-raped in Judges 19; the daughters of Shilo are raped en masse by the Benjaminites in Judges 21. But 2 Samuel 13 is different. In this narrative a brother rapes his sister. And this is not just any brother and sister—they are the "first family," part of David's royal family!

Like all biblical narratives, the Tamar text is brief but to the point and does not deviate to discuss irrelevant issues.[2] It is a story of incest, rape, and fratricide.

> And it came to pass that after this Absalom the son of David had a fair sister whose name was Tamar. Amnon the son of David loved her. Amnon was so distressed that he fell sick for his sister, Tamar, for she was a virgin. Amnon found it hard to contrive anything with regard to her.

But Amnon had a friend whose name was Jonadab, the son of Shimeah, David's brother. Jonadab was a very subtle man. He said to him, "Why are you, the king's son, so wasted from day to day? Will you not tell me?" Amnon said to him, "I love Tamar, my brother Absalom's sister." Jonadab said to him, "Lie down on your bed and feign to be sick. When your father comes to see you, say to him, 'I pray you, let my sister, Tamar, come and give me bread and prepare the food in my sight, that I may see it and eat it at her hand.'" So Amnon lay down and feigned to be sick. When the king came to see him, Amnon said to the king, "I pray you, let Tamar, my sister, come and give me bread and prepare the food in my sight that I may eat at her hand."

Then David sent to Tamar and said, "Go, now to your brother Amnon's house and prepare food for him." So Tamar went to her brother Amnon's house and he was laid down. She took flour and kneaded it and made cakes in his sight and baked the cakes. She took a pan and poured it out before him, but he refused to eat. Amnon said, "Cause everyone to leave me." So everyone left him. Amnon said to Tamar, "Bring the food into the room that I may eat from your hand." Tamar took the cakes which she had made and brought them into the chamber to Amnon, her brother. When she brought them to him to eat, he took hold of her and said to her, "Come, lie with me, my sister." She answered him, "No, my brother, do not force me. No such thing ought to be done in Israel. Do not do this shameful deed. I, where should I carry my shame? And as for you, you will be as one of the base men in Israel. Now, therefore, I pray you, speak to the king for he will not withhold me from you." But he would not listen to her voice. Being stronger than she, he violated her and laid [lit.] her.

Then Amnon hated her exceedingly so that the hatred with which he hated her was greater than the love with which he had loved her. Amnon said to her, "Arise, be gone." She said to him, "Do not add this greater wrong of sending me away to the other that you did to me." But he would not listen to her. Then he called his servant who ministered to him and said, "Put now this . . . out from me and bolt the door after her." She had a long-sleeved robe on her, for with such robes were the king's daughters who were virgins clothed. His servant brought her out and bolted the door after her. Tamar put ashes on her head and tore her long-sleeved garment that was on her, and laid her hand on her head, crying as she went. Absalom, her brother said to her, "Has Amnon, your brother, been with you? Keep silence, my sister; he is your brother. Take not this thing to heart." Tamar remained desolate in her brother Absalom's house. (2 Sam 13:1-20)

The opening verses of this tragic story set the scene by naming the three most important characters in the narrative—Absalom, Tamar, and Amnon—all of whom share the same father, King David (but two different mothers). Indeed, familial relationships are emphasized throughout the opening of the narrative, highlighting the theme of incestuous rape.

> The *son* of David had a fair *sister* whose name was Tamar. Amnon, the *son* of David . . . was so distressed that he fell sick for his *sister*. . . . Amnon had a friend . . . the *son* of Shimeah, David's *brother* . . . [who] said to him, "Why are you, the king's *son,* so wasted. . . . Amnon said to him, 'I love Tamar, my *brother* Absalom's *sister*." . . . Jonadab said to him, ". . . When your *father* comes to see you, say to him, "I pray you, let my *sister* . . . come. . . ." . . . When the king came to see him, Amnon said . . . "I pray you, let Tamar, my *sister*, come. . . ." David . . . said, "Go, now to your *brother* Amnon's house. . . ." So Tamar went to her *brother* Amnon's house. . . . Tamar took the cakes which she had made and brought them into the chamber to Amnon, her *brother*. . . . He took hold of her and said to her, "Come, lie with me, my *sister*." She answered him, "No, my *brother,* do not force me. . . ." Absalom, her *brother* said to her, "Has Amnon, your *brother,* been with you? Keep silence, my *sister,* he is your *brother*."

The narrator's emphasis on familial relationships in this narrative in effect replicate the familial references in an earlier account of rape. In the rape of Dinah (Genesis 34) familial relationships are highlighted: for example, Dinah is called the *daughter* of Jacob (v. 3) and the *sister* of Simeon and Levi (v. 25). These family ties are maintained throughout the story: Jacob heard that Shechem had defiled *his daughter* (v. 5); Shechem had done a disgraceful thing in defiling *Jacob's daughter* (v. 7); Shechem talked to *her father* and *brothers* (v. 11), who protested that they could not give their *sister* to one who is uncircumcised (v. 14); if their conditions were not met, Simeon and Levi threatened to take their *daughter* and be gone (v. 17—curiously, Simeon and Levi refer to Dinah in this verse as "our daughter" rather than "our sister." Perhaps it is because this verse is part of the negotiations that involve all of the "daughters" of Israel, Dinah included); Shechem had delight in *Jacob's daughter* (v. 19); *her brothers* slaughtered all the Hivite males (v. 25); and Simeon and Levi asked Jacob if Shechem should deal with their *sister* as with a whore (v. 31).

As if to highlight the brutality of Amnon's actions against Tamar, the narrator first tells us that Amnon ignored her pleas to be spared and "being stronger than she, he violated her and [literally] laid her." This is graphic language, to say the least. Indeed, in biblical Hebrew, the normal grammatical construct *šakab 'im* ("lie with") is used to convey cohabitation, a mutually agreed-upon act. However, *šakab* or *šakab et* ("lay") used with a direct object rather than a preposition) is the usual expression in the Hebrew Bible when the act is forced, a rape. Here, in 2 Sam 13:11 Amnon says: *šikbî 'immi* ("Come, lie *with* me, my sister"). And when she refuses, the narrator reports Amnon's violent acts: he "abused her and laid [no preposition] her [direct object]: *way'annehā wayyiškab 'ōtāh* (2 Sam 13:14). Since Tamar refused to be lain *with*, she is *laid*. And just as there had been an excess of love at the beginning of the narrative ("Amnon, the son of David loved [Tamar]. . . . Amnon was so distressed that he *fell sick for his sister*, Tamar, for she was a virgin. . . . Amnon found it hard to contrive anything with regard to her"), there is an excess of hate at the end.

Now the king's daughter is an object, and her half-brother's language emphasizes this. Amnon, who repeatedly called Tamar "sister" now tells his servant: "Put now *zō't* ['this'] . . . out from me." Amnon, son of a king and presumably respected by his father's subjects, has committed rape. As a result, Prince Amnon has earned the title "one of the base men in Israel."

Giovanni Francesco Barbieri's painting *Amnon and Tamar* portrays the "base" man quite graphically. Amnon's cruel violence and hatred is emphasized by his hands, balled up into fists like those of the spoiled child depicted in the narrative. All the while Tamar pleads with her brother for support. Although the biblical text describes her robe as long-sleeved, the kind worn by all the virgin daughters of the king, Barbieri, apparently unfamiliar with the biblical text, drapes her in a piece of mauve fabric. Amnon's nakedness is covered by a scarf of blue, and since there are no other colors in the painting, all the viewer's attention, like the reader's, is focused on the two figures, their body language, and the expressions on their faces.

Significantly, nothing is given of the mother-daughter relationship in this family constellation, and what is told about the father-daughter construct leaves much to be desired. David provides no direct communication with Tamar and even less evidence of warmth. King David visits his sick son in person, yet when his daughter is raped, the king neither visits nor comforts Tamar after she suffered the devastating violation.[3] For some inexplicable reason, although David becomes angry when he hears about the rape, he does nothing to punish Amnon. (Of course, having just "taken" [and impregnated] Uriah's wife, Bathsheba, and then sent Uriah to his death, David might not have felt himself to be on high enough moral ground to rebuke his son.) In any event, the rape victim's father does not respond.[4] Why not?

Not surprisingly, this narrative has been the subject of a great deal of interpretation. The rabbinic commentary on the Tamar episode revolves around two specific issues. The first area of concern for the sages is that of the possibility of a marriage between half-siblings suggested in Tamar's speech: "Please, speak to the king; he will not refuse me to you" (2 Sam 13:13). Although there is biblical precedent for such marriage between half-siblings (Sarah was the daughter of her husband Abraham's father but not that of his mother [Gen 11:29; 20:12]),[5] the sages believed that such marriages, although permissible prior to the giving of the Torah at Sinai, were no longer allowed during the monarchic time in which the narrative was set (Lev 18:9; 20:17; Deut 27:22). How then did they reconcile the discrepancy between Tamar's statement and biblical law? The rabbis resorted to the midrashic interpretation that Tamar's mother, Maacah, the daughter of King Geshur, had been taken captive by David (what a role model for Amnon, his son!)—and that she had conceived Tamar before converting to Judaism. Tamar would therefore have been permitted to marry Amnon according to Jewish law, because she was a non-Jew (Bronner 1994:122–23).

The second problem for the rabbis was the transformation of Amnon's passion from love to hatred, particularly in comparison to the Dinah/Shechem incident in which Shechem's desire for Dinah also had an element of love. Indeed, in the rape of Dinah narrative, the three verbs of force that describe her violation—"he took and laid [no preposition] and humiliated her" (*wayyiqqaḥ 'ōtāh wayyiškab 'ōtāh*)—so powerful in the Hebrew text, give way to an equally strong expression of endearment: "His soul clung to Dinah, the daughter of Jacob, and he loved the young woman, and he spoke to the heart of the young woman" (Gen 34:3).[6]

On the other hand, Amnon's rape of Tamar is characterized more by lust than love and ends with his loathing her. What motivated the change? *Why* does love—or even lust—turn to loathing? Modern theory about the nature of rape claims that rape is not the result of love or lust but of violence and hatred—a view this story certainly replicates. And the rabbis seemed to have shared the view that Amnon's behavior was violent and loathsome since they discuss at length what they consider to be Tamar's understandable desire for revenge. They even empower Tamar to punish Amnon by physically maiming him in such a way as to impair his virility (this certainly would explain why Amnon comes to hate Tamar so passionately!—quoted in Bronner 1994:123).

Significantly, the sages' empowerment of Tamar in her revenge displays a greater empathy for her than they feel for Dinah. They are cognizant of the fact that Tamar went innocently to her brother's home, at the request of her own father, and that she tried to safeguard her virginity but was overpowered by her attacker/brother. That is to say, the sages hold Tamar in higher regard than Dinah because in their eyes Tamar was not a gadabout. Moreover, she made her shame public and according to rabbinic opinion, thereby "helped prevent violence to others" (quoted in Bronner 1994:123). The sages claim that Tamar's contemporaries heard her cries and exclaimed that if such a crime could be done to the daughter of a king, how much more vulnerable were the daughters of ordinary men. As a result, the rabbis credit Tamar's response to her violation as bringing about the introduction of the "worthy institution of *yihud*," the laws that prohibit private meetings between the sexes.

Another interesting reference to the Tamar story occurs in the Mishnah. It appears in a discussion in which a contrast is drawn between love of a man for a woman versus love (friendship) between two men:

> All love which depends on some material cause, if the material cause ceases, the love ceases. Love which does not depend on some material cause, never fails forever. What love is that which depends on some material cause? This is the love of Amnon and Tamar. And that which does not depend on some material cause? This is the love of David and Jonathan. (quoted in Bronner 1994:124)

The verses contrast love that depends on self-gratification, carnal love, to another love that is unselfish and seeks only the good of the one loved. This analysis views the love of a man for a woman as changing with outward appearance or outward fortune, whereas love between two men is timeless and endures forever. The passage appears to offer a negative evaluation of the male-female relationship in contrast to male friendship, which is described in glowing colors. Such an extreme attitude would be rather unusual in rabbinical writings, which usually emphasizes marriage as the highest human state. Is it possible that this

mishnaic reference is the closest the rabbis could get to a condemnation of the use of women as sex objects?

The story of violence among David's children does not end here.
Although Amnon may have tried to negate any familial bonds, his
half-brother Absalom cannot. Upon seeing Tamar in deep humiliation, with ashes on her head, her clothing torn, crying, holding her
head, Absalom knows immediately that it was Amnon, their brother,
who raped Tamar, their sister.

> Absalom spoke to his brother Amnon neither good nor bad because
> Absalom hated Amnon because he had violated his sister.
>
> It came to pass after two full years that Absalom had sheepshearers in
> Baal-hazor, which is near Ephraim. Absalom invited all the king's sons.
> Absalom came to the king and said, "Behold, now. Your servant has
> sheepshearers. Let the king, I beseech you, and his servants go with your
> servant." The king said to Absalom, "No, my son. Let us not all go now
> lest we be a burden to you." He pressed him, but he would not go and
> he blessed him. Then Absalom said, "If not, I pray you, let my brother
> Amnon go with us." The king said, "Why should he go with you?" But
> Absalom pressed him that he let Amnon and all the king's sons go with
> him. Absalom had commanded his young men, saying, "Mark, now,
> when Amnon's heart is merry with wine and I say to you, 'Smite
> Amnon.' Then kill him. Fear not. Have I not commanded you? Be
> courageous and be valiant." The servants of Absalom did to Amnon as
> Absalom had commanded. Then all the king's sons arose and every man
> rode on his mule and fled.
>
> It came to pass, while they were on the way, that the report came to
> David, saying, "Absalom has slain all the king's sons and there is not one
> of them left." The king arose and tore his garments, and lay on the earth,
> and all his servants stood by with their clothes rent. (2 Sam 13:22-31)

What began as an incestuous rape culminates in fratricide. Absalom's hatred of his brother festers for more than two years before he
avenges his sister's abuse. While Absalom no longer refers to Amnon as
"brother," perhaps a subconscious attempt to deny any familial tie, the
relationship of brother–sister–brother cannot be removed. Indeed,
Absalom's reason for hating Amnon is precisely *because* "he had violated his sister" and the pronoun "his" connects *both* men with Tamar,
and marks *both* men as Tamar's brothers. Just as Cain had lured Abel
into the open, uninhabited country to kill him (see pp. 149–55), so
too does Absalom manage to persuade David to send Amnon to a fatal
sheepshearing at Baal-hazor. But I see more to this story. Under the
surface of this tale of incestuous rape is a deeper Freudian theme of sib-

ling rivalry, an enmity that rests on the child's assumption that paternal love is scarce.

Amnon's initial love for Tamar turns quickly into rivalry with Absalom because Amnon realizes the futility of obtaining David's love. From Amnon's perception, the *real* object of Amnon's desire—*David's love*—is reserved solely for Absalom. As a result, the very sight of Tamar is a reminder of that failure, and Amnon now loathes his sister. "Amnon hated her exceedingly so that the hatred with which he hated her was greater than the love with which he had loved her" (2 Sam 13:15). Amnon's blending of hatred and love, so explicit in his emotional reversal, is typical of what psychoanalysts refer to as "displacement." Amnon's love for David becomes Amnon's hatred of Tamar; incest with Tamar becomes rivalry with Absalom. And the object of desire, paternal love, is denied.

Cain and Abel: The "Meat" of the Text

Why, you might ask, would I include Cain and Abel in this chapter rather than in chapter 6 in which I discuss the brother/brother construct and its attendant rivalries? After all, as I discuss below (see p. 154), there are many readings of this text that portray the conflict between Cain and Abel as centering on the brothers' love for their parents, especially their mother. Hence, chapter 6 would seem a more logical choice. However, several rabbinical writings center around *female siblings* of Cain and Abel, sisters whom the Genesis narrative does not mention. Thus, I have included the sad tale of the first offspring of humans in this chapter. As in the brother/brother relationships I discuss in chapter 6, love turns to hatred. I would like to begin this section with a general overview followed by two alternative readings. The first reading is based on Freud's brother/brother theories, which place Momma in the center of the conflict. The second reading examines the text in light of the rabbinical material that includes a third sibling—Sis.

Crime and Punishment

The story of the very first set of brothers in the Hebrew Bible is an extreme example of sibling rivalry.[7] The story is quite brief:

> The man knew Eve his wife, and she conceived and bore Cain, saying, "I have gotten a man from YHWH." And again, she bore his brother Abel. Abel was a keeper of sheep, and Cain a tiller of the ground. In the

course of time it came to pass that Cain brought of the fruit of the
ground an offering to YHWH. And Abel, he also brought of the choicest of the firstlings of his flock and of the fat parts thereof. YHWH had
respect for Abel and to his offering, but for Cain and his offering he had
no respect. Cain was very angry and his face fell. YHWH said to Cain,
"Why are you angry, and why has your face fallen? If you do well, will
you not be accepted? And if you do not do well, sin is couching at the
door; to you will be its desire. Yet you may rule over him." Cain talked
to Abel his brother . . . and when they were in the field, Cain rose up
against his brother Abel, and killed him. Then YHWH said to Cain,
"Where is Abel your brother?" He said, "I do not know; am I my
brother's keeper?" And he said, "What have you done? The voice of your
brother's blood is crying to me from the ground. And now you are
cursed from the ground, which has opened her mouth to receive your
brother's blood from your hand. When you till the ground, it shall no
longer yield to you its strength; you shall be a fugitive and a wanderer on
the earth." Cain said to YHWH, "My sin/punishment[8] is greater than I
can bear. Behold, you have driven me this day from the face of the earth,
and from your face I shall be hidden; and I shall be a fugitive and a wanderer on the earth, and it will come to pass that whoever finds me will
kill me." Then YHWH said to him, "Therefore, whoever kills Cain,
vengeance will be on him sevenfold." And YHWH put a mark on Cain,
lest any who came upon him should kill him. (Gen 4:1-16)

This sad tale begins innocently enough. The two sons, Cain and
Abel, subsisted through the toil of their hands (unlike their parents in
Eden). For some reason, Cain decides to bring an offering to God, and
Abel apparently follows his example (that is, baby brother imitates big
brother). Their offerings are based upon their respective occupations.
Not surprisingly, Cain becomes jealous of Abel because his younger
brother's offerings are pleasing to God (their father-figure) while *his*
offerings are rejected without comment. As a result, Cain commits
fratricide.

This text is fraught with unanswered questions, beginning with why
the Deity inexplicably rejects Cain's offerings. Traditional scholars say
that the reason for God's reaction can be inferred from the descriptions
of the offerings: Abel's is characterized as being "the *choicest* of the
firstlings of his flock" while Cain's are termed simply as coming "from
the fruit of the soil" without further detail. Sarna, for example, writes,
"Abel appears to have demonstrated a quality of heart and mind that
Cain did not possess. Cain's purpose was noble, but his act was not
ungrudging and openhearted" [?] (1989:32). This explanation is similar to that of the rabbis:

CAIN BROUGHT OF THE FRUIT OF THE GROUND: Of the inferior crops (this is deduced from the fact that it does not say, of the first of the fruit), he being like a bad tenant who eats the first ripe figs but honors the king with the late figs (the former were esteemed a special delicacy; v. Isa XXVIII, 4; Jer XXIV, 2). AND ABEL, HE ALSO BROUGHT OF THE FIRSTLINGS OF HIS FLOCK AND OF THE FAT THEREOF (IV, 4). (Midrash *Genesis Rabbah* 22:5)

Rather than praising Cain for his unsolicited offering, or even explaining his lack of enthusiasm for the sacrifice, the Deity rebukes Cain saying, "If you do well, will you not be accepted? And if you do not do well, sin is couching at the door; to you will be its desire. Yet you may rule over him." This part of the text bristles with difficulties. What must Cain *do* to "do right"? *Who* has done wrong? *Who* has rejected *whom?* What would have happened if God had accepted *both* Cain's and Abel's offerings rather than choosing just one? God's response to Cain's sense of devastation suggests either that Cain has *already* done something wrong (even before he has) or some unstated resentment of this firstborn son. All we know for sure from the narrative is that Cain is bringing his father-figure a gift and the gift is rejected—for no apparent reason.

After being rebuked by God, the narrative tells us that "when they were in the field, Cain rose up against his brother Abel, and killed him."[9] But once again, the conversation between the boys *prior* to Cain's act as reported in the narrative is troublesome. Verse 8 says, literally, "Cain said to his brother Abel . . ." with the three-dot ellipsis drawing attention to the lacuna. Because the text is indeterminate, the Aramaic Targums, like the Greek, Syriac, and Latin versions, add: "Come, let us go into the field." (This is also the reading of the Samaritan text, the Oxford Study Bible and the Ramban.) On the basis of the usage in Exod 19:25 and Esther 1:18, many Jewish commentators took the unexpressed object of the verb to be the foregoing words of God. Others took *wayyōmer* to mean, "He had words with him." Ibn Ezra, Bekhor Shor, Radak, Sforno refer to foregoing words. Saadiah and Rashi take the third view. But all we know from the biblical text itself is that Cain spoke with his brother. *What* the older boy said to the younger is pure conjecture.

Interestingly, some of the rabbis give reasons other than jealousy over God's preference for Abel's sacrifices as a motive for Cain's fratricide. To quote Midrash *Genesis Rabbah* 22:7, Rabbi Simon asks the question:

About what did they quarrel (the Midrash assumes that SPOKE means that they had a legal argument)? "Come," said they, "let us divide the world." One took the land and the other the movables. The former said, "The land you stand on is mine," while the latter retorted, "What you are wearing is mine." One said: "Strip"; the other retorted: "Fly [off the ground]." . . . R. Joshua of Siknin said in R. Levi's name: Both took land and both took movables, but about what did they quarrel? One said, "The Temple must be built in my area," while the other claimed, "It must be built in mine."

Another interesting reading is that of Midrash *Genesis Rabbah* 22:8:

CAIN ROSE UP AGAINST HIS BROTHER ABEL, etc. R. Johanan said: Abel was stronger than Cain, for the expression ROSE UP can only imply that he [Cain] lay beneath him (they had already quarreled and Abel had thrown Cain down). He [Cain] said to him, "We two only are in the world: what will you go and tell our father [if you kill me]?" At this he was filled with pity for him; straightway he rose against him and slew him.

Setting aside Cain's motives temporarily, after the murder, without a break in the narrative, the Deity confronts Cain with a question that is more of a cry of horror than a fact-finding mission: "What have you done?" In a dramatic exclamation the Deity continues: "The voice of your brother's blood is crying to me from the ground. And now you are cursed from the ground, which has opened its mouth to receive your brother's blood from your hand. When you till the ground, it shall no longer yield to you its strength; you shall be a fugitive and a wanderer on the earth" (Gen 4:10). The terminology is potent. Abel's blood is crying (*so'ăqîm*) to God, an expression that throughout the Hebrew Bible is suffused with poignancy and pathos, with moral outrage and soul-stirring passion. For example, the Deity heeds the outcry (*s'ăqah*)[10] of the Hebrews against the harsh slavery of Egypt in Exod 3:7; his "anger blazes forth" when he hears the "outcry" of the ill-treated widow and orphan in Deut 22:21-23; and to the prophet Isaiah an "outcry" is the absolute negation of justice and righteousness.[11] But against *whom* was Abel's blood an "outcry"? Was the Deity blaming Cain? On the other hand, is it possible that the Deity was blaming *himself* for having caused Abel's death because he rejected Cain, the less-favored child? In other words, does the Deity's favoritism of Abel in this narrative foreshadow Isaac's favoritism of Esau discussed in chapter 6?

Not surprisingly, Cain's reaction, like that of Esau, is emotion-laden: "My *'āwōn* is greater than I can bear. Since you have driven me this day away from the ground; and from your face I shall be hidden." Significantly, Cain's cry has two meanings since *'āwōn* means both sin—and its penalty! Which is the more difficult for Cain to bear? Perhaps they are equally onerous. In this narrative, like that of Isaac and his two sons, sibling rivalry results because of a father's favoritism.

Remarkably, some (of the more generous) aggadists describe Cain as one who *repented* of his crime and was forgiven by God. For example, according to *Genesis Rabbah* 22:13, when Adam asked Cain what doom had been decreed against him, his son answered that his repentance had propitiated God: "Adam met him and asked him, 'How did your case go?' 'I repented and am reconciled,' replied he. Thereupon Adam began beating his face, crying, 'So great is the power of repentance, and I did not know!'"

Most other aggadists, however, see an unrepentant Cain and say that wherever Cain went as a fugitive, the earth quaked under him and that animals tried to attack him to avenge the innocent blood of Abel. Rather than seeing the sign of Cain as a protective device, they write that it is a sign of shame and an example for murderers. As a result, Cain's punishment is more severe than death, even worse than the death of Abel who died instantly (*Exodus Rabbah* 31:17). A similar explanation is given by Philo (*De virtutibus* 200) and is reflected in the Septuagint rendering of the words "a fugitive and wanderer" as "groaning and trembling." According to other rabbinic writings, when Cain could bear it no longer, God gave him a dog for protection, or, according to another opinion, made him horns that caused the animals to fear him:

> Rab said: He gave him a dog. Abba Jose said: He made a horn grow out of him. Rab said: He made him an example to murderers. R. Hanin said: He made him an example to penitents. R. Levi said in the name of R. Simeon b. Lakish: He suspended his judgment until the Flood came and swept him away, as it is written, And He blotted out every living substance, etc. (*Genesis Rabbah* 22:12)

Of course, the story of Cain and Abel has inspired many extra-biblical/extra-rabbinical literary works, possibly because of the complex character of Cain. Surprisingly, however, in medieval mystery plays, where characters are usually portrayed as positive and negative stereotypes, Cain is never wholly evil (see, for example, *Mactatio Abel* [Gassner 1963:57–71]).

Reading One: Cain, Abel, and Eve—Momma Again!

The extra-biblical literary depictions that I find most interesting for purposes of this book are those that portray the conflict between the brothers as centering on the brothers' love for their parents, especially their mother, and those that say that the conflict was over an unnamed sister. For example, according to Judah b. Rabbi: "Their quarrel was about . . . Eve" (Midrash *Genesis Rabbah* 22:7), thus a very early example of the Oedipal conflict! More recently, in Gabriel Legouvé's version, *La mort d'Abel* (*The Death of Abel,* 1792), Cain hates his brother, again because Abel is preferred by Eve. Similarly, in Wilhelm Hegeler's novel *Pastor Klinghammer* (based on Cain and Abel), rivalry—over Momma—culminates in the murder of one of the brothers. This same theme forms the central core of the plot in a section of *A Sleep of Prisoners* (1951) by the English playwright Christopher Fry.

Certainly, William Blake's *Adam and Eve Discovering Abel* shows an inconsolable Eve weeping over the body of her son, Abel, and Cain's facial expression suggests to me that the son is more concerned with his mother's reaction than with his murderous deed.

Reading Two: Cain, Abel, and Their Sisters

As mentioned on p. 149, several rabbinical writings center around *female siblings* of Cain and Abel, sisters whom the Genesis narrative does not mention. For example, Rabbi Joshua b. Karhah says: "Only two entered the bed [Adam and Eve], and seven left it: Cain and his twin sister, Abel and his two twin sisters": "An additional twin was born with Abel, and each claimed her. The one claimed: 'I will have her, because I am the firstborn'; while the other maintained: 'I must have her, because she was born with me'" (Midrash *Genesis Rabbah* 22:7). And Adam (according to the Talmud) sided with Cain:

> R. Akiba said: Come and hear! Why did not Adam marry his daughter? [Or why could not Adam have married his daughter? Eve's offense should have been followed by her death, and as to Adam, he could have found a help-meet in his daughter (Tosaf.)] So that Cain should marry his sister. . . . Therefore, it was an act of grace on Adam's part to deny himself his sister; or, as Rashi states, God commanded Adam to deal graciously with Cain, so that Cain, by marrying her, should build up the world. But otherwise, she would have been forbidden (to Cain)? — Once however that it was permitted, it remained so. R. Huna said: A heathen may marry his daughter. But should you ask, If so, why did not Adam marry his daughter? — In order that Cain might marry his

> sister, that the world might be built up by grace. Others give this version: R. Huna said: A heathen may not marry his daughter; the proof being that Adam did not marry his daughter. But that proof is fallacious: The reason was that Cain should marry his sister, so that the world should be built up by [Adam's] grace. (*b. Sanhedrin* 58b)

Thus, at least for some of the rabbis, incestuous jealousy appears as the driving motive for the fratricide in the story of Cain, whether the object of desire was the mother or displaced onto her daughter, Cain's and Abel's (unnamed) sister.

Rivalry and Gender Identification

It is not surprising that there are few tales of sisters in the Hebrew Bible, a text that chronicles genealogies and relationships between men. Women are absent from the lists of begetters and begotten with only one exception: in Gen 4:19 a descendant of Cain named Lamech takes two wives, Adah and Zillah. The women are each given credit for having sons who founded dynasties responsible for various aspects of human civilization (dwelling in tents, raising cattle, playing music, forging instruments of bronze and iron, etc.). One daughter is also mentioned by name, Naamah (4:22).

The rest of the Hebrew Bible, however, defines women and *their* relationships from a male perspective. As a result, we see only two outstanding cases of sisters: Leah and her sister Rachel in Genesis and the daughters of Zelophehad in Numbers. What is interesting to me about these sister relationships is that, while virtually all of the narratives of brothers involve sibling rivalry, these tales of sisters do not.

In the case of Rachel and Leah there is strife, to be sure. Certainly Rachel and Leah compete. But unlike traditional sibling rivalry that involves envy, jealousy, and competition for *parental love* (in this case, the love of Laban), the contention between Leah and Rachel is over Jacob's seed. Indeed, in the scene leading up to the departure of Jacob and his household from Laban's land (Gen 31:4-16), Jacob reviews with his wives all that has happened to them, tells them of a vision he had that promised him much of Laban's flocks, and of God's message that the time had come to return home. The sisters make clear that their allegiance is to Jacob, their husband, and not Laban, their father. Bitterly and poignantly, the daughters *together* describe themselves in the relationship to their father as exploited and dispossessed slaves, treated as foreign women unrelated to him:

Then Rachel and Leah answered him, "Is there any portion or inheritance left to us in our father's house? Are we not regarded by him as foreigners? For he has sold us, and he has been using up the money given for us. All the property which God has taken away from our father belongs to us and to our children; now then, whatever God has said to you, do." (Gen 31:14-16)

In the second case, that of Zelophehad's daughters, *together* the sisters present to Moses their special situation: according to the rules (Num 26:52-56), no one from their deceased father's family will receive an inheritance in the new land and they will be destitute. Rather than competing with each other to succeed *within* the existing set of laws or striving against each other for a blessing and boon from two father-figures (Moses and the Deity), the girls work together to change the system, and their initiative constitutes a unique success story for women, perhaps the first feminist revolution in recorded history. Mahlah, Noah, Milcah, Hoglah, and Tirzah come forward to speak publicly to Moses, and they challenge both Moses and the direct decree of the Deity: "Why should the name of our father be taken away from his family, because he had no son? Give to us a possession among our father's brethren" (Num 27:4). The narrative is dramatic and suspenseful. What will Moses' response be? Furthermore, how will the challenged Deity react? Strikingly, the ruling is generalized to show that henceforth, in cases where there is no son, daughters will inherit: "The daughters of Zelophehad are right; you shall give them possession of an inheritance among their father's brethren and cause the inheritance of their father to pass to them. And you shall say to the people of Israel,—If a man dies, and has no son, then you shall cause his inheritance to pass to his daughter." The second part of this narrative appears in Numbers 36, which addresses the male relatives' concern that the land should not leave their tribe. Moses then promulgates an additional law to protect the integrity of the tribal land holdings: female inheritors were not to be allowed to marry out of their tribe. The book of Joshua records the allotment of territory to the daughters of Zelophehad as part of the general description of land distribution to the tribes (Josh 17:3).

The sages of the Talmud, following their scriptural exemplar, praise rather than criticize Zelophehad's daughters for their bold behavior. Indeed, the rabbis vie with each other in the effort to praise them. Bronner examines some of these rabbinic texts and pays particular attention to the varied social attitudes displayed in them (1994:126–29). The midrashic sources are particularly fascinating because in them men, through words that they place in the mouths of women, strongly criticize the mores of the society that they themselves dominate.

Conclusion

In sum, contrary to the narratives of sisters, the relationships of Cain and Abel, Esau and Jacob, Absalom and Amnon, Joseph and his brothers, as well as of Jehoram and his brothers are far from harmonious. Sadly, these brother fall within Freud's construct of the powerful elemental effect of the sibling conflicts. Indeed, throughout the Hebrew Bible, brothers *do* seem to be the first potential rivals. And brother–sister relations? Hmm. . . .

Afterwards: After Words

All of this having been written, so what? Since there can be no doubt that my readings of these biblical narratives are somewhat idiosyncratic, why read my readings?

First, I hope that I have conveyed the idea that biblical narratives cannot be discussed in any absolute sense. Certainly, my reading is no closer to the true meaning than any other interpretation. As I discuss in chapter 1, I view interpretation to be a *reader's* response, necessarily based on a *reader's* personal input, assumptions, and biases. For example, I take my own feminist stance as an explicit starting point. As such, I attend to the issue of gender and accord a privileged status to the experience and interests of the female biblical characters. I am aware, however, that this particular bias has implications with which biblical scholars who follow a different approach might disagree. But if I have been successful, then all of our readings can coexist.

Second, I approach the Hebrew Bible as a literary work rather than a holy text. As such, I treat the biblical characters in the same way I would discuss Shakespeare's *Hamlet,* Sophocles's *Oedipus,* or Ford's *Giovanni,* again unlike many theologians who treat the text and all the characters therein as sacred. What I have tried to show throughout this book is that the traditional approach to biblical criticism is not the only way of reading the Hebrew Bible. For this reading, traditional questions do not apply.

Third, my literary approach is clearly informed by psychoanalytic theory. What I have tried to do throughout this book is to read psychoanalytic theory and the Bible concurrently; rather than reading the Bible *in light* of Freud and Lacan, I have been examining biblical narratives *while reading* the works of psychoanalysts. Therefore, I hope that I have shown that it is possible to juxtapose psychoanalytic literary theory and the biblical text without agreeing with all of Freud's or Lacan's views, particularly their views of women.

Finally, as many others have stated, it is not easy to read the Bible without the burden of other interpretations and commentaries obscuring our vision. What I have tried to do throughout this book, however, is to show that we *also* invest Scriptures with our own characteristic clusters of wishes—our fantasies—and transform these fantasies into the kind of significance we find meaningful: intellectual, social, moral, and/or aesthetic. In other words, my relation to Noah and Ham, Lot and his daughters, Adam and Eve, Moses, Cain and Abel, Absalom and Amnon and Tamar, and the entire litany of biblical characters (including, in particular, the Deity) has something to do with the murky complexities of my everyday relations with the people around me. As a reader, I do not simply identify with a character and then live through the plot with him or her; my *form* of identification and, consequently, my view of the characters changes as the plot develops. All Hebrew Bible characters exhibit human frailties and make mistakes—perhaps that is enough for *me* to have learned.

Notes

1. Psychoanalytic Theory and the Hebrew Bible: What Hath Freud Wrought?

1. See Rashkow 1993:15–25.

2. See Rollins 1999 for a complete discussion of psychological biblical criticism in the twentieth century, particularly chapter 3.

3. For a number of different perspectives on the current state of the debate between feminists and various kinds of psychoanalysis, see Wright 1984.

4. See Carmichael (1997:1–3).

5. See, e.g., Graves and Patai (1983:240); Fox (1974:557–96); Sarna (1966:131–33); de Vaux (1961:46–48).

2. Sin and Sex, Sex and Sin: The Hebrew Bible and Human Sexuality

1. Freud's principal work on the sexual life of human beings are his *Three Essays on the Theory of Sexuality* (1905d:135–243) and *Some Psychical Consequences of the Anatomical Distinction between the Sexes* (1925j). For recent representative neo-Freudian reviews and critiques of Freud's ideas, see Mitchell (1975:1–131) and Irigaray (1977:34–67).

2. See Carmichael (1997:1–3).

3. In this book the word *rabbis* refers to the particular group of Jewish religious leaders known technically as "the rabbis." The rabbis flourished from the second until approximately the end of the sixth centuries in Palestine and Babylonia. Growing out of a particular sect of first-century Judaism, their cultural hegemony over the masses of Jews grew during this period, in which the major literary productions of rabbinic Judaism—the midrashim and Talmuds—were produced. Their closest historical cognates are, therefore, the church fathers.

4. Incest within this context consists of acts of sexual intercourse performed either by consent, rape, or trickery between persons related either as blood kin or as marriage kin.

5. This contradiction played an interesting role in the history of England, a country whose incest laws were based on the biblical proscriptions. Tyndale attempted (unsuccessfully) to dissuade Henry from divorcing Catherine of Aragon, and his contention was that marriage with a deceased brother's wife is not unlawful. He condemned the divorce on two grounds, theological and political, although the distinctions blur. The theological involved a discussion on the reconciling of these two biblical texts: Lev 18:16, which forbids a marriage with a brother's wife, and that which mandates the levirate marriage, Deut 25:5. Coverdale, however, used his knowledge of Hebrew to address the issue of Henry's divorce, and his solution put him in the monarch's favor. Rather than translate *yᵉbāmāh* in Deut 25:5 as "her husband's brother," the literal translation used by Tyndale, Coverdale used, with great political acuity, "kinsman," changing the nature of the precept. It was no longer

Henry, Arthur's brother, who had the duty to "raise up seed," but some more remote "kinsman." For a further discussion of this issue, see Rashkow (1990:43–65).

6. The Hittite Code represents legal thinking in Hatti between 1450–1200 BCE. Parallels to the Hittite Code in ancient Israel appear mainly in Leviticus 17–26 and Deuteronomy 12–26. These parallels are especially clear in the code's use of similar technical terms. For example, the terms *brother* and *brother-in-law* identify citizens who are covenant partners, rather than simply individuals who are kin to one another by birth. So too in Deut 25:5-10 where the term *brother-in-law* means a legal guardian.

7. The Code of Hammurabi is a treatise on legal theory, political science, and social organization. Hammurabi, king of Babylon from 1792–1750 BCE, published this document to endorse legal thinking and moral values of his government. In the Hebrew Bible, the Covenant Code (Exod 21–23), the Holiness Code (Lev 17–26), and the Deuteronomic Code (Deut 12–26) are parallel to the Code of Hammurabi.

8. A modern Arab village near Hebron might shed some light on the story of David and Bath-Sheba. In the mountain villages, it is customary even today to spend the hot summer nights in a round, open verandah that is built on a roof. The king's palace was probably located in the highest place in the city, allowing him to see what was happening on the rooftops below.

9. For portrayals of cultic functions carried out by naked priests, see *Ancient Near Eastern Texts* (1958), plates 597, 600, 603, 605. Cf. Leick (1994:30–41, 48–54). Among the representations of male Canaanite gods catalogued by Negbi, however, very few have visible genitalia (1976).

10. The Middle Assyrian Code was published by Tiglath-Pileser I, king of Assyria from 1115–1077 BCE. A major section of the code is devoted to case laws that clarify guilt and responsibility.

11. Compare the Genesis 38 story of Judah ordering his daughter-in-law to be burned (*hôśî 'ûhā wᵉtiśśarēp*) when told that "Tamar played the harlot" (*zēnᵉtāh tāmār*).

12. See, also Deut 5:9; cf. Num 5:14.

13. For views on homosexuality in ancient Greece, see Kenneth Dover (1989:60–68, 81–109); and David Cohen (1987:6–21).

14. See also D. S. Bailey (1975).

15. In some instances in the Masoretic text, the object of *shakab* has been vocalized to suggest a direct object of a transitive verb, as in the English slang "to lay her" (see, e.g., Lev 15:24; 2 Sam 13:14). See p. 144 and Rashkow (1990:100–102) for a discussion of this verb form.

16. See Rashkow 1993, particularly chaps. 4 and 5.

17. The Story of Lillith from the Alphabet of Ben Sira 23 A-B. This is a narrative, satirical work, written probably in the geonic period (approximately 600–1040 CE) in the East and is one of the earliest, most complicated, and most sophisticated Hebrew stories written in the Middle Ages. Maimonides and other authorities attacked the work vigorously, but it was accepted generally as part of the midrashic tradition, to the extent that a circle of Ashkenazi Hasidic mystics in the twelfth and thirteenth centuries attributed some of their mystical compilations to works and theories received from Joseph b. Uzziel, who inherited the wisdom of Ben Sira and Jere-

miah. The anarchistic and heretical elements in the work went unrecognized, probably because of the censorship exercised by copyists, who prevented the full version
from being known to readers.

18. Eunuch (*sᵉrîs*) need not necessarily be incapable of marital relations. Kugel
(among others) notes that the term *eunuch* has a much broader range of meanings in
Greek usage and can mean someone stricken with infertility (1990:75–76). No
understanding of the term is without problems, and it should be noted that while the
Septuagint translates it to mean eunuch, Targum Onkelos uses officer. Kugel sum-
marizes the issue succinctly: "Since Potiphar is generally identified by early exegetes
with 'Potiphera' in Genesis 41:45, the father of Aseneth, Joseph's future wife. . . .
How could a eunuch be the father of Aseneth? . . . Various ways around this apparent contradiction were found: Potiphar had become a eunuch only after Aseneth's
birth; Potiphar was called Potiphera because he had been punished with castration
(again, after Aseneth's birth); Aseneth was not Potiphar's real child; etc." (1990:75).

19. Lerner (1986) traces male control of female sexuality from its locus within the
patriarchal family to regulation by the state.

20. Some modern commentators (e.g., Bright 1980:31; Holladay 1986:144–45)
omit *šādûd* ("destroyed") for two reasons: first, it is not found in the Septuagint version where Jer 4:30 begins, "And you, what are you doing?" and second, it is a masculine predicate adjective, while the subject "you" is feminine. On the other hand,
Thompson accepts its presence, translating it as "despoiled" (1980:231) as do most
earlier commentators (see, e.g., Skinner 1930:37; Driver 1907:26; Streane 1805:43).
The lack of gender agreement may be explained by noting that certain "inconsistencies in gender and even number are not uncommon in biblical Hebrew" (Barré
1986:614, 616). The Masoretic version of Jer 4:30 certainly contributes to the
imagery of Israel as harlot.

21. See Fewell and Gunn (1991) and Niditch (1989a) for recent discussions of
the Jael-Sisera narrative.

22. Milgrom has rejected this interpretation because the Hebrew term for kid
(*gād*) is asexual, meaning it refers to both female and male kid [1985:51]. But Milgrom overlooks the fact that the word *gād* is a masculine noun.

23. Although *şōra'at* is often translated as "leprosy," it has none of the major
symptoms of that malady (Preuss 1978; Sawyer 1976; Hulse 1975).

24. Juliet Mitchell points out that psychoanalysis can hardly avoid being phallocentric in a society organized along patriarchal lines: "if psychoanalysis is phallocentric, it is because the human social order that it perceives refracted through the individual human subject is patrocentric" (1975:xv).

3. Throw Momma from the Garden a Kiss: Or Paradise Revisited

1. As Iser writes, "Whatever we have read sinks into our memory and is foreshortened. It may later be evoked again and set against a different background with
the result that the reader is enabled to develop hitherto unforeseeable connections"
(1978:125).

2. There is, of course, a variety of applications of the term *myth* in contemporary
usage, including any widely held fallacy. As used in this book, myths are defined as a

system of hereditary stories believed to be true by a particular cultural group, and
that serve to explain (in terms of the intentions and actions of deities and other
supernatural beings) why the world is as it is and things happen as they do. Myths
also provide a rationale for social customs and observances and establish the sanc-
tions for the rules by which people conduct their lives. It is useful here to consider
the definition of myth given by Barthes: "Myth does not deny things, on the contrary, its function is to talk about them; simply, it purifies them, it makes them innocent, it gives them natural and external justification, it gives them clarity . . . "
(1975:156).

3. See Norman O. Brown's translation of Hesiod's *Theogony* for a particularly
readable version and commentary.

4. The Hebrew expression *tōhû wābōhu* designates a totally chaotic state. The
term *tōhû* also appears in 1 Sam 12:21; Isa 49:9; Job 26:7; Ps 107:40; and in all of
these places expresses nonentity, vacuity, and confusion.

5. Cf. Cassuto (1975:71–102).

6. Anath, daughter of El and sister of Baal, is both a warrior and a fertility goddess whose cult spread from Canaan to Egypt in the eighteenth and nineteenth
dynasties. In a temple built in the time of Rameses II (thirteenth century BCE) a pillar is dedicated to Anath queen of heaven and mistress of all the gods (Cassuto
1971:18).

7. The *Epic of Gilgamesh* is an important literary work written in cuneiform on
twelve clay tablets about 2000 BCE. This poem is named for its hero, Gilgamesh, a
tyrannical Babylonian king who ruled the city of Uruk, known in the Hebrew Bible
as Erech (Gen 10:10; Ezra 4:9) and now as Al Warkâ', Iran. According to the myth,
the gods respond to the prayers of the oppressed citizenry of Uruk and send a wild,
brutish man, Enkidu, to challenge Gilgamesh to a wrestling match. When the con-
test ends with neither as a clear victor, Gilgamesh and Enkidu become close friends
(is it possible that biblical writers modeled their account of the friendship of David
and Jonathan on the relationship between Gilgamesh and Enkidu?). They journey
together share many adventures, and accounts of their heroism and bravery in slay-
ing dangerous beasts spreads to many lands. For a particularly readable translation,
see Sanders 1984.

8. Freud's position is that this statement is particularly significant in the development of female children. Chodorow (1978), however, claims mother-attachment is
equally significant for boys.

9. Other arguments were raised against the reading that God took counsel with
someone or something. Rhetorically, this reading conflicts with the central thought
of the section, that is, God *alone* created the entire world. Further, the expression
na'ăśeh is not one of consultation. In 2 Sam 24:14, for example, we find, "We shall
fall into the hand of the Lord . . . but unto the hand of man I shall not fall." Since a
negation is expressed at the end of the verse, the self-exhortation no longer applies,
and consequently the singular form appears. Rabbis also refute other interpretations,
for example, that there is a reference here to various elements within the godhead, or
that there is an echo in the Torah of related pagan myths.

10. The Oedipus myth, which Sophocles followed rather closely in his dramati-
zation, relates that Oedipus, the son of Laius, king of Thebes, and his wife, Jocasta,

was exposed immediately after birth because an oracle had revealed to the father, eager for offspring, that he was destined to be killed by his son. The infant, once exposed, is rescued by shepherds and grows up as a prince in another court until, unsure of his origin, he consults the oracle and is advised to avoid his homeland lest he become his father's murderer and his mother's husband. Upon leaving his new home, he encounters King Laius, his unrecognized father, and kills him. He arrives in Thebes, solves the riddle of the sphinx that is bringing doom to the city, and is rewarded by the Thebans with the remuneration reserved for the liberator of the city: he is made king and receives the hand of the queen, his mother, Jocasta, in marriage. For a long time, he reigns peacefully and with honor; he has two sons and two daughters by his mother. A plague breaks out in the city, and the Thebans, inquiring of the oracle how they can be freed from the plague, are informed by the messengers that the plague will cease as soon as Laius's murderer is banished from the land. Eventually, it is revealed that Oedipus himself is the murderer of Laius but is also his son and the son of Jocasta. Overwhelmed by the terrible act he has unwittingly committed, Oedipus blinds himself and leaves his homeland.

11. The Oedipal model doesn't end with expulsion of Adam and Eve from the garden. Indeed, narrative after narrative describes YHWH chastising Israel for backsliding to *earlier female deities*. As I discuss in chapter 4, elsewhere in the Hebrew Bible Israel eventually becomes a construct of the deity's (male) offspring. Hearing the father's voice, what Freud calls the "superego" and what Lacan (in a play on words) calls *le nom/non-du-père* ("the name/no-of-the-father"), the son, as an embodiment of all the males of the community, identifies with the father image, that of the male deity. By doing so, Israel becomes a "kingdom of priests."

12. For alternate Lacanian readings of this forbidden fruit as phallus, see Piskorowski (1992), Fodor (1954), and Parker (1999), as described on p. 8.

13. As Frye writes, "the chief point made about the creation of Eve is that henceforth man is to leave his parents and become united with his wife. That parent is the primary image . . . that . . . has to give way to the image of the sexual union of bridegroom and bride" (1982:107).

14. Some interpreters take this to mean that before eating the fruit Adam and Eve are not aware of their sexuality. But that negates the divine command to procreate. James Barr points out (1992) that there was no reason, given the acceptance of sexuality as normal in ancient Hebrew culture, for the couple to abstain. In the noncanonical book of Jubilees (3:6), Adam and Eve have sexual relations as soon as God introduces them, literally, "love at first sight." The first sex act described in the Bible comes after the departure from Eden: *wᵉhā'ādam yāda' 'et-hawwāh 'ištô*. And Adam knew Eve his wife (Gen 4:1) (*yāda'*—to know—being a euphemism for sexual intercourse), and she conceived and bore Cain (*wattahar wattēled 'et-qayin*). As Barr notes, intercourse is here described for the first time because it is the first time that a child is produced. Adam and Eve then have a second son, Abel, and when Adam is 130 years old he "knows" Eve again, fathering Seth. How many times Adam knows Eve after that, or how many more wives Adam knows is unstated, but he begets "sons and daughters" for eight hundred more years.

15. Although John Otwell argues (1977) that the verb in the final clause of Gen 3:16 (*māšāl*) can mean "to liken" as well as "to rule," and that the object of the verb

in this verse is governed by a preposition easier to relate to this meaning, this form of the verb is generally used in contexts that would not support Otwell's claim. Rather, a *nûn* would have to be added to the verb form *nim šal* for the meaning to become "to speak metaphorically" or to liken or compare."

16. See chap. 5 for a discussion of other father/child incest narratives. This section appears here rather than there because the narratives discussed in that chapter involve episodes of a father drinking wine to excess, having an *actual* sexual encounter with his offspring, and subsequently condemning not his offspring but his grandchildren.

17. According to Freud, the mother becomes the original seducer, the original erotic manipulator of the infant, both male and female. "The fact that the mother thus unavoidably initiates the child into the phallic phase is, I think, the reason why, in phantasies of later years, the father so regularly appears as the sexual seducer" (Freud 1931:238).

18. The person shamed often feels the need to take revenge for his or her humiliation, to "save face." By "shaming the shamer," the situation is reversed, and the shamed person feels triumphant (Horney 1950:103).

19. Although the word *bat* ("daughter") appears with some frequency, all things are relative: as one might expect in a patriarchal society, the word *ben* ("son") appears ten times more often. This explains, perhaps, why little attention had been given to the daughter role. As Leah Bronner discusses, the meaning of the word *bat* and the contexts in which it appears vary greatly. The word is used to refer alternatively to actual persons, to poetic personas or characterizations adopted by speakers in poetic texts, and to collectives or to abstract qualities. As a metaphor, *bat* is often used in the Hebrew poetry of scriptures as a figure of purity and moral value to personify nations and peoples (Bronner 1994:111).

4. Oedipus Wrecks: The Covenant of Circumcision

1. Cf. Gen 46:8-27, which lists all the male descendants of Jacob through his wives and handmaids (Leah 33; Zilpah 16; Rachel 14; Bilhah 7). See also Exod 1:5, which states that "the total number of persons that were of Jacob's issue came to seventy, Joseph being already in Egypt." The discrepancy in the Genesis 46 account is a result of the inclusion of Judah's sons Er and Onan, who died in Canaan, as well as Joseph and his two sons, Manasseh and Ephraim, who were already in Egypt. It appears that in Exod 1:5 (and in Deut 10:22, which repeats the same figure) "seventy" is a round number, used to evoke the idea of totality, comprehensiveness on a large scale, rather than literality. Another example of the rhetorical use of seventy is Genesis 10, where precisely seventy nations issue from the three sons of Noah, and these constitute the entire human family.

2. In linguistic terms, however, this may not be correct; rather, some scholars view this usage as an expression of a semantic universal that taboo body parts are subject to a spatial displacement by a more or less contiguous organ. As Vasvari (1990) discusses, the two legs above the knee, forming an angle that is the "lap," have been charged with genital meaning, the thighs connoted the sex organ.

3. Friedrich Gesenius calls this form the plural of "local extension," that is, an indication of a place or an area (1910:407). Genesis 28:11, for example, (. . . and placed

them "under" his head) uses this construction to describe the "place" of Jacob's head. Trible concludes that *marg⁽e⁾lōtāyw* in Ruth 3:4, 7, 8, 14 functions as a euphemism for the genitals (1978:199). Campbell views this usage as a rhetorical device, an intentional ambiguity about just how much of Boaz was to be uncovered (1975:121). See also Rashkow 1990:119–52 for a further discussion of the use of *marg⁽e⁾lōtāyw* as a euphemism for male genitalia in the book of Ruth.

4. See also Steinmetz (1991) and Williams (1991).

5. See, for example, Sarna (1989:396–97); Cross (1983:4–43); Alt (1967); Haran (1965:51–52); Hyatt (1955).

6. As Freud wrote (1926:211), "mythology may give you the courage to believe in psychoanalysis."

7. Of course, I am not the first to return Moses to Egypt. See, for example, Freud's *Moses and Monotheism* for a different reading of the Moses/Egyptian connection (1939).

8. See Lichtheim (1976) for a compilation of hymns dedicated to the cults of Isis and Osiris, and Downing (1981) for examples of Egyptian art devoted to the enormous dimensions of the wooden Phallus.

9. Danna Nolan Fewell has reminded me that *maṭṭeh* also includes the meaning "tribe," lending further weight to its procreative connotation. That is to say, God's "rod" produces the "tribes" of Israel.

10. The Hebrew *ḥarṭummim* (magicians) derives from an Egyptian title meaning chief priest (Sarna 1991:37); since the cults of Osiris and Isis were the most popular, it is likely that these so-called magicians were part of the cult of Isis and Osiris.

11. Both Freud and his follower Ernest Jones insisted that although there are vast numbers of symbols, the objects or ideas symbolized are limited in number. Psychoanalytic symbols are restricted to the body and its functions (particularly the sexual ones), family members, birth, and death.

12. Pardes also sees interesting (but different) echoes of the Isis and Osiris myth in this incident with Zipporah, viewing the brief passage as an example of monotheistic censorship and a "repressed cultural past." According to Pardes, the well-known story of Osiris and Isis is retold in the circumcision scene, and Isis (as a character) is "wrenched apart as her role of midwife-mother-sister-wife is divided among Shiprah, Puah, Yocheved, Miriam, Pharaoh's daughter, and Zipporah" (1992:93).

13. See, for example, Graves and Patai (1983:240); Fox (1967:557–96); Sarna (1970:131–33); de Vaux (1961:46–48).

14. There are thirty-six instances of this formula in the Torah, all listed in *Mishnah Keritot* 1:1. This punishment is peculiar to ritual texts and is largely confined to offenses of a cultic and sexual nature. Since there is no biblical definition of *karat* ("cut off"), and in most texts, the impersonal, passive form of the verb is used *nikr⁽e⁾tāh* (as here), not only the type of punishment but also the executive authority is uncertain.

15. See Rashkow (1993) for an elaboration, particularly with reference to Genesis narratives.

16. Contra Boyarin, who posits that "circumcision is a male erasure of the female role in procreation" (1992:476).

5. Daddy-Dearest and the "Invisible Spirit of Wine": Theme and Variations

1. William Shakespeare's full quote reads: "O thou invisible spirit of wine, if thou hast no name to be known by, let us call thee devil" (Cassio, in *Othello*, 2.3). Perhaps this is one meaning of the French saying, "Nothing equals the joy of the drinker, except the joy of the wine in being drunk."

2. See chap. 4 for a brief synopsis of Sophocles's work as well as a more detailed explanation of Freud's theory.

3. It should be noted that the Levitical prohibitions are against "uncovering" one's father's nakedness, not merely "seeing" his genitalia. See chap. 2 for a further discussion of the Levitical and Deuteronomical prohibitions.

4. See also, Anthony Phillips (1980:39–40) and the comments of S. D. Kunin (1995:173–75). Stanley Brandes's position is that anthropological evidence suggests that in many cultures fathers make every effort to ensure that they do not reveal their genitals to their sons (1980:99).

5. This is the first example of the genre of parental blessing and cursing. See all of Genesis 49 and Gen 27:4, 29 as examples.

6. See, for example, the Wakefield Pageant "The Deluge" in J. Gassner 1972:72–87.

7. This play was adapted by Richard Rogers and Peter Stone and renamed "Two by Two"; it appeared on Broadway in 1970.

8. A *mishteh* ("feast," "banquet") is usually an occasion for drinking. See, e.g., 1 Sam 25:36; Isa 5:12; Esther 2:18; 5:14; 8:17; 9:19.

9. Bronner does offer three possible explanations: (1) the rabbis' silence may reflect deep revulsion on their part, a sentiment that comes to full expression only centuries later in the writings of the medieval commentators; (2) the rabbis, like modern commentators, saw homosexuality as the greater evil and therefore saw no point in castigating Lot in his no-win choice; (3) the Talmud does describe in great detail the depraved social, religious, and moral practices that prevailed in Sodom, and it is in the context of these descriptions that the rabbis hint at Lot's degeneracy (Bronner 1994:115).

10. See also Mieke Bal's analysis of Freud's essay in connection with the story of the sacrifice of Jephthah's daughter in Judges 11 (Bal 1988:72–73).

11. Vawter argues that "this story, tenuously connected with the preceding narrative, obviously had little to do with the Sodom and Gomorrah saga and owes its preservation to other concerns" (1977:242).

12. See, for example, R. W. Medlicott (1967) and Ernest Jones (1938).

13. The Italian word for the children who appear in paintings as allegorical creatures or little wingless angels.

14. Although no interpretation of the names of Judah's son is given in the text, a midrash and Targum Jonathan connect it with the Hebrew (*'ariri*—"childless"). Given that Er is "displeasing to YHWH" (Gen 38:7), his name may be a wordplay on the Hebrew *ra,* "evil."

15. The basic root meaning of the Hebrew is uncertain, but it may be "to procreate" (Sarna 1989:266). In Deut 25:7, the brother of the deceased husband is called the *yavam*—"progenitor."

16. *Genesis Rabbah* 55:5-6 understands this verse as Onan practiced a primitive form of birth control through coitus interruptus. Another tradition (*b. Yeb. Yevamoth* 34b) interprets the act as "unnatural intercourse."

17. See Rashkow 1993 for an elaboration.

6. Boys Will Be Boys: Sibling Rivalry and the Fear of Castration

1. In chaps. 2 and 3 of *Beyond the Pleasure Principle* (1920), Freud raises two serious difficulties with the wish-fulfillment theory of dreams. First, people who have experienced a shock regularly dream about the trauma, and second, there are dreams that bring to conscious memory the earliest years of childhood, which are linked to painful impressions of anxiety, prohibition, disappointment, and punishment. In both of these cases, Freud questions the wishful impulse that could be satisfied by going back to distressing experiences. He attempts to resolve the issue by claiming that there must be *some* wish-fulfillment of which neither the analyst nor the patient is aware, but which can be discovered over time.

2. Psychoanalysts treat "daydreams" and "night dreams" quite differently, asking different questions about them and using different language to describe them. Generally speaking, in discussing daydreams, analysts look for conflicts among the dreamer's id, ego, and superego. In night dreams (like the ones in Genesis 28 and 32), however, analysts look for conflicts between conscious and unconscious ideas. Freud discusses this model of dream theory principally in chapter 7 of *The Interpretation of Dreams* (1900), and in the chapters on dreams in the *Introductory Lectures on Psychoanalysis* (1916–17). Because Jacob's dreams in Genesis are night dreams, this is the model I explore in this chapter. See Arlow and Brenner (1964) for a general description of, and distinction between, these two theories of dream analysis.

3. See, e.g., Oppenheim (1956) and Niditch (1989b).

4. This has been described as the acetabulum, the cup-shaped socket in the hipbone that receives the head of the thighbone.

5. The first explanation is that of Rashi, the second is by Ramban.

6. Cf. 1 Sam 9:9; 1 Kgs 14:1-5; 2 Kgs 8:8; 22:18. In 2 Kgs 1:2-5 the same technical expression is used in connection with a pagan god.

7. *Mimmē'ayik* —literally, "from your innards"—denotes emotions that are very deeply felt by men *and* women, such as passion, deep distress, or pity, and is generally not used to refer to reproductive organs (see, for example, Songs 5:4; Isa 16:11; Jer 31:19).

8. The reference is to the offspring of Lamech and Adah: "Adah bore Jabal; he was the father of those who dwell in tents and have cattle" (Gen 4:20).

9. Interestingly, the author of *Jubilees* was apparently distressed by Rebecca's close relationship with her younger son (perhaps an early Freudian?). (*Jubilees*—called variously the *Book of Jubilees,* the *Lesser Genesis,* the *Apocalypse of Moses,* and the *Testament of Moses*—is a book of the Pseudepigrapha, a midrashic-type commentary on the book of Genesis.) *Jubilees* 19:16 reads, "And *Abraham* loved Jacob, but Isaac loved Esau" (emphasis added). Not only is the order of the clauses changed, but by substituting *Abraham* for *Rebecca*, Abraham, the consummate patriarch, becomes Jacob's patron, with Isaac's love for Esau as somewhat of a "consolation prize."

10. The stories of Anat, part of the literary lineage of Ugarit have many parallels to motifs in the Hebrew Bible. A particularly significant one for purposes of this chapter is the story in which Anat's mother tries to take away his inheritance.

11. The hegemony of the older brother in the ancient world is widely attested (see, in particular, Mendelsohn 1959). It is taken for granted, for example, in a

Sumerian hymn to Enlil extolling the fact that in the city of Nippur "the older brother honors the younger, acts humanely toward him" (*ANET* (1958:574). The right of the firstborn to a double share of the inheritance is documented at Mari (*ANET* 1958:545) and Nuzi (*ANET* 1958:220), in the Middle Assyrian laws (*ANET* 1958:185), and in biblical law (Exod 13:2, 12-15; 22:28; 34:19f.; Lev 27:26f.; Num 3:5-13; 8:5-19; 18:15-17; Deut 15:19; 21:17).

12. Despite the tone of his words, Isaac lives on for many years. The relevant texts about Isaac's age are Gen 25:20, 26; 26:34; 31:38.

13. For this usage of the Hebrew *šōma'at* ("to be listening"), cf. Gen 18:10.

14. Cf. 1 Sam 23:18 and the reverse in Josh 6:26.

15. When Rebecca asks, "Why should I be bereaved of you both in one day?" "both" may refer to the two sons since Esau would either be judicially condemned to death for murder or struck down in an act of private revenge. Cf. 2 Sam 14:7.

16. In connection with the transference of the birthright from one son to another, this practice was proscribed only by later Pentateuchal legislation.

> If a man has two wives, the one loved and the other disliked, and they have borne him children, both the loved and the disliked, and if the first-born son is hers that is disliked, then on the day when he assigns his possessions as an inheritance to his sons, he may not treat the son of the loved as the first-born in preference to the son of the disliked, who is the first-born, but he shall acknowledge the first-born, the son of the disliked, by giving him a double portion of all that he has, for he is the first issue of his strength; the right of the first-born is his. (Deut 21:15–17)

We know, however, that it was part of the social custom and legal practice in the Near East in the second millennium BCE. One document from the city of Nuzi reads: "Concerning my son Zirteshup, I at first annulled his relationship, but now I have restored him to sonship. He is the elder son and shall receive a double portion" (Speiser 1930:39). Another document records the purchase of the birthright by a younger brother for the price of three sheep, while a tablet from Alalakh actually deals with the prenatal conferral of the birthright (Mendelsohn 1959:38–40).

17. The sole instance of a biblical condemnation of Jacob's usurpation of Esau's inheritance comes from Hosea, who deprecates Jacob's attempt to supplant Esau even as early as in the womb. However, Hosea amends the Genesis version by placing the struggle with the angel at Beth El (discussed on p. 119ff.) before his servitude to Laban instead of at Penuel on the way home, and has the angel weep and implore Jacob (Gen 12:4-5). As in the case with later polemic treatises, it is likely that Hosea is reinterpreting the Genesis traditions for his own didactic purposes.

18. The aggadah (or haggadah) is often defined in a negative manner, as that portion of rabbinic teaching that is not halakhah, i.e., that is not concerned with religious laws and regulations. The aggadah is for the most part an amplification of those portions of the Bible that include narrative, history, ethical maxims, and the reproofs and consolations of the prophets.

19. Although this is reported or hinted at only in late midrashim, it may be an allusion to the notorious case of matricide committed by Nero, who contrived the murder of his mother Agrippina (Suetonius, "Nero" 34:5; Tacitus, *Annals* 14:1–13; Jos. *Ant.*, 20:153; War, 2:250).

20. Jacob's meeting with Esau after his return from Aram is embellished similarly with numerous rabbinic comments whose gist is that Esau retained his undying hatred, so that Jacob had good reason to be afraid of him. The messengers sent by Jacob to Esau (Gen 32:3) were in reality angels, and then Esau's reconciliation with Jacob (Gen 33:4) was unreal. In fact, Esau had tried to bite his brother's neck(!), but was thwarted because it had become like marble (*Genesis Rabbah* 78:9; Esau's poor teeth!).

21. The noun that is used here (*sullām*) is unique to this narrative. Etymologically, the root, "to heap up, raise," suggests a ramp or a solid stairway. Archaeologically, the Mesopotamian ziggurats were equipped with flights of stairs leading up to the summit. Yet the traditional "ladder" is such a frequent translation that it seems pointless to replace it.

22. Linguistically, the term "climb" or "mount" is used in a sexual sense par excellence: the German expression "*den Frauen nachsteigen*" ("to run [lit. "climb"] after women") and "*ein alter Steiger*" ("an old rake" [lit. "climber"]) are prime examples.

23. As discussed in chap. 1, Jacob's marriage to two sisters is specifically prohibited by the Levitical laws against incest: "And you shall not take a woman as a rival wife to her sister, uncovering her nakedness while her sister is yet alive" (Lev 18:18). Although Carmichael argues that this rule is not about incest based on the issue of rivalry as the ground of the prohibition (1997:46), I agree with Kunin (1995) who states that the rule *is* about incest, because a man who marries one sister automatically creates a kin relationship with the other. It should be noted, however, at Qumran, Lev 18:18 was understood differently and read, "And you shall not take a woman as a rival wife to another" etc. Rachel and Leah, aside from being sisters, are also Jacob's first cousins, but that particular degree of consanguinity is not prohibited.

24. Freud relates an interesting case in which "a patient dreamed that '*his uncle gave him a kiss in an automobile.*' He went on at once to give me the interpretation, which I myself would never have guessed: namely that it meant 'auto-eroticism'" (1900:408–9).

25. In Gen 24:3, for example, Abraham wants his slave to fetch a wife for Isaac, and he commands the slave: "*sîm-nā' yād°kā yahat y°rēkî*"—"Put your hand under my thigh." This action has been viewed as euphemistic expressions of an earlier swearing-ceremony made while grasping the phallus. There is also etymological evidence for this in German (cf. *Zeu Genesis* ["beget"] and *Zeuge* ["witness"].

26. There is, however, a certain tension between the dreamer and a reader, between a hermeneutics of correspondence and a method of association or displacement (see Frieden 1990). A dreamer interpreting his or her own dream searches for similar dream thoughts that lie behind dream contents in a condensed yet corresponding form. Drawing from the associative approach, a reader, like a psychoanalyst, uses connections provided by the dreamer that relate to the dream contents by contiguity, not by resemblance. These two interpretive models stand opposed, yet they also tend to blur into each other. The opposition has heuristic value here, as does the related distinction between metaphor and metonymy (see, e.g., Jakobson and Halle 1975:72–76, 90–96; for a discussion of the unstable interactions between metaphor and metonymy, see de Man 1983:12-15).

According to Freud, one of the primary aspects of dream-work entails displacement, a relationship by *contiguity*. Freud writes that "the individual dream thoughts are represented in the dream by multiple elements" (1900:318). Moreover, "the elements in the dream content which stand out as the essential components by no means play the same role in the dream thoughts" (1900:340). Disparities are even more compelling when the dream contents have been displaced and have received a completely new center of interest.

27. This is Weber's descriptive term, which calls attention not only to the scenic, theatrical aspects of the dream, but to its narrative moment as well (1982:171 n.1).

7. My Sister, My—Hmmm . . . : Brother–Sister Incest and Sibling Rivalry

1. See Rashkow 1993, chap. 2.

2. A full literary analysis is presented in Bar-Efrat (1989); see also Fewell and Gunn (1993); and Rashkow (1990) for recent discussions of this story.

3. See Phyllis Trible for a chilling discussion of this relationship (1984:53–54).

4. As in Tamar's case, the sad case of Dinah's rape reflects little paternal involvement or reaction. Indeed, it certainly seems as though Simeon and Levi are referring unconsciously to their father when they ask, "Shall he treat our sister like a whore?" (Gen 34:31). And when Jacob angrily responds "You have troubled me . . . ," he provides a purely utilitarian argument in his words of reproof ("I being few in number, they will gather themselves together against me, and I shall be destroyed, I and my house"; Gen 34:30).

5. On the theme of sister marriage, see Skinner 1930:237; Rashkow 1993.

6. The first verb, *wattidbaq,* indicates a permanent bond, not a temporary infatuation. Genesis 2:24, for example, explains that "a man leaves his father and his mother, clings (*dabaq)* to his wife, and they become as one flesh." Similarly, the psalmist says "my soul clings (*dabaq)* to you" when referring to God. And Ruth's steadfastness to Naomi is emphasized by the repetition of the word *dabaq*—a leitmotif in that narrative. The narrator also reports that Shechem "spoke to the heart" of Dinah, an expression that appears in the Hebrew Bible only eight other times, each time in situations putting or showing the speaker in a positive or favorable light. To "speak to the heart" is to "comfort," "appease," or "soothe" (see, for example, Judg 19:3; Hos 2:16; 2 Sam 19:8; 2 Chron 30:22; 32:6; Isa 40:2; Gen 50:21; Ruth 2:13).

7. The stories of Anubis and Bata, nineteenth Egyptian dynasty (1307–1196 BCE), relate a tale that parallels that of Cain and Abel. These stories, however, focus the sibling rivalry on their mutual desire for children, which leaves them both infertile.

8. See p. 153.

9. The Hebrew *śadeh* is used throughout the biblical text to refer to the open, uninhabited country away from settled areas (although, of course, one of the many inconsistencies in this narrative is that there can be no "settled" areas, since at this point in Genesis there are only four humans!). Because it is considered "far from society," the *śadeh* often is the scene of a crime (as can be inferred in Deut 22:25 and 2 Sam 14:6).

10. The Hebrew stems are dialectical variants of each other.

11. Isaiah 5:7 reads: "He hoped for justice, but behold! Injustice! Righteousness, but behold! An outcry!"

Works Cited

Aeschylus. 1967. *The Eumenides*. Trans. Richmond Lattimore. Chicago: University of Chicago Press.

Alexander, Franz. 1948. *Fundamentals of Psychoanalysis*. New York: Norton.

Alt, A. 1967. *The God of the Fathers: Essays on Old Testament History and Religion*. Trans. R. A. Wilson. Garden City: Doubleday.

Ancient Near Eastern Texts. 1958. Ed. James B. Pritchard. Princeton: Princeton University Press.

Arlow, Jacob A., and Charles Brenner. 1964. "Psychoanalytic Concepts and the Structural Theory." *Journal of the American Psychoanalytic Association* 35:16–94.

Bach, Alice. 1990. "The Pleasure of Her Text." In *The Pleasure of Her Text: Feminist Readings of Biblical and Historical Texts,* ed. Alice Bach, 25–44. Philadelphia: Trinity Press International.

Bailey, Derrick Sherwin. 1955. *Homosexuality and the Western Christian Tradition*. Hamden: Archon.

Bal, Mieke. 1988. *Death and Dissymmetry: The Politics of Coherence in the Book of Judges*. Chicago: University of Chicago Press.

———. 1994. "Head Hunting: 'Judith' on the Cutting Edge of Knowledge." *Journal for the Study of the Old Testament* 63:3–34.

Bar-Efrat, Shimon. 1989. *Narrative Art in the Bible*. Sheffield: Sheffield Academic.

Barr, James. 1992. *The Garden of Eden and the Hope of Immortality*. Minneapolis: Fortress Press.

Barré, Michael. 1986. "The Meaning of *l' šybnw* in Amos 1:3—2:6." *Journal of Biblical Literature* 105:611–31.

Barthes, Roland. 1975. *The Pleasure of the Text*. Trans. Richard Miller. New York: Hill and Wang.

Bassett, F. W. 1971. "Noah's Nakedness and the Curse of Canaan. A Case of Incest?" *Vetus Testamentum* 21:236–74.

Berlin, Adele. 1985. *The Dynamics of Biblical Parallelism*. Bloomington: Indiana University Press.

———. 1989. "Lexical Cohesion and Biblical Interpretation." *Hebrew Studies* 30:29–40.

Bloom, Harold. 1976. "Poetic Crossing: Rhetoric and Psychology." *The Georgia Review* 30:495–526.

Boose, Lynda E. 1989. "The Father's House and the Daughter in It: The Structures of Western Culture's Daughter-Father Relationship." In *Daughters and Fathers,* ed. Lynda E. Boose and Betty S. Flowers, 19–74. Baltimore: Johns Hopkins University Press.

Boyarin, Daniel. 1992. "'This We Know to Be the Carnal Israel': Circumcision and the Erotic Life of God and Israel." *Critical Inquiry* 18:474–505.

Brandes Stanley. 1980. *Metaphors of Masculinity: Sex and Status in Andalusian Folklore*. Philadelphia: University of Pennsylvania Press.

Brenner, Athalya. 1997a. "The Hebrew God and His Female Complements." In *Reading Bibles, Writing Bodies: Identity and the Book*, ed. Timothy K. Beal and David M. Gunn, 56–71. London; New York: Routledge.

———. 1997b. *The Intercourse of Knowledge: On Gendering Desire and 'Sexuality' in the Hebrew Bible*. Leiden: Brill.

Bright, John. *Jeremiah*. Anchor Bible. Garden City: Doubleday, 1980.

Bronner, Leila Leah. 1994. *From Eve to Esther: Rabbinic Reconstructions of Biblical Women*. Philadelphia: Westminster/John Knox.

Broome, Edwin C. 1946. "Ezekiel's Abnormal Personality." *Journal of Biblical Literature* 65:277–92.

Campbell, E. F., Jr. 1975. *Ruth*. Anchor Bible 7. New York: Doubleday.

Carmichael, Calum M. 1997. *Law, Legend, and Incest in the Bible: Leviticus 18–20*. Ithaca: Cornell University Press.

Carroll, Robert P. 1986. *Jeremiah: A Commentary*. Old Testament Library. Philadelphia: Westminster.

Cassuto, Umberto. 1971. *The Goddess Anath: Canaanite Epics of the Patriarchal Age*. Trans. Israel Abrahams. Jerusalem: Magnes.

———. 1975. "The Israelite Epic." *Biblical and Oriental Studies* 2.

———. 1978. *A Commentary on the Book of Genesis*. Trans. Israel Abrahams. Jerusalem: Magnes.

———. 1983. *A Commentary on the Book of Exodus*. Trans. Israel Abrahams. Jerusalem: Magnes.

Chodorow, Nancy. 1978. *The Reproduction of Mothering: Psychoanalysis and the Sociology of Gender*. Berkeley: University of California Press.

Clines, David J. A. 1990. *What Does Eve Do to Help? and Other Readerly Questions to the Old Testament*. Journal for the Study of the Old Testament Supplement Series. Sheffield: Sheffield Academic.

Coats, George W. 1988. *Moses: Heroic Man, Man of God*. Sheffield: JSOT Press.

Cohen, David. 1987. "Law, Society, and Homosexuality in Classical Athens." *Past and Present* 117:6–21.

Cole, W. G. 1959. *Sex and Love in the Bible*. New York: Association.

Con Davis, Robert, ed. 1983. *Lacan and Narration: The Psychoanalytic Difference in Narrative Theory*. Baltimore: Johns Hopkins University Press.

Conrad, Joseph. 1912. *A Personal Record*. New York, London: Harper & Brothers.

Coogan, Michael D. 1978. *Stories from Ancient Canaan*. Philadelphia: Westminster.

Cross, Frank Moore. [1973] 1983. *Canaanite Myth and Hebrew Epic*. Cambridge, Mass.: Harvard University Press.

Daube, David. 1986. "Old Testament Prohibitions of Homosexuality." *Zeitschrift der Savigny-Stiftung für Rechtsgeschichte* 103:20–93.

Day, John. 1985. *God's Conflict with the Dragon of the Sea: Echoes of a Canaanite Myth in the Old Testament*. Cambridge: Cambridge University Press.

de Beauvoir, Simone. 1961. *The Second Sex*. Trans. H. M Parshley. New York: Bantam.

de Man, Paul. 1983. *The Rhetoric of Blindness*. London: Routledge.

de Vaux, Roland O. 1961. *Ancient Israel: Its Life and Institutions*. New York: McGraw-Hill.

Douglas, Mary. 1975. *Implicit Meanings*. London: Routledge.

Dover, Kenneth J. 1989. *Greek Homosexuality*. Cambridge, Mass.: Harvard University Press.

Downing, Christine. 1981. *The Goddess: Mythological Images of the Feminine*. New York: Crossroad.

Driver, S. R. 1907. *The Book of the Prophet Jeremiah*. New York: Scribner.

Eilberg-Schwartz, Howard. 1990. *The Savage in Judaism: An Anthropology of Israelite Religion and Ancient Judaism*. Bloomington: Indiana University Press.

Feldman, Yael S. 1994. *Freud and Forbidden Knowledge*. New York: New York University Press.

Felman, Shoshana, ed. 1980. *Literature and Psychoanalysis: The Question of Reading: Otherwise*. Baltimore: Johns Hopkins University Press.

Fewell, Danna Nolan, and David M Gunn. 1991. "Controlling Perspectives: Women, Men, and the Authority of Violence in Judges 4 & 5." *Journal of the American Academy of Religion* 58:389–411.

————. 1993. *Narrative in the Hebrew Bible*. Oxford Bible Series. New York: Oxford University Press.

Fishbane, Michael J. 1991. "The Holy One Sits and Roars: Mythopoesis and the Midrashic Imagination." *Journal of Jewish Thought and Philosophy* 1:1–21.

Fodor, A. 1954. "The Fall of Man in the Book of Genesis." *American Imago* 11:203–31.

Fokkelman, J. P. 1987. "Genesis." In *The Literary Guide to the Bible,* ed. Robert Alter and Frank Kermode, 36–55. Cambridge, Mass.: Harvard University Press.

Fox, Michael V. 1974. "The Sign of the Covenant: Circumcision in the Light of the Priestly 'Ôt Etiologies." *Revue biblique* 81:557–96.

Fox, Robin. 1974. *Kinship and Marriage*. 1967. Harmondsworth: Penguin.

Freud, Sigmund. 1894. "The Neuro-Psychoses of Defense." In *The Standard Works of Sigmund Freud,* ed. and trans. James Strachey, vol. 3, *The Aetiology of the Neuroses,* 43–86. London: Hogarth and Institute of Psychoanalysis.

————. 1896. *The Aetiology of the Neuroses*. Vol. 3 of *The Standard Works of Sigmund Freud*.

————. 1900. *The Interpretation of Dreams*. Vol. 4 of *The Standard Works of Sigmund Freud*.

————. 1905. *Three Essays on the Theory of Sexuality*. Vol. 7 of *The Standard Works of Sigmund Freud*.

————. 1909. "On Infantile Sexual Theories." *Collected Lesser Writing on Neurosis*. Vol. 2 of *The Standard Works of Sigmund Freud*.

————. 1913. *Totem and Taboo*. Vol. 13 of *The Standard Works of Sigmund Freud*.

———. 1914. *On the History of the Psycho-Analytic Movement*. Vol. 14 of *The Standard Works of Sigmund Freud*.

———. 1915. "Repression." In *The Standard Works of Sigmund Freud*, 14.143 60.

———. 1916–17. *Introductory Lectures on Psycho-Analysis*. Vol. 15 of *The Standard Works of Sigmund Freud*.

———. 1920. *Beyond the Pleasure Principle*. Vol. 18 of *The Standard Works of Sigmund Freud*.

———. 1925. *Some Psychical Consequences of the Anatomical Distinction Between the Sexes*. Vol. 19 of *The Standard Works of Sigmund Freud*.

———. 1926. *The Question of Lay Analysis: Conversations with an Impartial Person*. Vol. 12 of *The Standard Works of Sigmund Freud*.

———. 1928. *Dostoevsky and Patricide*. Vol. 21 of *The Standard Works of Sigmund Freud*.

———. 1931. *Female Sexuality*. Vol. 21 of *The Standard Works of Sigmund Freud*.

———. 1937. *Analysis Terminable and Interminable*. Vol. 23 of *The Standard Works of Sigmund Freud*.

———. 1939. *Moses and Monotheism: Three Essays*. Vol. 23 of *The Standard Works of Sigmund Freud*.

Frieden, Kenneth. 1990. *Freud's Dream of Interpretation*. Albany: State University of New York Press.

Fry, Christopher. 1951. *A Sleep of Prisoners*. London: Oxford University Press.

Frye, Northrop. 1982. *The Great Code: The Bible and Literature*. New York: Harcourt.

Frymer-Kensky, Tikva. 1992. *In the Wake of the Goddesses: Women, Culture, and the Biblical Transformation of Pagan Myth*. New York: Fawcett Columbine.

Gallop, Jane. 1989. "The Father's Seduction." In *Daughters and Fathers,* ed. Lynda E. Boose and Betty S. Flowers, 97–110. Baltimore: Johns Hopkins University Press.

Gassner, John, ed. 1963. *Medieval and Tudor Drama*. New York: Bantam.

———. 1972. "The Deluge." In idem, *Medieval and Tudor Drama*. New York: Bantam.

Gesenius, Friedrich W. 1910. *Hebrew Grammar*. Oxford: Clarendon.

Gimbutas, Marija Alseikaite. 1982. *Goddesses and Gods of Old Europe*. Berkeley: University of California Press.

Good, Robert M. 1982. "Metaphorical Gleanings from Ugarit." *Journal of Jewish Studies* 35:55–59.

Graves, Robert, and Raphael Patai. 1983. *Hebrew Myths: The Book of Genesis*. New York: Greenwich House.

Griffiths, J. G. 1980. *The Origins of Osiris and His Cult*. Leiden: Brill.

Gunn, David M. 1980. *The Fate of King Saul*. Sheffield: JSOT Press.

Halperin, David J. 1993. *Seeking Ezekiel: Text and Psychology*. University Park: Pennsylvania State University Press.

Hamilton, V. P. 1990. *The Book of Genesis: Chapters 1–17*. Grand Rapids: Eerdmans.

Haran, M. 1965. "The Religion of the Patriarchs." *Annual of the Swedish Theological Institute* 4:51–52.

Harris, R. 1976. "Woman in the Ancient Near East." *The Interpreter's Dictionary of the Bible*. Nashville: Abingdon.

Hegeler, Wilhelm. 1904. *Pastor Klinghammer*. Berlin: Fleischel.

Heine, Susanne. 1989. *Matriarchs, Goddesses, and Images of God: A Critique of Feminist Theology*. Trans. John Bowden. Minneapolis: Fortress Press.

Herman, Judith Lew, and Lisa Hirschman. 1981. *Father-Daughter Incest*. Cambridge, Mass.: Harvard University Press.

Herodotus. 1920. *Historia*. Loeb Classical Library. Trans. A. D. Godley. Cambridge, Mass.: Harvard University Press.

———. 1987. *The Histories. Book 2*. Trans. David Grene. Chicago: University of Chicago Press.

Hesiod. 1953. *Theogony*. Trans. Norman O. Brown. New York: Macmillan.

Holladay, William. 1986. *Jeremiah 1: A Commentary on the Book of the Prophet Jeremiah*. Hermeneia Series. Philadelphia: Fortress Press.

Horney, Karen. 1950. *Neurosis and Human Growth*. New York: Norton.

Hulse, E. V. 1975. "The Nature of Biblical 'Leprosy' and the Use of Alternative Medical Terms in Modern Translations of the Bible." *Palestine Exploration Quarterly* 107:87–105.

Hyatt, J. P. 1955. "Yahweh as the God of My Father." *Vestus Testamentum* 5:130–36.

Irigaray, Luce. 1977. *Ce Sexe Qui N'en Est Pas un (This Sex Which Is Not One)*. Trans. C. Porter and C. Burke. Ithaca, N.Y.: Cornell University Press.

Iser, Wolfgang. 1978. *The Act of Reading: A Theory of Aesthetic Response*. Baltimore: Johns Hopkins University Press.

Jakobson, Roman, and Morris Halle. 1975. *Fundamentals of Language*. 2d ed. The Hague: Mouton.

James, Edwin O. 1959. *The Cult of the Mother-Goddess*. London: Thames & Hudson.

Jobling, David. 1986. *The Sense of Biblical Narrative, II*. JSOT Supplement Series 7. Sheffield: JSOT Press.

Jones, Ernest. 1938. *Papers on Psychoanalysis*. Baltimore: William Wood.

———. 1949. *Hamlet and Oedipus*. London: Victor Gollancz.

Joüon, Paul. 1923. *Grammaire de l'Hébreu Biblique*. Rome: Pontifical Biblical Institute.

Knight, George A. F. 1981. *Theology in Pictures: A Commentary on Genesis, Chapters One to Eleven*. Edinburgh: Handsel.

Kugel, James L. 1981. *The Idea of Biblical Poetry: Parallelism and Its History*. New Haven: Yale University Press.

———. 1990. *In Potiphar's House: The Interpretive Life of Biblical Texts*. San Francisco: HarperSanFrancisco.

Kunin, Seth Daniel. 1995. *The Logic of Incest; A Structuralist Analysis of Hebrew Mythology*. JSOT Supplement Series 185. Sheffield: Sheffield Academic.

Lacan, Jacques. 1958. "Les Formations de l'Inconscient." *Bulletin de Psychologie* 12:250–56.

———. 1977a. *Écrits*. Trans. Alan Sheridan. New York: Norton.

———. 1977b. *The Four Fundamental Concepts of Psycho-Analysis*. Trans. Alan Sheridan. London: Tavistock.

Landy, Francis. 1983. *Paradoxes of Paradise: Identity and Difference in the Song of Songs*. Sheffield: Almond.

Lang, Bernhard. 1983. *Monotheism and the Prophetic Minority: An Essay in Biblical History and Sociology*. Sheffield: Almond.

Leach, Edmund. 1983. *Culture and Communication: The Logic by Which Symbols Are Connected*. Cambridge: Cambridge University Press.

Legouvé, Gabriel. 1800. *La Mort d'Abel*. Paris: Mérigot.

Leibowitz, Nehama. 1981. *Studies in Bereshit (Genesis): In the Context of Ancient and Modern Jewish Bible Commentary*. Jerusalem: Magnes.

Leick, Gwendolyn. 1994. *Sex and Eroticism in Mesopotamian Literature*. London: Routledge.

Lerner, Gerda. 1986. *The Creation of Patriarchy*. New York: Oxford University Press.

Levine, Baruch. 1989. *Leviticus*. The Jewish Publication Society Torah Commentary. Philadelphia: Jewish Publication Society.

Lévi-Strauss, Claude. 1967. *Structural Anthropology*. Trans. Claire Jacobson and Brooke Grundfest Schoepf. New York: Anchor.

Lichtheim, Miriam. 1976. *Ancient Egyptian Literature II: The New Kingdom*. Berkeley: University of California Press.

Mace, David. 1953. *Hebrew Marriage: A Sociological Study*. New York: Philosophical Library.

Maimonides, Moses. 1904. *The Guide for the Perplexed*. Trans. M. Friedlander. New York: Dutton.

Matthews, Victor H., and Don C. Benjamin. 1997. *Old Testament Parallels: Laws and Stories from the Ancient Near East*. New York: Paulist.

McClelland, David C. 1964. *The Roots of Consciousness*. Princeton: Van Nostrand.

McKnight, Edgar V. 1988. *Post-Modern Use of the Bible: The Emergence of Reader-Oriented Criticism*. Nashville: Abingdon.

Medlicott, R. W. 1967. "Lot and His Daughters." *Australian New Zealand Journal of Psychiatry* 1:134–39.

Mendelsohn, I. 1959. "On the Preferential Status of the Oldest Son." *Bulletin of the American Society of Oriental Research* 156:38–40.

Midrash Rabbah: Genesis. 1983. Ed. H. Freedman and I. Epstein. Trans. H. Freedman. London: Soncino Press.

Milgrom, Jacob. 1985. "You Shall Not Boil a Kid in Its Mother's Milk." *Bible Review* 1:48–55.

Miscall, Peter D. 1983. *The Workings of Old Testament Narrative*. Philadelphia: Fortress Press.

Mitchell, Juliet. 1975. *Psychoanalysis and Feminism*. New York: Random House.

Moss, Donald. 1989. "On Situating the Object: Thoughts on the Maternal Function, Modernism and Post-Modernism." *American Imago* 46:353–69.

Muller, John P., and William J. Richardson. 1982. *Lacan and Language: A Reader's Guide to Écrits*. New York: International Universities Press.

Müller, Wilhelm. 1856. "The Legend of the Swan Knight." *Germania* 1:418–40.

Negbi, Ora. 1976. *Canaanite Gods in Metal*. Tel Aviv: Institute for Archaeology.

Niditch, Susan. 1982. "The 'Sodomite' Theme in Judges 19-20: Family, Community and Social Disintegration." *Catholic Bible Quarterly* 44:365–78.

———. 1989a. "Eroticism and Death in the Tale of Jael." *Gender and Difference in Ancient Israel*. Ed. Peggy L. Day. Minneapolis: Fortress Press.

———. 1989b. *The Symbolic Vision in Biblical Tradition*. Harvard Semitic Monographs 30. Chico, Calif.: Scholars.

Ochshorn, Judith. 1981. *The Female Experience and the Nature of the Divine*. Bloomington: Indiana University Press.

Odets, Clifford. 1954. *The Flowering Peach*. New York: Dramatists Play Service.

Oppenheim, A. Leo. 1956. "The Interpretation of Dreams in the Ancient Near East." *Transactions of the American Philosophical Association* 46.

———. 1964. *Ancient Mesopotamia: Portrait of a Dead Civilization*. Chicago: University of Chicago Press.

Otwell, John. 1977. *And Sarah Laughed: The Status of Woman in the Old Testament*. Philadelphia: Westminster.

Ozick, Cynthia. 1983. "Notes Toward Finding the Right Question." In *On Being a Jewish Feminist: A Reader,* ed. Susannah Heschel, 120–51. New York: Schocken.

Pardes, Ilana. 1992. *Countertraditions in the Bible: A Feminist Approach*. Cambridge, Mass.: Harvard University Press.

Parker, Kim Ian. 1999. "Mirror, Mirror on the Wall, Must We Leave Eden, Once and for All? A Lacanian Pleasure Trip through the Garden." *Journal for the Study of the Old Testament* 83:19–29.

Parkinson, R. B. 1991. *Voices from Ancient Egypt: An Anthology of Middle Kingdom Writings*. London: British Museum.

Patai, Raphael. 1967. *The Hebrew Goddess*. New York: Avon.

Phillips, Anthony. 1980. "Uncovering the Father's Skirt." *Vestus Testamentum* 30:39–40.

Philo. 1971. *Questions and Answers on Genesis: Translated from the Ancient Armenian Version of the Original Greek*. Supplement I of *Philo in Ten Volumes*. Trans. R. Marcus. London and Cambridge, Mass.: William Heinemann and Harvard University Press.

Piers, Gerhart, and Morton B. Singer. 1953 [reprint 1971]. *Shame and Guilt: A Psychoanalytic and a Cultural Study*. New York: Norton.

Piskorowski, Anna. 1992. "In Search of Her Father: A Lacanian Approach to Genesis 2–3." In *A Walk in the Garden: Biblical, Iconographical and Literary Images of Eden,* ed. Paul Sawyer and Deborah Morris, 310–18. Sheffield: JSOT Press.

Pitt-Rivers, Julian. 1977. *The Fate of Shechem*. Cambridge: Cambridge University Press.

Plaskow, Judith. 1990. *Standing Again at Sinai: Judaism from a Feminist Perspective* San Francisco: Harper & Row.

Plutarch. 1936. *Moralia: Vol. 5*. Trans. Frank Cole Babbitt. Loeb Classical Library. Cambridge, Mass.: Harvard University Press.

Pope, Marvin. 1977. *Song of Songs*. Garden City: Doubleday.

Preuss, J. 1978. *Biblical and Talmudic Medicine*. Ed. and trans. F. Rosner. New York: Sanhedrin.

Ragland-Sullivan, Ellie. 1986. *Jacques Lacan and the Philosophy of Psychoanalysis*. Urbana: University of Illinois Press.

Rank, Otto. [1912] 1992. *The Incest Theme in Literature and Legend: Fundamentals of a Psychology of Literary Creation*. Trans. Gregory Richter. Reprint; Baltimore: Johns Hopkins University Press.

———. 1932. *The Myth of the Birth of the Hero*. Trans. Mabel E. Moxon. New York: Vintage.

Rashkow, Ilona. 1990. *Upon the Dark Places: Anti-Semitism and Sexism in English Renaissance Biblical Translation*. Sheffield: Sheffield Academic.

———. 1993. *The Phallacy of Genesis: A Feminist-Psychoanalytic Approach*. Louisville: Westminster/John Knox.

Robertson, J. M. 1900. *Christianity and Mythology*. London: Watts.

Rollins, Wayne G. 1999. *Soul and Psyche: The Bible in Psychological Perspective*. Minneapolis: Fortress Press.

Rose, Jacqueline. 1982. "Introduction." In *Feminine Sexuality*. New York: Norton.

Sanders, N. K. 1984. *The Epic of Gilgamesh*. New York: Penguin.

Sanhedrin: Hebrew-English Edition of the Babylonian Talmud. 1969. London: Soncino.

Sarna, Nahum. 1966. *Understanding Genesis*. New York: McGraw-Hill.

———. 1970. *Understanding Genesis: The Heritage of Biblical Israel*. New York: Shocken.

———. 1989. *Genesis*. The Jewish Publication Society Torah Commentary. Philadelphia: Jewish Publication Society.

———. 1991. *Exodus*. The Jewish Publication Society Torah Commentary. Philadelphia: Jewish Publication Society.

Sawyer, J. F. A. 1976. "A Note on the Etymology of Sara't." *Vetus Testamentum* 26:241–45.

Schiller-Tietz, Nikolaus. 1892. *The Consequences, Significance, and Nature of Blood Relationship in the Life of Humans, Animals, and Plants*. Berlin: Heusers.

Setel, T. Drorah. 1985. "Prophets and Pornography: Female Sexual Imagery in Hosea." In *Feminist Interpretation of the Bible*, ed. L. M Russell. Philadelphia: Westminster.

Shakespeare, William. 1936. *The Tragedy of Othello, The Moor of Venice*. In *The Complete Works of Shakespeare*, ed. William Aldis Wright. Garden City: Doubleday.

Silverman, Kaja. 1992. "The Lacanian Phallus." *Differences* 4:84–115.

Skinner, John. 1930. *A Critical and Exegetical Commentary on Genesis*. Edinburgh: T. and T. Clark.

Smith, Joseph H. 1986. "Primitive Guilt." In *Pragmatism's Freud: The Moral Disposition of Psychoanalysis,* ed. Joseph Smith and William Kerrigan, 52–78. Baltimore: Johns Hopkins University Press.

Soler, Jean. 1979. "The Dietary Prohibitions of the Hebrews." Trans. Eilberg Forster. *New York Review of Books* 26:24–30.

Speiser, E. A. 1930. *Annual of the American Society of Oriental Research* 10.

———. 1964. *Genesis*. Anchor Bible. Garden City: Doubleday.

Spiro, Melford E. 1961. "An Overview and a Suggested Reorientation." In *Context and Meaning in Cultural Anthropology,* ed. Francis I. K. Hsu. Homewood: Dorsey.

Steinmetz, Devora. 1991. *From Father to Son: Kinship, Conflict, and Continuity in Genesis*. Louisville: Westminster/John Knox.

Stone, Merlin. 1976. *When God Was a Woman*. New York: Dial.

Streane, A. W. 1805. *The Book of the Prophet Jeremiah, Together with Lamentations*. Cambridge: Cambridge University Press.

Thompson, J. A. 1980. *The Book of Jeremiah*. Grand Rapids: Eerdmans.

Torok, M. 1964. "'L'envie du Pénis Sous la Femme." *La Sexualité Féminine: Nouvelle Recherche Psychanalyse*. Paris: Payon.

Trible, Phyllis. 1978. *God and the Rhetoric of Sexuality*. Philadelphia: Fortress Press.

———. 1984. *Texts of Terror: Literary-Feminist Readings of Biblical Narratives*. Overtures to Biblical Theology. Philadelphia: Fortress Press.

Vasvari, Louise O. 1990. "A Tale of 'Tailing' in the Libro De Buen Amor." *Journal of Interdisciplinary Literary Studies* 2:13–41.

Vawter, Bruce. 1977. *On Genesis: A New Reading*. Garden City: Doubleday.

Vermeule, Emily. 1979. *Aspects of Death in Early Greek Art and Poetry*. Berkeley: University of California Press.

Voltaire. 1906. *Ezekiel*. Trans. William F. Fleming. Vol. 4 of *Philosophical Dictionary*. Akron: Werner.

Weber, Samuel. 1982. *The Legend of Freud*. Minneapolis: University of Minnesota Press.

Weinsheimer, Joel. 1979. "Theory of Character: Emma." *Poetics Today* 1:1–2.

Wenham, Gordon J. 1979. *The Book of Leviticus*. Grand Rapids: Eerdmans.

Williams, James G. 1991. *The Bible, Violence and the Sacred*. New York: Harper-Collins.

Winnicott, D. W. 1971. "Mirror-Role of Mother and Family in Child Development." In *Playing and Reality*. London: Tavistock.

Wolfson, F. 1987. "Circumcision, Vision of God, and Textual Interpretation: From Midrashic Trope to Mystical Symbol." *History of Religions* 27:189–215.

Wright, Elizabeth. 1984. *Psychoanalytic Criticism: Theory in Practice*. London: Methuen.

Zeligs, Dorothy F. 1988. *Psychoanalysis and the Bible: A Study in Depth of Seven Leaders*. New York: Human Sciences.

Index

Biblical Passages

Authors and Artists

Subjects